A Study of Philip Roth

An American Bestseller Novelist

A Study of Philip Roth

An American Bestseller Novelist

Shuchi Agrawal

GNOSIS

Nurturing the Aspirations

Worldwide Circulation through Authorspress Global Network
First Published 2011
by
GNOSIS
E-35/103, Jawahar Park
Laxmi Nagar, Delhi-110 092
e-mail: authorspress@yahoo.com

An Imprint of Authorspress

A Study of Philip Roth: An American Bestseller Novelist
ISBN 978-93-81030-07-3

Printed in India at Tarun Offset, Delhi.

Sheer Playfulness and Deadly Seriousness are my closest friends.

– Philip Roth

Preface

The galaxy of the Jewish novelists in America since the Second World War includes luminaries like Saul Bellow, Norman Mailer, Isaac Bashevis Singer, Bernard Malamud and Philip Roth. They are among the most celebrated American writers. These novelists primarily deal with the clash of psychological forces at the pressing points of character and explore erotic cravings, taboos and inhibitions.

Philip Roth turns these into the very topics of his penetrating and perceptive investigation. He assiduously fathoms frustrated yearnings and paralyzed desires, probes the enigmas of sex and scruples and pursues the relentless search for meanings and solutions in the labyrinth of lost longings, ferocious marital strife, grim inner conflict, turbulent and tortured emotions, libidinal yearnings, love, conflicting moods, repressed wishes and the unconscious. Thus Roth indefatigably explores the innermost recesses of psyche and true to unravel its depths and secrets.

So far little work has been done to highlight and critically analyze Philip Roth as a relentless explorer of the deep layers of human psyche with reference to his novels *Letting Go, When She was Good, Portnoy's Complaint, Our Gang, The Breast, The Great American Novel, My Life as a Man and The Professor of Desire.*

Shuchi Agrawal

Acknowledgements

'Thanks'—these six letters seem to be very simple to be used and said, but my vocabulary and language fail to find any other word than be so precise and expressive in extending my gratitude and indebtedness as these six golden letters. I really feel today that the most difficult job is 'Thanks giving' and wish that had there been a parameter / estimate of one's feeling, my work would have been easier and I would have had no difficulty in showing my warm and sincerest feeling for everybody with the help and support of whom I was able to undertake this endeavour successfully.

At the outset, I place on record my deeply felt gratitude to my guide and mentor, Dr. O.S. Gupta, Retired Head of the English Department, Meerut College, Meerut, who is the primal impulse behind orientation in research, and the fountainhead of strength during the conception and completion of this work.

I am extremely thankful to the Librarian and the Library Staff of the American Centre and British High Commission, Delhi, which were a source of inspiration and guidance during the gestation period of this venture.

I also want to pay homage to my father, Mr. G.L. Agrawal, who encouraged me and helped me in arranging the required books and material. I should also like to record my debt to my soul-mate, Mr. Abhinav Agrawal, C.A., without whose cooperation this book might never have seen the light of day. My heartiest thanks to my brother, Mr. Nikhil Agrawal, for the pains he took in the typing of this manuscript. My ardent thanks to Ms. Poonam Bhola, Lecturer (English), R.D.S. Public Girls College, Rewari, for her support and motivation. Moreover, my heartiest thanks to my publisher who showed interest in my work and obliged me.

Shuchi Agrawal

Introduction

Central social transformations over the past century provided the American novel with a continuously replenishing supply of vital materials, and always their vitality has depended in very large measure on the factor of novelty. Many circumstances gave social dislocation – as the rise of the mercantile middle class out of the collapsing feudal order. Ethnic, rural, regional and sexual subcultures also emerged in which the initial struggle out of feudalism of the middle class is recapitulated in the struggle for freedom, acceptance and personal autonomy of Jews, Blacks, provincial southern or midwesterners, women or homosexuals – in short, groups, that have become newly conscious of themselves and the special nature of their minority or regional experiences.

The history of the twentieth-century novel in this country may be described as an evolutionary development in which emerging social situations become important for the novelist rather than imaginative material. Thus racial, ethnic, regional, or sexual perspective because of its newness or its bizarre character, gave a fertile ground for the novel.

In the early nineteenth century and the years following world war I we have had the new England novel of Hawthorne and Melville: the novel of the developing Western frontier of James Fennimore Cooper; the more deeply Western novel of Mark Twain; the international and New York novel of James. Many works after the turn of this century dramatized the plight of the midwestern and southern adolescent struggling to escape the suffocations of the small town; other works explored the usually destructive consequences of the adolescent's escape – to New York, Long island, Paris and the south France. Later during the thirties, there were large numbers of novels dealing with the new depression created subculture of the economically dispossessed. After World War-II the racial and ethnic novel came into authority as the Anglo-Saxon mid-western experience ceased to be the typifying experience of most American writers.

An obsessive hunger for new experience and a disposition to seek it in the actualities of the social world rather than to produce it imaginatively—these have been highly visible characteristics of our writers. If in the traditional European novel, characters tend to move in an environment of custom, experience for Americans is an entity sought as destination and quarry, a dynamic and elusive state. So the European novel came to rest in serenity and reconciliation reminding us that solution may perhaps be found only in an enlightened personal desire with public necessity. The American novel tends, by contrast, to remain in a state of uncompromised adversary motion. Twentieth century has been remarkable for the accelerating vengeance with which novelists throughout their works have carried on the process of demystifying experience. For, we now suffer from a surfeit of negation and an apparent failure of understanding of just what values have been negated, what were the illusions we once mistook for truth. So this moral consciousness has profoundly affected the nature of life in America at this time. Today, most of the novels make a serious claim upon our attention to the extent that they hardly contain any realistic celebrities made recognizable by the regular appearance of their faces.

The physical dislocation of the individuals from direct relation to his social and public experience has its correlative. Our attitude toward sex is necessarily ambivalent in this age when the old taboos that once restricted opportunity and performance have been replaced by freedom and liberty often degenerating into licence and gay abandon. On the one hand, sex for us is the last of the intimately personal experiences to carry on with ever-renewing freshness of sensation in a never deadening world. It is also what we have left of a possibility for transcendence, the discovery of new adventure, the conquest of a continuously reconquerable frontier. It is undoubtedly true that sex obsesses us today to the extent that opportunities for extra sexual levels of relationship have died out, to the extent that, locked as we are inside our narcissism, we are forced to make up through our sexuality for the "depletion" of other socially interactive resources. The result, however, is not a humanization of our sexual impulse but rather its further mechanization. The final result of this interest is pornography. Many novels have instructed us over the past several years in the mysteries of other people's sexuality, a knowledge of which we hope will help illuminate our own and we have been enlightened about what it is like to be a male heterosexual, a male homosexual, a male rapist, a male masturbator and middle aged male lover of little girls.

It is conventional to notice that the growth of the novel form has been accompanied in modern times by a steadily increasing emphasis upon individual consciousness, the inward-turning, preoccupations of the imperial self. There is particular relation established in the classic modern novel between individual consciousness and the physical or social environment in which it is set down. Self-consciousness functions more and more as the medium as well as the substance of narrative. Monologue, in short, is the natural "solipsistic" form, just as "paranoia" is the inevitable solipsistic condition. Saul Bellow, Philip Roth, Walker Perry and Joseph Heller have all written monologistic novels. But the case of Roth is of particular interest, because in a sense, his whole career up to now has represented a sustained and sedulous effort to deal creatively with some of the circumstances in contemporary life that have helped to produce the current obsessiveness with the monologistic form. Monologistic novel is, in the very nature of things, inward looking, peeping into and penetrating the innermost layers of psyche—conscious, subconscious and unconscious.

In 1961, Roth published a remarkable essay entitled "Writing American Fiction" which attracted considerable attention at the time and has since come to be regarded as something of a classic critical statement. What impresses one most in rereading it today is the accuracy with which Roth was able to diagnose and pinpoint the more serious problems confronting the writer of fiction.

Roth cited Mailer's "Advertisements for Myself" as the expression of "a despair so great that the man who bears it, or is borne by it, seems for the time being… to have given up on making an imaginative assault upon the American experience and has become instead the champion of kind of public revenge." Later in the essay he criticized Salinger for creating characters whose sole response to the contemporary world is to have heroes who breakdown and succumb or commit suicide or retreat into a specious mysticism, while Malamud's characters seemed to him to be people who exist outside the rude realities of the current historical situation and who function as metaphors for general human possibilities rather than as representations of existing social types.

Philip Milton Roth was born in Newark, New Jersey, in 1933, the son of American born parents and the grandson of European Jews who were part of the nineteenth century wave of immigration to the United States. He grew up in the city's lower middle class section of Weequahic and was educated in Newark Public Schools. He later attended Bucknell University, where he received his B.A., and the University of Chicago, where he completed his M.A. and taught English. Afterwards, at both Iowa and Princeton, he taught creative writing and for many years he taught comparative literature at the University of Pennsylvania. He retired from teaching in 1992.

For the last half century, the novels of Philip Roth have renergized American fiction and redefined its possibilities. Roth's comic genius, his imaginative daring, his courage in exploring uncomfortable and unpalatable truth and his assault on political, cultural and sexual orthodoxies and his insight in exploring and fathoming the innermost recesses of human psyche caught in the of paroxysms and paradoxes of excruciating passions have made him one of the most perceptive writers of our time and his insight in exploring and fathoming the innermost recesses of human psyche caught in the vortex of paroxysms and paradoxes of excruciating passions.

His first book was *Goodbye, Columbus (1959)* a novella and five stories that use wit, irony, and humour to depict Jewish life in post-war America. The book won him critical recognition, including the National Book Award for fiction, and along with that, condemnation from some within the Jewish community for depicting what they saw as the unflattering side of contemporary Jewish American experience. His first full-length novel was *Letting Go (1962),* a Jamesian realistic work that explores and examines many of the societal and ethical issues of the 1950s. This novel was followed in 1967 by *When She Was Good,* another novel in the realistic mode that takes as its focus a rare narrative voice in Roth's fiction: a young Midwestern female.

He is perhaps best known-notoriously so, to many-for his third novel, *Portnoy's Complaint (1969*), a wildly comic representation of his middle class New York Jewish world in the portrait of Alexander Portnoy, whose possessive mother makes him so guilty and insecure that he can seek relief only in elaborate masturbation and sex with forbidden *shiksas*. For readers of that hilarious novel eating liver would never be the same. *Portnoy's Complaint* was not only the New York Time's best seller for the year 1969, it also made a celebrity out of Roth, an uncomfortable position that he would later fictionalize in such novels as *Zuckerman Unbound (1981) and Operation Shylock (1993).* Following the publication of *Portnoy's Complaint,* Roth experimented with different comic modes, at times outrageous, as illustrated in the works *Our Gang (1971),* a parodic attack on Richard Nixon; *The Breast (1972*), a Kafkaesque rendering of sexual desire; *The Great American Novel (1973*), a wild satire of both Frank Norris's novelistic quest and the great American pastime, baseball; and short story "On The Air".

In *My Life As A Man (1974),* Roth not only introduces his most developed protagonist, Nathan Zuckerman but for the first time his fiction becomes highly self-reflexive and postmodern. One of his most significant literary efforts is the Zuckerman trilogy: beginning with *The Ghost Writer (1979), Zuckerman Unbound, and The Anatomy Lesson* (1983) and wrapped up with a novella epilogue, *The Prague Orgy* (1985). These novels trace the development of Roth's alter ego, Nathan Zuckerman, from an aspiring young writer to a socially compromised, and psychologically besieged, literary celebrity. In *The Counterlife (1986)* perhaps his most ambitious and meticulously structured novel, Roth brings a temporary end of his Zuckerman writings. It is also the first time that the author engages in a sustained examination of the relationship between American and Israeli Jews.

His next four books—*The Facts* (1988), *Deception*(1990), *Patrimony* (1991), and *Operation Shylock*-explore the relationship between the lived world and the written world, between "fact" and "fiction". Through his protagonist in these works, also named Philip Roth, the author questions the genres of autobiography and fiction, and the mischievously encourages the reader to become caught up in this literary game. The other three are subtitled as either an autobiography *(The Facts),* a memoir or "true story" (*Patrimony),* or a confession *(Operation Shylock*). The most elaborate of these, *Operation Shylock,* is arguably Roth's finest work, leading fellow writer Cynthia Ozick to call it in one of the interviews, "the Great American Jewish Novel" and Roth "the boldest American writer alive."

Roth's next novel, *Sabbath's Theater* (1995), is a return to the outrageous psycho-sexual (and tragicomic) form that entertained and outraged so many in *Portnoy's Complaint*. Its "hero", over the hill puppeteer Mickey Sabbath, is nothing if not a character portrait of transgressive behavior. However in his next three novels, what is called his American Trilogy, Roth relies once again on Nathan Zuckerman as his agent of focus. *American pastoral(1997), I Married a Communist (1998),* and *The Human Stain* (2000) can be read as novels that reflect key moments in late twentieth-century American experience—in the 1960s, 1950s and 1990s, respectively—and each is chronicled by an older Zuckerman, no longer the mischievous and sexually adventurous young writer he once was. In this later trilogy, the aged writer has become somewhat of a recluse who devotes himself exclusively to his writing, and through this writing reveals the stories of memorable individuals who, in many ways, represent the social, political, and psychological conflicts that define post-war America.

In *The Dying Animal (2001),* Roth revisits the life of David Kapesh, the protagonist of *The Breast* and *The Professor of Desire (1977).* As in the earlier novels, Kapesh is concerned with the erotic side of experience and as he puts it, "emancipated manhood". Yet even though its focus is explicitly sexual, this novel, like almost all of Roth's other works, has as its theme the ways in which individuals—specifically men—live with desire in the larger sense of the word. One of the ha. marks of Roth's fiction is the ways in which sexual, communal, familial, ethnic, artistic, and political freedoms play themselves out on the field to contemporary existence.

His most recent novel, *The Plot against America,* takes Roth into fresh literary territory. It is an alternative history whose premise is the 1940 election of Charles A. Lindbergh to the White House. What, Roth asks, would America have been like had isolationist and anti-Semitic Lindbergh defeated F.D.R., reached a cordial "understanding" with Adolf Hitler, and kept the United States out of the Second World War? Reminiscent of the four works preceding it, the new novel appears to continue the author's exploration of American identities and American psyche, national as well as individual, within the context of its history.

In addition to his novels and short stories, Roth has also proven to be an accomplished essayist. In collections such as *Reading Myself and Others* (1975) and the more recent *Shop Talk (2001),* his focus is on the act of writing, both his own and that of other authors. The lengthy interviews that make up *Shop Talk* first appeared in such publications as the *New York Times Book Review, the New York Review of Books, the New Yorker,* and the *London Review of Books*. The pieces themselves are testament to Roth's unwavering and ongoing admiration of some of the most significant writers in the last half of the twentieth-century. Until 1989 he was the General Editor of the Penguin book service "Writers form the other Europe", which he inaugurated in 1974. The series helped to introduce American audiences, to among others, Milan. Unlike many prolific novelists, whose productive qualities may tend to wane over time, Roth has demonstrated a unique ability not only to sustain his literary output, but even surpass the scope and talent inherent in his previous writings. His later fiction is his best work, as demonstrated by the succession of awards he received in the 1990s (and a Nobel Prize in Literature a very likely possibility). He has lived in Rome, London, Chicago, and New York. He currently lives in Connecticut. His awards and honours include:

1) Aga Khan, Paris Review, 1958
2) Houghton-mifflin Literary Fellowship, 1959
3) National Book Award for Fiction for *Goodbye, Columbus,* 1960
4) National Institute of Arts and Letters Grant,1959
5) Daroff Award, Jewish Book Council of America for *Goodbye, Columbus,* 1960
6) Second Prize in the O. Henry Prize Story Contest for "Defender of the Faith", 1960
7) Guggenheim Fellowship, 1960
8) For Foundation Grant in Playwriting, 1965
9) Elected to National Institute of Arts and Letters, 1970
10) American Book Award Nomination for *The Ghost Writer,* 1980

11) National Book Critics Circle Nomination for *The Anatomy Lesson,* 1983
12) National Book Critics Circle Nomination for *The Anatomy Lesson,* 1984
13) National Book Critic Circle Award for *The Counterlife,* 1987
14) National Arts Club Medal of Honor, 1991
15) National Book Critics Circle Award for *Patimony,* 1992
16) Pen/Faulkner Award for Fiction for *Operation Shylock,* 1993
17) Time Magazine's Best American Novel of the *Year for Operation Shylock,* 1993
18) Jewish Cultural Achievement Award in the Arts, 1993
19) Karl Capek Prize (Czech Republic), 1994
20) National Book Award for Fiction, *Sabbath's Theater,* 1995
21) National Book Critics Circle Nomination for American Pastoral, 1997
22) National Book Award Nomination for *American Pastoral,* 1997
23) Pulitzer Prize for Fiction Nomination, *American Pastoral,* 1997
24) Ambassador Book Award, English-speaking Union, for *I Married a Communist,* 1998
25) National Medal of Arts, 1998

The salient feature of Jewish novelists in America since Second World War is their sheer numerical presence and their persistent upward mobility. They include Saul Bellow, Norman Mailer, Isaac Bashevis Singer, Bernard Malamud and Philip Roth. They take their place among the most distinguished American writers and to bracket them together is to be aware of both their place in American Literature and the vastly varied gamut they occupy collectively. For these novelists it is the clash of psychological forces at the pressure points of character which is crucial and which determines their stance toward sex, love and wedded life. Their fiction deals with the erotic longings, taboos and inhibitions. However, Philip Roth turns them into the very topics of his investigation.

From this standpoint his novels broadly indicate four stages in his evolution as an explorer of human psyche, which will be discussed and evaluated in the successive chapters.

Contents

1

First Stage: Ethical Jewhood and Failed Renunciation

Roth's early novels comprise a tale of failed renunciation. They depict the psychology of repressed and driven characters. Their heroes repress desires which, naturally, refuse to jettison them and instead doggedly plague them in the form of compulsive and irrational behaviour. For example in *Letting Go,* the reciprocal renunciation of Gabe Wallach and Libby Herz precedes six hundred pages of vacillation (his) neurasthenia (hers) muddle, and sudden irrational tantrums and paroxysms (theirs).

Letting Go is Philip Roth's first novel and second book. His first, *Goodbye Columbus* was a collection of short stories published three years ago when Mr. Roth was only 26. It made him famous and won him no less than four awards: A Houghtan Mifflin Literary Fellowship, the National Book award for fiction, a prize for the year's best book of Jewish interest from the Jewish book council of the National Jewish Welfare Board, and one of the eighteen $1500 awards given by the National Institute of Arts and Letters. Seldom has a new writer's debut been greeted with such acclaim.

Letting Go is further proof of Mr. Roth's astonishing talent. This is a clumsily constructed novel, but a morbidly fascinating one. Its psychological insight convinces that he has a phenomenal ear for colloquial dialogue. He is an effective story-teller, although he prefers to tell many separate stories rather than one definite story. He is as true and incisive with feelings of minor characters as he is with his protagonists. This last, of course, is regarded as a literary virtue in some circles.

Letting Go is the story of a few years in the lives of four persons. Part of it is told in the first person by Gabe Wallach, a wealthy, intelligent, well intentioned, indecisive college teacher of English. The rest in alternating chapters is told by Mr. Roth in the conventional third person. Gabe is sorry for other people's troubles. But he sincerely tries to be helpful. But he cannot see why he should become deeply involved, why he should let go and become responsible for the health, happiness and economic security of others. But life and people sometimes demand total and uninhibited participation. His understandable reluctance haunts his conscience. Not having serious troubles of his own, he feels guilty. Probably he feels guiltier than he has any cause to feel, but that is a point which is here to be widely discussed.

The three persons into whose lives Gabe feels himself deeply embroiled are Paul Herz, fellow English teacher, desperately poor, tout, earnest, apprehensive, good and kind; Libby Herz, Paul's wife born a Catholic but converted to Judaism in a futile effort to appease Paul's offended parents, neurotic, hysterical, unreasonable, loitering on the brink of mental collapse; and Martha Reganhart, divorced, a mother of two children, Gabe's mistress, hearty, healthy, sloppy, generous and bitter.

Sex is the crudest element which obsesses everybody. But money, religion, family, children, love are also matters of concern, and a dozen other crucial matters also preoccupy all of them. Few novels are so deep in *squalour*, anxiety and emotional tumult as *Letting Go*. And few ones explore and come to terms with the lives of noisy desperation led by a large proportion of mankind.

In addition to being a long and intimate study of its four unforgettable principals, *Letting Go* a is harshly satirical account of many other characters in many different walks of life. Mr. Roth is amusing and touching and shocking by nature. He writes with a fine combination of sympathy and mockery about middle-class New York Jews, Gabe's and Paul's relatives. He is savagely satirical about academic appointments. He is adroit and amusing in his thumbnail sketches of American types: loathsome old men washed into a dreadful removing house by a tide of misery; an abortionist; a Negro Hipster; a pregnant girl of 19 (Theresa Haug), mentally subnormal; a bellicose, suspicious, ignorant and dishonest factory worker out of job (Mr. Bigoness).

Letting Go seethes with life. It is disorderly and much too long (630 pages). It is nasty in spots because Mr. Roth is still so young he wants to shock. But it is not pretentious, mannered or clogged with sterile symbolism. He writes out of his passionate interest in his fellow human beings. He is probably the most talented novelist under 30 in America.

Set in 1950s Chicago, New York and Iowa city, *Letting Go* presents as brilliant a fictional portrait as we have of a mid-century America defined by social and ethical norms and by moral compulsions conspicuously different from those of today.

Newly discharged from the Korean War army, reeling from his mother's recent death, freed from old attachments and voraciously seeking others, Gabe Wallach is drawn to Paul Herz, a fellow graduate student of literature, and to Libby, Paul's capricious and intensely sensitive wife. Gabe's desire to be connected to the ordered "World of feeling" that he finds in books is just tested vicariously by the anarchy of the Herzes' struggles with responsible adulthood and then by his own eager love affairs. Driven by the desire to live seriously and act generously Gabe meets an impossible test in the person of Martha Reganhart, a spirited, outspoken, divorced mother of two, a formidable woman who, according to critic James Atlas, is masterfully portrayed with "depth and resonance."

The complex liaison between Gabe and Martha and Gabe's moral empathy for the trials and tribulations of others are at the heart of this tragically comic work.

Gabe Wallach is a second lieutenant in Oklahoma and his one connection with the world of feeling is not the world itself but Henry James. In his grief (because his mother has recently died) and confusion, he promises himself that he would do no violence to human life, not to another's, and not to his own.

It is a year later that Gabe hands the book to Paul Herz who looks to be hailed a young man rapidly losing contact with his own feelings. They both are enrolled as graduate students at the University of Iowa. At that time, Gabe lives alone in a small apartment near the campus and is having troubles of his own.

He is about ready to find somebody to complain to. In the very first meeting with Libby Herz, he feels that there is something wrong with her; later he also comes to know her real problem, that is, she cannot conceive and she is desperately in need of a child because only a child can make her life complete and meaningful. Without a child, there is emptiness in her life. Gabe's mother has departed two years ago. Even then he cannot be normal. He wants to go away from his father, that is why instead of getting admission in New York, he comes to Iowa city, so that he can live away from his father.

Libby is a hysterical girl and she breaks down suddenly. She is unpredictable and irrational; she generally spoils the dinner parties and social meetings. When Gabe is invited for dinner by Herzes, at that time also she quarrels with Paul. She also spoils the dinner when she goes to the Hawalian House. Gabe wants some solace in the relationship with Majorie Howells. She wants to stay with Gabe, but Gabe has no serious emotional attachment with her. He consideres her sweet, empty-headed girl. But when Gabe goes to meet his father the girl badly misses him and he asks her to leave his house. He never feels that he should meet her. He feels no strong sentiment for the girl.

Gabe is taller and heavier like his mother, his father is a dentist. His father has been chairman of an organization of doctors and lawyers in New York City. Immediately after the death of his mother, Gabe finds himself blaming his father for having been unworthy of her. But the reality is just the opposite, because it is she who has ruined his father's life as his mother herself admits in a letter to Gabe.

"He never once admits that I've done him an injustice being his wife. He holds my hand fifty times a day.... All through out marriage I've been improving his life for him...."[1]

Paul marries Libby against the wishes of his parents. He is the only son of his parents and even his uncle Asher is against his decision of marrying Libby. The reason is that Libby is a catholic and she also suffers from cold. Each and every person advises and argues against this marriage but Paul defying the well-considered advice of all, marries her because he really loves her.

Gabe is highly sympathetic towards Paul and Libby. When Libby tells him about her miscarriage, he is deeply moved.

"The girl was not a nut and she was not a liar, and that knowledge produced in me a feeling of helpless that was almost a presence in my limbs."[2]

After some gap, Herzes reappears in Gabe's life. Now Paul is reputed to be one of the most reasonable young men. Now the story introduces us to another family of Martha Reganhart and her two kids: Cynthia, a seven-year-old girl, and Markie, a four-year-old boy. She is divorced and works as a waitress to support her family and takes courses. A lawyer named Sid Jaffer helps her a lot in getting her divorce from her husband Dick Reganhart, who is a painter. Sid wants to marry Martha but she does not respond positively to his proposal. She feels that this time she will do it for love.

She is a kind and solicitious mother, who is highly dutiful towards her kids because it is only she who is supporting her family, not Dick Reganhart. He never sends a penny to support the kids. So she is highly calculative and rational.

At first, Paul lives with Libby without marriage. Later they marry when Paul is 21 and Libby is 19. His father has disappointed him and Paul feels his love for Libby flowing again. Libby is positively pregnant. But they cannot have a child as it is dangerous to the life of Libby in conceiving a baby because of her week kidneys. So against Libby's wish, who wants to become a mother, they get the child aborted. But Paul's love for Libby does not abate as he waxes eloquent about his fervent, ardent and profound love for her:

"I love you. I want you to know I love you, Libby, I love you I'll do anything for you, Lib, I love you."[3]

Gabe's father grows interested in a widow, Fay Silberman, who is divorced and a smoker. But Gabe cannot give her the place of his mother. He does not like her continuous drinking and smoking. But Mr. Wallach is highly impressed by her. He feels forlorn and wants to mitigate his desolation in the company of Silberman who herself has kids. First his father gets engaged to her and then after Christmas they get married.

A new chapter starts in the life of Gabe who feels enchanted to Martha. He telephones her when he is in Brooklyn with his father and his party:

> Martha Reganhart began to loom in my head and subsequently in my heart too as a green, watery spot in a dry land. Why I had called her now seemed perfectly clear.[4]

Now the scene shifts to Hawalian House, Martha's apartment. She is busy with the preparations because Sid is coming that evening for dinner. Sissy is Martha's paying guest. The tragedy in Sissy's young life is that she has been married for eleven months to a man who is impotent. Now she is involved with Blau Stott who is a Negro.

For nearly four years now Martha has been pretending to be two parents and not half a set. She abhors her ex-husband Dick Reganhart who leaves her in the lurch. She hates him so much that she will never forgive him. It is nearly three years since sent a penny to support his children. Sid is forty-one years old and he articulates his desire to Martha: "I want to sleep with you."

But Martha does not love him and never can. In fact, she wants to maintain the dignity of a mother. That's what she says to Sid:

> If I let everybody's hands go travelling down my blouse. What kind of mother would I be?[5]

Her demands are no more complicated or unusual than any other girl's. Since her return to Chicago, two other proposals have come Martha's way.

One is from Andy Rathen, a Rush street musician and another from Billy Parlino, who at the time is the husband of her best friend Bev.

Martha is not mean, bitchy, immoral, selfish, stupid or dishonest—all the words Dick has hinted at her when she flees finally from Mexico with the children. "It could not be she who was the betrayer of their children."[6]

That is the day to meet Martha. Gabe wants to call Martha and verify their dinner date but by mistake he dials the Herzes and maintains a dumb silence and hangs up. That evening he meets Paul and Libby, and realizes:

> I was even willing to believe that he(Paul) was not Libby's misfortune but that she was his. Perhaps the truth was not Libby was a girl with desires nobody could satisfy; perhaps they weren't even desires but the manifestation of same cellular disorder... I was willing to believe that Libby either did not need to be rescued or was impossible to rescue.[7]

Gabe also finds that Libby is badly in need of a child. She is suffering from cold. So she cannot leave the job and stay at home alone as she says:

> "Oh, I want a baby or some thing". She moaned "I' want a dog or TV Paulie, I can't do anyting."[8]

Gabe says to Paul, "Then give her a child. Have a child." At this Libby rebukes Gabe, she loses her temper. She is hysterically shattered; she is in tantrums. Due to her lousy kidneys, she cannot give birth to a child.

Gabe is invited by Martha to her apartment. That night, they become one. Gabe is very tired and wants to sleep but Martha does not allow him to do so.

"I felt a strange and separate pleasure. I felt called for, labored over. I felt used. Above, she was me now, and below I was her. Man, woman, mother, child all distinction melted away."[9]

Gabe's health deteriorates. He cannot even move for many days, so he starts living with her, and she starts taking care of his needs. He is looked after and in this way Gabe comes close to Cynthia and Markie. He says to Martha:

> Martha, you're a generous, competent, warm-blooded, splendid girl.[10]

Sissy leaves the house in a huff because she is angry with Martha as she never allows her to lie with Blaiei in her house and Gabe is allowed. Gabe loves her seriously, selflessly but Martha needs Gabe to fulfil her carnal as well as emotional needs:

> Every goofy girl in the street has some one who can stay all night, but mine has to leave at three in the morning, does that seem fair?[11]

She turns on her knees, takes Gabe's face in her hands and says:

> Gabe, just tell me, do I seem selfish and mean? There's them, but then there's still me, isn't there? stay and live with me.[12]

But she does not want to marry Gabe: "I don't need a husband, sweetheart—just a lover."[13]

She needs a passionate lover, not a husband. After some days they begin to quarrel over money. Gabe pays her half amount of boarding and loading. He has to leave Martha's house. After being separated from Martha, it occurs to him that he should never marry. But he finds that he cannot live without her, He calls her:

> Martha, it's me, Martha, I have missed the hell out of you, I made a damn weak, silly error.[14]

Martha replies:

> Oh, you're drunk baby—but come, come anyway."[15]

They again start living together. One day they invite Paul and Libby but Libby and Martha spoil the meeting. Paul and Libby decide to adopt a baby from an agency but it takes too much time. Gabe suggests them the name of a lady, Theresa Haug, is 19 years old, married woman, who does not want the child. So it decided that Herzes will bear all the expenses of doctors and hospitals of Haug and after delivery they will get her child.

Herzes calls the baby girl "Rachel".

Dick Reganhart marries June and he wants his kids back. He gets a great success and takes Cynthia and Martha with himself. Markie dies and Martha wants to marry Sid Jaffe. Gabe is ready to pay a cheque of worth $500 to Mr. Bygones so that all the legal formalities regarding the adoption of Rachel would be complete.

Paul realizes that he is not a man of feeling; it occurs to him that if he is anything at all it is a man of duty. He faces many vicissitudes—abortion, adoption, familial excommunication. He arrives at Blooklyn after abandoning his wife. If he hasn't left Libby, it must be that he really has come east to see his father and assuage his mother. If it is not for his parents' sake that he has come east then it is for something else and he does not want to think about that right now. If he has actually left Libby, then she must be dead. He has given up everything for her but he does not know whether he loves her or not, though often he remembers her even being away from her. He almost decided to leave Libby. So marital conflict is also depicted in this novel. He himself confesses:

> The marriage hasn't worked out.[16]

The reason behind the marital conflict is that Paul does not make love to Libby. His sexual abstinence can be ascribed to the apprension that there in the fear that Libby would turn-up pregnant again, which will inevitably be followed by abortion and its concomitant horrors. So he is hesitant and reluctant for sexual unison with her. In fact, he lavishes abundant care and attention upon the precaution itself, more than what is expected from most young men. Paul has had some inclination for sacrifice and even some power to deal with it.

He cares less for his own pleasure and more for Libby's health. Then Libby becomes sick and out of what seems on the surface a sheer lack of energy. Then it begins to appear that perhaps in his new job lies his salvation. His students are generous and responsive. Then his father dies. He reaches Brooklyn cemetery.

Martha is employed now at the university as secretary to Clude Delse, the director of the summer quarter. She starts avoiding Gabe who wants to leave Chicago for good.

Gabe goes to meet Cynthia and Markie but at that time Markie is in hospital and Cynthia enjoys herself with him in water. Cynthia inwardly thinks about him—"she had never liked him; now she remembers how he had made her mother unhappy. If it had not been for him, her mother would have married her father again."[17]

Gabe does not know where to go. He is trying to find life in others' happiness. He does a lot for others but gets no reward. His altruistic nature does not earn dividends for him. He has two applications to still fill out later, one for a job teaching American Literature in Greece, another for a position in Istanbul. He is certain that he cannot stay much longer in Chicago. It is one of the few things he is certain of, that there is no chance of even a little peace and happiness. He would only make out the applications and wait to see what happens.

Seeing Paul and Libby happy Gabe is brought around again to thinking of himself as a husband and a father. Libby gives him the news that Sid Jaffe is getting married. When Gabe meets Martha, she refuses to be kissed by him, because she is selfish. She is only a mother. She comes to know that Dick has divorced his second wife, June. Then she gets ready to marry Sid to get back her child. She says to Gabe:

> Sid Jaffe happens to be a fine man. He is not jelly either he is going to get my baby back do you know that? And them I am going to have an orderly life—don't try to get me in bed again. You![18]

He tries his best to help Herzes in getting the child legally adopted. But he is unsatisfied with a just invitation card sent by Libby to invite him on Rachel's first birthday. He does not want to get in touch with Herzes.

The novel thus highlights ethical Jewhood. All the characters have their ethical norms and they live for their ethics, and these ethics emerge as the root cause of their traumas and excruciating dilemmas.

Thus I find that at the centre of *Letting Go* is, ostensibly, Gabe Wallach, affluent, goodlooking, with a fondness for Henry James's *Portrait of a Lady*. Like Isabel Archer, Gabe has recently lost a parent (his domineering mother), and the novel follows his pursuit of several potential mates as he rejects one feminine ideal after another. He resembles his emotionally unresponsive mother and seeks a sense of vitality through his involvement in the lives of those whose circumstances are more difficult and more constricted than his own. His difficulty lies in his inability to become emotionally attached to others. So the desires, frustrations, and, above all, torments and tribulations of the other major characters truly form the centre of the novel.

The theme of the novel is unfolded with Gabe's response to his mother's death. His mother confesses to "doing things for another's good" and "pushing" and "pulling" to shape others' lives into the form she values.[19] She effectively bullies Gabe's father into living a "decent" life, despite his more romantic inclinations.

The novel's subplot follows the tortuous realationship beetween Catholic Libby De' 'itt (Herz) and Jewish Paul Herz. Young college students, the couple decides to marry against their parent's strong objections to a "mixed marriage." Their families disown them, and they are pitted against social ostracism, an unwanted pregnancy, Libby's poor health, financial strains, and frustrated career ambitions. Paul coerces Libby into an abortion; Libby becomes ever more dependent on Paul and uses guilt to bind him to her. In order to shape the lives of others, Gabe is drawn to the Herzes's—Phonetically suggestive of "hurts"—suffering. He hopes both to allay their pain and to colour his somewhat pallid and drab existence with their intense emotions. When Libby confides her troubles to Gabe, he kisses her, and both recoil out of loyalty to Paul.

Shortly thereafter, Gabe has an affair with an entirely different sort of woman, the young divorcee and mother, Martha Reganhart. She is good-humoured, capable, warm and direct a foil to Libby. None the less, Martha cannot decide whether she wants a man who will help to support her two children or a playboy who will give her a taste of youthful freedom; her ambivalence drives Gabe and her apart. Even as they share a desire for emotional freedom, neither can escape a sense of i npropriety in having an affair in a home with children.

Much has been made of men's relationships to their fathers in *Letting Go*, but the novel might easily be read as an exposure of patriarchy from the perspective of daughters. Though we know Paul is a writer, we never learn what Libby's major career goals are. The only insight we get into her aspirations are from Paul's perspective.

For instance, as Libby dresses up for dinner with Paul's uncle, Paul inspects her with misgivings, "what he found [——] was something that bothered him, something that he could only think of as aspiration."[20] A victim of the "feminine mystique," Libby aspires to become an ornamental wife; pleasing others, especially Paul, and she is devastated when she fails to do so.

To win over Paul, his uncle and cousin, for example, Libby spends an exorbitant amount on an elegant hairdo. It works. Paul's cousin concludes, "She' s so charming, and so alive and so pretty. Her skin, her hair."[21] Paul is disturbed by the implications of her expensive and ostentatious display. He may have been attracted to her delicate beauty. Gabe Wallach notes her pale, translucent skin and the "tiny purple vein tapping at her temples; something there to remind the rest of us how delicate and fragile is a woman."[22]

But Paul knows he can't maintain such a woman. He's bothered by the thought, "now she was all his!"[23] After the dinner, Libby senses Paul's disapproval and discomfiture, and seeks to undo it by undoing her hair and tearfully apologizing and not only the expense but now the waste of eight—dollars on hairstyle:; "regretting not only the expense but now the waste of eight dollars."[24]

Libby mistakenly believes that if she succumbs and abases herself each time she displeases Paul, she will win back his approval and love; instead, she reveals her dependency, which Paul increasingly comes to see as a burden and liability. He wonders, "Trying to improve her had he only made a monkey of her?"[25]

Libby represents a traditional ideal of womanhood as ornamental, other centred, and her failure is not simply a result of her displacement to a poorer family but also of Paul's ambivalence toward the role of patriarch; unlike her father, he does not consistently want to play the role of patriarch.

In rejecting her appeal to him, Libby's father outlines his patriarchal expectations of his daughter:

> I can only reiterate that neither aid nor good wishes can be expected, now or in the days to come, from this quarter, Obligations are reciprocal, and when one party has failed another, the cessation of obligatory feelings from the injured can be designated with no word other than Justice; certainly with none of the words you suggest. My obligations, Mrs. Herz, are to sons and daughter, family and Church, Christ and country, and not to Jewish housewives in Detroit. [——] You have defied your father, your faith, and every law of decency, from the most sacred to the most ordinary.[26]

In fact, she loves Paul because he has "made a woman of her," and she uncritically accepts his proprietary attitude toward her. Paul believes he has "lifted her up from childhood with him"[27] and then confesses, " In courting her he had changed her, he had worked at changing her."[28]

Paul repudiates his Uncle Asher's *Playboy* view of woman as well as his Uncle Jerry's sentimental view, but after he marries Libby and moves to Detroit to build up their bank account he cannot quite transcend the proprietary view of his own father, who has pleaded with Paul to consider the expense of a sickly woman.

Paul rejects his father's language until he discovers Libby is pregnant. He wants her to have an abortion, but does not want to appear to force her:

> There are probably I don't know how many every day of the years Peo-ple like us, in our circumstances, unprepared for a child. There's no reason why we shouldn't at least inquire

> about a way out. I don't see why every rotten thing that falls our way has to be accepted. Don't you agree? You don't have to say a word, Lib. You don't have to say a thing. When we come out, you say no, that's fine with me. All right? Is that all right?[29]

Paul makes it clear that he views a baby as "a rotten thing" that will interfere with his plans to go graduate schools, but he wants to appear to give Libby a choice. Despite her desire to please, she is appalled at the idea of an abortion and argues that a baby could "be a pleasure for us."[30]

Paul's insincerity in giving Libby a choice is confirmed when they meet with the abortionist. Because abortions were illegal in the 1950s, the operation is risky for Libby, and the meeting takes place in an atmosphere of shame and secrecy.

Paul monopolises the discussion with the doctor who exclusively addresses Paul, referring to Libby only as "your wife" and recommending that "if you want let her stay off her feet the next day, and that's it. You have nothing to worry about."[31]

When Paul questions the cost of the abortion, the doctor reminds him: "You can find somebody for a hundred and fifty if you want to look down dark alleys. But this is your wife were dealing with. I should think you would want the best."[32]

Then the men shake hands to confirm the deal. Like Libby's father, Paul often sees his realationship to Libby in terms of contractual obligations and presumes the right to make decisions for her.

Like many victims of "feminine mystique," Libby is torn between her desire to be beautiful, charming and deferential, and her perception that she does not receive the traditional compensations for such a performance. Her husband fails to either protect or revere her.

She moves pathetically when the fatherly old man down the hall compliments her, "Oh, your're pretty as Levy says. A yiddisher maydele."[33]

She hasn't received such uninhibited and unusual adoration for years and urges Paul to help the man. When they move from Detroit to Iowa Chick, she responds to her dilemma by alternately reaching out to the wealthy Gabe Wallach and recoiling from the temptation he poses. She is thus impaled on the horns of a crude and cruel dilemma which eventually renders her vulnerable to schizophrenia and hysterical breakdown.

Gabe and Libby meet when Paul begins a master programme at the University of Iowa. Gabe is immediately drawn to Paul, both for his familiar Jewish background and his unfamiliar poverty. His response to Libby is more ambivalent—only when Libby shares the story of their misfortunes does Gabe fall in love with her. He wants to protect her, lends her his car, lifts her out of her abasement. Paul senses their mutual attraction and leaves them alone, thinking, "Libby. My Libby. Fuck my Libby. Take Libby. Take Libby away!"[34]

Paul no longer wants to be the patriarch; he wants Gabe to take on the responsibility of protecting the emotionally crippled Libby.

Libby believes: "Gabe can give her the life Paul can't. Gabe's father won't reject his only son for marrying a shiksa. Gabe can afford to provide eight-dollar hairdos, college tuition, and a running car." But in the most satisfying moment of their relationship, it is Gabe, not Libby, the two enjoy decorating. Gabe runs in to Libby as he's trying to find a "real man's hat"[35]

She laughs and they delight in choosing, not the manly, restrained fedora he had planned on but a homburg and extravagant items like "puce gloves," stockings and garters, and finally a "scarlet smoking jacket."[36]

Gabe is the feminized consumer, a turnabout permitting them to momentarily enjoy a fantasy. Libby yearns for the beautiful clothes that would win her praise at home and in a crowd. Gabe wants to satisfy her but can only do so by humiliating Paul. The scene ends with Libby tearing herself away. Then returning, touching "my new-our new gloves,"[37] and then imploring Gabe to contact Paul's parents.

When Gabe's mission with the parents fails, Libby becomes progressively more hysterical. She resembles many pre-feminist heroines in her inability to reconcile her ornamental role with the rude and raucous realities of her life as an adult and a worker. Lily Bart, the heroine of Edith Wharton's *House of Mirth,* falls from a high polite society to a working class life and, unable to imagine a "dingy" life for herself takes an overdose of sleeping pills. The unnamed narrator of Charlotte Perkings Gilman's "The Yellow wallpaper," cannot reconcile her understanding of herself as a deferential, spiritual woman with the sexual and physical realities of marriage and motherhood. She too falls a victim to bouts of weeping, sleeplessness and circuitous arguments with men who have little understanding of the conflicts she faces. So it is with Libby.

She feels "Indecent" and powerless to regain the affections or respect of her estranged husband. Her world is limited to her husband and Gabe. She is torn between the two conflicting loyalties and in turn gets disintegrated with a split personality. In one of the scenes in which she falls apart, Paul and Gabe pick her up at the office where she's a typist:

> Libby was hunched over the machine, wearing for all that the radiator was bubbling and steaming away across the room her polo coat and her red earmuffs; her face was scarlet and her hair was limp, and moving in and out of her mouth was the end of handkerchief, upon which she was chewing. Stencils were strewn over the desk and wadded on the floor, and from her throat came a noise so strange and eerie that it struck me as prehistoric, the noise of an adult who knows no words. Yearning and misery and impotence—She was like something in a cage or a cell——.[38]

She is a pathetic victim of emotional dichotomy, disintegration of personality and torments. This misery she cannot express in words. Paul has repeatedly berated her for "complaining" which leads to her physical breakdown. Unlike Paul, the writer, Libby cannot even copy the words of others correctly. A hysteric, she has lost the power of ventilating her emotional suffering in words, and so her body speaks it through her symptoms, which range from uncontrollable weeping to lethargy to mysterious fevers. Searching for a way out of her suffering, for some means of demonstrating her value, she says, "Oh I want a baby or something. I want a dog or a TV. Paulie, I can't do anything."[39] Recognizing motherhood as the traditional vocation for woman, Paul and Gabe eagerly latch on to her vague request as a panacea. Because Libby's health doesn't allow her to have children, they eagerly search for a baby to adopt, never considering the possibility that she will be no more capable of raising a child than typing a stencil.

Ironically, Gabe should be sceptical of motherhood as a recipe for Libby's unhappiness, for it is Martha Reaganhart's role as a 1950s mother that thwarts her plans for self-actualization. But Gabe initially cannot see this because of his own pleasure in being mothered by Martha. If Libby calls forth Gabe's urge to be a patriarchal protector, Martha calls forth his desire to be his mother's little boy. He is initially attracted to Martha as a straight talking, confident, lusty woman. She has little tolerance for the pretensions of his English department colleagues, and she manages to support her two children on a waitress's salary through clever management and extraordinary energy. Gabe calls her a supermom. He calls on her, Thanksgiving Day when on his widowed father first introduces him to Faye, the father's new fiancée. Smarting under his sense of being orphaned, he seeks comfort from Martha and confesses, "Strangely, I found myself wanting to believe that I had some rights to her total concern and attention."[40]

His relationship with Martha takes a more serious turn when he falls ill and she lavishes attention upon him. While he is recovering in bed, he fondly recalls childhood illnesses:

> I lay in bed, listening to the radio, and choosing from amongst those offered me only the most ancient of programs. [-----] Yes, there harassing the air-waves were those same luckless couples who had struggled through my childhood for then too a radio had glowed beside my convalescent's bed and who turned out to be struggling still. And recovering from a minor ailment, I discovered [-----] it was all as cocoonish and heartwarming on the south side of Chicago as it had been fifteen years before on the west side of New York.[41]

Enjoying his role as a favourite child, Gabe decides to move into Martha's apartment. But the relationship deteriorates as he comes to expect Martha to keep house as his mother did (her medicine chest and closets, he says, are "shameful") and as Martha increasingly expects him to pick up household expenses. Both value traditional gender roles even as they chafe under the restrictions implied by them.

Although Gabe ultimately does not want to be father to Martha's children, he does want her to continue being defined by her motherhood. She explains to Gabe why she's willing to give her ex-husband the custody of her children. She has longed to go back to college and has spent many afternoons watching the activity on campus with her young son in town.

"Then I got ashamed and picked myself up and went off to the playground where I belonged. But I don't have too much love for that playground, I've got to admit it."[42]

Martha wants what Gabe has, a career and the freedom to come and go as an unencumbered adult. Once her husband has the kids, she leaves her job as a waitress on the night shift, takes an office job, and resumes coursework toward her undergraduate degree.

But she changes her focus at the cost of Gabe. She rightly recognizes that in allowing her husband custody of the children she has sacrificed Gabe's respect. More than that, she feels disappointed in herself and breaks up with Gabe. When her youngest child dies in her husband's custody, she gives up the large apartment she had shared with her children and moves in to a boarding house as a kind of penance, represented by the spare meal of raw carrots and the neat closet Gabe sees when he visits her.

Even while Martha sees through the cultural mystique surrounding the role of housewife and mother, she sees that her only alternative, from Gabe's perspective and her own, is to be the cold, selfish career woman and she likes this even less. Martha takes up again with the lawyer Sid Jaffe, a venerable family man who is too conventional for Martha to passionately love, but who, Martha says, promises to "get me my baby back."[43]

Martha sees little possibility of "having it all" and chooses the well-travelled road of motherhood over that of career woman. Although Roth draws poignant pictures of two women dissatisfied with the "pleasures" their culture insists women derive from an exclusive focus on husbands, children, and housekeeping, neither find a successful alternative. Libby fails to visualise one and desperately throws herself into the role of devout Jewish mother to demonstrate her "decency." Martha, as clear headed as ever, settles for middle class propriety with Sid Jaffe over self-censorship and social disapproval. The woman's failure is by no means the man's success. Paul is nearly crushed by Libby's demands and her dependence on him. Gabe enjoys

Martha's irreverence and intelligence but still wants the services of a far more domestic woman. In neither case do the men fully embrace the patriarchal roles they have nevertheless chosen.

Thus *Letting Go* is a Jamesian realistic work that explores many of the societal and ethical issues of the 1950s. In this novel, Roth portrays the moral dilemmas of young people cast precipitously into adulthood and in the process describes a skein of social and family responsibilities as they are brought into focus by issues of marriage, abortion, adoption, friendship and career. The novel's expansiveness provides a wide scope for Roth's gift for vivid characterization and psychological analysis and, in his protagonist Gabe Wallach, he creates a nuanced portrait of a responsive young academic whose sense of morality draws him into the ordeals of others with unforeseen consequences.

Thus *Letting Go* is young Philip Roth's first attempt at a big, serious novel in the mode of Henry James. Written in a self-consciously literary and earnest style that Roth was later to discard, he explores the psyche of three characters: Gabe Wallach (a young Jewish Literary intellectual from the east coast; in other words, a stand in for Roth), the struggling writer Paul Herz and Paul's troubled wife Libby. It is somewhat of an academic novel, as most of the story takes place first at the University of Iowa and later at the University of Chicago (two schools at which, Roth, like Gabe, spends time as an instructor). But the university settings are really a minor backdrop for the troubled and rather incestuous relationships that develop amongst these three primary and a large assortment of secondary characters and psychological tensions, paradoxes and dichotomies that ensue from these tortuous complex interactions.

Although Roth's style was to change and evolve rather dramatically over the years, in this first novel, we see several themes and motifs that ramify throughout his career. These include:

> The autobiographical narrator, a precursor of Nathan Zukerman and David Kapesh, who serves as a prism through which we see the larger events of the novel. A troubled relationship with a parent—in this case his father, who is widowed and lonely back in New York. Romantic difficulties with emotionally unstable women, resulting in

> horrific arguments. Ambivalence about his Jewish heritage marked by a desire to both please his family and establish his own identity.

Of Roth's early work, Saul Bellow says:

> Unlike those of us who came howling into the world, blind and bald, Mr. Roth appears with nails, hair and teeth, speaking coherently. At twenty-six he is skillful, witty and energetic and performs like a virtuoso. [44]

Bellow was commenting specially on *Goodbye, Columbus* and Five Short stories, but his words are equally applicable to *Letting Go*. As much growth as we see in the phenomenal growth of Roth's work over the past 40 plus years, it is easy to forget that he has retained a remarkably high level of artistic quality and psychological acumen right from the start. In fact, since turning 60, an age when most renowned writers start having trouble, Roth has written, arguably, four of his finest novels.

When She was Good is the trenchant portrait of Lucy Nelson, a young midwestern woman whose perception of her own suffering turns her into a ferocious force, "enemy-ridden and unforgivingly defiant", as Roth would later describe her.

In this mesmerizing, funny, chilling novel, the setting is a small town in the 1940s midwest; the subject is the heart of a wounded, lacerated and truculently moralistic young woman, whose "goodness" is a terrible disease.

When she was still a child Lucy Nelson had her alcoholic father thrown in jail. Ever since she has been trying to reform the men around her, even if that ultimately means destroying herself in the process. With his unerring portraits of Lucy and her helpless, childlike husband, Roy, Roth has created an uncompromising work of fictional realism, a version of provincial American piety, yearning and discontent that is at once callous and compassionate.

Willard, the grandfather of Lucy, wants only civilization, "Not to be rich, not to be famous, not to be mighty, not even to be happy, but to be civilized that was the dream of his life". His own father was a fierce and ignorant man, a trapper, a lumberman and at the end of his life, a watchman at the iron mines. His mother was a hardworking woman with a slavish nature. When Willard was seven, his sister Ginny was one. Willard's father was very cruel to Ginny. She lived with her parents until the end of her mother's life. At the age of 18, Willard had decided to go on journey out into the civilized world. He went to liberty centre and became a postal clerk there. Willard's son-in-law Whitney is a good-for-nothing fellow who does not settle himself in any job; rather his wife Myra gives piano lessons to students. Bertha, the wife of Carroll, takes care of the four persons at home.

Now the quarrel starts between Myra and Whitney who is alive eating Willard's food. In fact, Whitney loves Myra, adores her and adulates her-, of which he does not articulate to Myra. When Lucy was a child she called up the police to take him away, but her grandparents were angry at her:

> We are civilized people in this house and there are some things we do not do and that is number one. We are able to settle out own arguments and conduct out own affairs and we don't require the police to do it for us.[45]

Lucy's parents don't act like parents. Her father is a drunkard who always keeps on running away from his liabilities and responsibilities. But Lucy makes a whole household into a public scandal. Whitney wants her to be a college graduate, but she wants to marry Roy, because she is pregnant with his child at eighteen. She goes ahead and marries the wrong person for the wrong reason.

Whitney is used to hitting Myra with a belt. Lucy comes to know of it and asks her mother to protect herself before he kills her. According to her, Whitney is beyond hope, beyond everything, an incorrigible and irreclaimable fellow. Whitney watches his pregnant eighteen-years old daughter driving shut the bolt against his entering into the house.

When young Roy Bassart comes out of service in the summer of 1948, he does not know what to do with his future. In the army, Roy had developed an interest in drawing and he wants to become a professional artist. He is under the influence of Uncle Julian. His mother and his aunt Irene are sisters. He has also an interest in poetry.

> The water is like time itself,
> Running... Running...

The water is like time itself,
Flowing... flowing...[46]

Roy's usual interest in girls run to the ones who are a little more serious and sedate about things. Bev Collision has more and less been his private property during the senior year and is now a junior in elementary post at the University of Minnesota.

He has always respected her a lot. Actually it is because of his respect for her that he has never tried to make her go all the way. Although he tries his best to have sexual intercourse with her, yet she does not acquiesce to him.

The cheerleader Roy is somewhat interested in a girl named Mary Little Field though everybody calls her Monkey. She is only a junior who Roy thinks, is probably too young for him now. Roy loves adventures; he would never be satisfied unless he is doing something creative.

Over the years Myra, Lucy's mother, has somehow managed to save two thousand dollars for Lucy's education; plus Lucy's own eleven hundred dollars in savings, plus the living aid scholarship. But Lucy is against accepting the money not only because it would continue to bind her to home but because she knows how it has been paid out to her mother. When she was small, she told her friends that it was actually her grandparents who lived with them in their house and not the other way around. From the age of ten, she had no friend in whom she could confide. Not even Kitty Egan; whom she discovered in her second year of high school and who for four months was as intimate a companion as Lucy had ever had. Kitty's older sister Angelica called "Saint Teresa's little way of spiritual childhood". So Lucy dedicates herself to a life of submission, humility, silence and suffering until the night her father pulls down th shade and upends the pan of water in which her mother is soaking her beautiful fret feet. After calling upon Saint Teresa of Lassie and Our Lord and getting no reply she calls the police. Now she starts hating suffering as much as she hates those who make her suffer. She has nothing to confess to father Damroch:

People can call me all the names they want—I don't care!

I have nothing to confess, because I am right and they are wrong and I will not be destroyed![47]

Then Lucy becomes a perfect part of the band of Mr. Valero, but she has to leave the band because her college starts: oh how she would miss the band! How she would miss Mr. Valero!

Roy is going to be twenty-one. What is Roy going to become? An artist? A businessman? Or is he going to ship out and really give Sweden a chance? Lucy and Roy now fall in love. He calls her 'Angel'. He takes Lucy into his confidence and goes all the way with her. A week before Lucy's graduation the news arrives that Roy had been accepted at the Britannia School of Photography and Design. Truthfully there are a lot of important ways in which she is discovering that she does n't like Roy that much. She simply cannot bear him when he sings songs into her ear. He is so childish sometimes, even if he is twenty-one.

After graduation she begins her summer schedule at the Daily Bar. Then one day they have the worst argument they have ever had with each other. It is about the place in Fortkean where Roy has to live, she still thinks that he is a little coarse with his language.

Lucy's personal education goals are to develop a logical mind, self-discipline, increase her general fund of knowledge, learn more about the world we live in and learn more about herself. Lucy does not like Roy talking about her parents, Whitey and Myra. Ellie, Roy's cousin comes to know the secret of her father, Mr.Sowerby, his fickleness which she shares with Lucy but does not let her mother know.

Originally, Lucy could not stand to watch Roy smoke a cigar or drink a beer. Ellie admires Lucy's courage, her pride, her strength. Lucy and Roy drive down with a cartful of luggage to begin their schooling in Fort-Kean. There Lucy learns that she is pregnant. She goes to a doctor for abortion, but the doctor refuses to oblige. She tells him:

> He (Roy) says things, but he does not even know what! Doctor--please, you are right I don't want to marry him. I don't want to lie to you. I hate liars and I don't lie and what's the truth![48]

First Roy procrastinates the matter of marriage, then he decides to marry her. Lucy has to marry him against her real wishes because something is happening which she is helpless to stop!

Something is growing inside her body and without her permission.

> I don't want to marry him.[49]

> She didn't want to marry him! He was the last person in the world she would ever want to marry![50]

She does not want to live Myra's life again—submission and silent suffering. Finally, Roy and Lucy are married. To her surprise hardly a Sunday passes when they do not travel up to Liberty Centre to visit his family. One day she gets the news that her father had blackened her mother's eye. Then she swears to herself that her child will never know what life is like in a fatherless house. She will not repeat her mother's life nor will her offspring repeat.

They have now undergone six months of marriage marked by happiness and harmony. All the premarital uncertainty have ended. Then Edward is born—a pale little baby with blue eyes and white hair with the sweetest, mildest and most severe disposition. Just before Edward's first birthday, uncle Julian hires Roy to come up to the house to take the pictures at Ellie's painting party. The next day Roy begins to talk about leaving his job and opening a studio of his own. He actually gives the order of his own studio's visiting cards without opening it. She asks "When are you going to grow up?"[51]

He talks to her of temporary separation so they both calm down. When they do quarrel, Edward locks himself up in the bathroom, sitting under the washbasin, holding a washcloth over his face. He sobs hysterically. She wants Roy to understand that his behaviour is disturbing Edward's mental peace. Roy realizes:

> She was the most important person in his life, now as always. She was so strong, so good. She was probably one of the most incredible girls for her age there had ever been. He wanted her to know that it was her courage in the face of her father's behavior that he had always admired. She knew right from wrong. There was none in the world like her. He felt privileged and honored to be her husband.[52]

He also admits that the idea of separation is not his, but his uncle's. But hardly after a week, Roy leaves the job of Hopkins and Mr.Sowerby's lawyer telephones Lucy saying that he is representing Roy for getting a divorce from her.

But Roy comes back and now he decides to start anew with a clean state. She says she will not forgive him unless he promises never to speak to Julian Somersby again as long as he lives. Then she tells Roy what Ellie has overheard her father talking the telephone. Lucy sees him pretending now nearly all the time, so as to avoid the clashes that have recurred almost weekly after the first six months of the marriage. Even since the disappearance of her husband, Myra starts aging, there are Sundays when she seems less a woman in her early forties than a woman into her sixties. Lucy disdains her father, she is not worth a moment of her thought, of her pity.

On Christmas Eve, when three years have elapsed since Whitney had forsaken Myra, Blanched Muller asks Myra to divorce her husband on the ground of desertion and become his wife. Lucy's mother hasn't yet given Mr. Muller a definite answer to his proposal.

One night, Roy conveys to Lucy his desire to have a little girl, Linda Sue. In that deep winter silence, listening to what he had said, she thinks that, maybe, at long last he isn't mouthing words for the sole purpose of pleasing. He seems not to be pretending. She finds authenticity in his voice. She feels that he is expressing a genuine feeling, a real desire. In the next few weeks Roy does not mention Linda Sue again.

Lucy is pregnant again with her second child, but she does not break the news out even to Roy. She thinks that Roy is no longer childish and irresponsible, no longer feigning. Thanks to her influence he is now a changed man. But suddenly her ill luck again overtakes her when she comes to know that Whitney is back in jail on the charge of theft. At this Myra says to her:

> He's where you always wanted him to be.[53]
>
> She became mentally disturbed: "I will not be accused, I will not be held responsible."[54]

In such a disturbed state of mind, she again quarrels with Roy:

> You worm! Don't you have any guts at all? Can't you stand on your own two feet eve? You leech! You Sponge! You'll never change![55]

Then Roy takes Edward to Sowerbys and tells Lucy that now Eddie hates her like poison. She wants to have her family back in Fortkean but no one helps her—not even Daddy Will. She goes to Sowerbys but they all prevent her from meeting Roy and Edward, her husband who should be protecting her, defending her, shielding her, guarding her but instead stands between her and her child, her and her home, between her and the life of a woman.

She always wants to make her father a father, her husband a husband but cannot do so. When she tells Roy about her pregnancy he calls her mad. She wants to bid goodbye to all protectors:

> You are no longer needed, you are no longer wanted—alas, you have been revealed what you are. Farewell, farewell, philanderers and friends, cowards and weaklings, cheaters and liars. Father and husbands, farewell![56]

And finally she dies. It is some months after the funeral that the letters from the prison begin to come directly to the house.

Sandwiched between his enormously successful collection of short stories, *Goodbye, Columbus*, and the critically acclaimed *Portnoy's Complaint*, *Letting Go* (1962) and *When She was Good* (1967) have drawn comparatively little attention because of their perceived failures. *Letting Go* Includes brilliant scenes but also appear somewhat ponderous and overwritten. *When She was Good* is written in a midwestern idiom that can seem lugubrious to readers who enjoy the verve and flamboyance of Roth's other works.

In fact, the novels represent a sustained, if ambivalent, engagement with the emerging woman's rights movement of the 1960s, the "second wave feminism" that began with Simone de Beavoir's *The Second Sex* (1949) and Battery Friedman's *The Feminine Mystique* (1963). Both novels develop forceful critiques of patriarchy that should delight feminist readers. But they don't. Even as his heroines overturn abusive, manipulative, or weak fathers and husbands, they emerge so damaged, so filled with angst, self-disgust, rage, and bitterness that they are even more crippled than the patriarchs they have defeated. Their inability to imagine a new community order makes their fight seem worse than futile; their struggles are so destructive that in the later novel the narrator leads the reader to feel relief in the humiliating and improbable demise of Roth's recalcitrant and defiant heroine.

The three heroines, Libby Herz, Martha Reganhart and Lucy Nelson are initially presented as victims of patriarchy. Libby's greatest aspiration is to please her husband by being beautiful and charming, expensive qualities for a middle class woman. Her consumer expectations and ill health put enormous pressure on her poorly paid husband and leave her feeling "useless". Martha frees herself from two men, her father and her husband, who abuse the women in their families, only to find her hard-won independence lonely, stressful, and unsatisfying. Despite Lucy's tirades against men, she consistently acts in a way as to force them to discharge their patriarchal "duty."

All the three free themselves from oppressive father figures and begin attending college, only to drop out and marry. All attach themselves to men pursuing their career ambitions, while the women languish in dead-end jobs or at home with children. All suffer from feelings of powerlessness and isolation. All are attracted to the "mystique of feminine fulfilment", the "pretty pictures of the picture of the American suburban housewife, kissing their station wagons of children at school, and smiling as they [run] the new electric waxer over the spotless kitchen floor". In *Letting Go*, Libby and Martha ultimately embrace this ideal, but Roth does not present their choices as recipes for their ennui. On the contrary, their decisions to devote themselves more fully to motherhood are depicted as compromises they make in the face of limited options. In the later novel, *When She was Good*, Lucy briefly rejects this ideal only to antagonize the men in the community so thoroughly that they doggedly and relentlessly pursue her through town in order to lock her up, and ultimately she freezes to death.

Martha Reaganhart of *Letting Go* and Lucy Nelson of *When She was Good* are as a single janus-faced character. Both are the daughters of alcoholic fathers. Both become pregnant in college, marry weak men, and have financially strained, failed marriages. Both bear a striking likeness to Roth's first wife, Martinson Williams, the "Maggie" to whom *Letting Go* was originally dedicated. Margaret was also the Gentile daughter of an alcoholic; she was a midwestern girl who leapt class barriers to take a few college classes before leaving the college to have children. All three women are working as waitresses when their future boyfriends/husbands meet them.

In *The Facts*, Roth's imaginative, masterly autobiography, he describes Margaret, whom he calls Josie, to mark his creative reconstruction of her as follows: "[S] he was actually a small town drunkard; angry daughter, a young woman already haunted by grim sexual memories and oppressed by an inextinguishable resentment over the injustice of her origins; hampered at every turn by her earliest mistakes and driven by fearsome need to bouts of desperate deviousness."[57] If Martha rises above her harrowing origins, neither Margaret nor Lucy Nelson, a character created after Roth's bitter separation from Margaret, could do so; both are depicted as women singularly lacking in self-awareness and overwhelmed by anger, resentment and desperation.

Roth and many of his critics have likened *When She was Good* to Gustave Flaubert's *Madame Bovary*. Both are the tales of women striving for an ill-defined, dimly sensed "something more." Both project their ambitions onto well-meaning but weak husbands who fail to satisfy them. Both lack the self-consciousness to realize the intrinsic irrationality of their demands and seem inevitably to meet tragic ends. However, Emma Bovary embodies an emerging consumer capitalist desire to achieve status through higher and higher levels of consumption. She is primarily an economic type, the insatiable consumer whose identity stems from how her possessions compare to those of others, Lucy, on the other hand, embodies the "ball breaker"[58], as Roy's Uncle Julian calls her. As such, she begins as a victim of a dysfunctional family and ends as a shrew and social pariah.

It is her grandfather's dignity, endurance, and solicitious compassion for the weaknesses in others that shapes Lucy's early home. "Daddy Will," as Lucy calls him, takes in his daughter Myra, son-in-law Whitey, and granddaughter, Lucy when Whitey loses his job. Over the next sixteen years Willard expects little from Whitey, who obliges by indulging in drinking bouts and losing every job Willard secures for him. In his caring solicitude for his son-in-law, Willard enables Whitey to remain a perpetual child and to humiliate Myra and Lucy. Lucy initially hopes to change the dynamics in her dysfunctional family by becoming the suffering martyr whose selflessness inspires others to similarly noble behaviour. Lucy's mother, Myra, has perfected this role. Willard reflects upon the effect Myra has had upon him. "Back when she was a child the very frailty of his daughter's bones could bring Willard almost to tears with awe[-----]. There were times when it seemed to him as though nothing in the world could so make a man want to do good in life as the sight of a daughter's thin little wrists and ankles."[59]

When Lucy tries to live upto this ideal, she discovers it to be utterly ineffective on her own father. Whitey returns home drunk one evening and sees Myra in the living room soaking her chronically aching feet. His feelings of guilt immediately threaten to overwhelm him and, instead of reforming himself, he deflects his anger away from himself and on to Myra Willard remembers: "Probably that Friday night he would at worst have weaved up the walk, thrown open the door, made some insane declaration, and dropped in to bed with his clothes on that and no more if circumstances, or fate, or whatever you wanted to call it, hadn't arranged for his first vision upon entering the house to be his wife Myra, soaking those fragile little feet of hers in a pan of water."[60]

Whitey is certain that Myra wields over him and also the neighbors. He storms over to Myra, grabs the pan of water and overturns it on the rug. He tells her she "might at least pull the shades down so that everybody who walked by didn't have to see what a suffering martyr she [is]."[61]

Lucy quickly sizes up the situation and tries first to pray to the Catholic martyr she has decided to emulate in life. Saint Teresa, as a Catholic nun, explains it to Lucy, "sought opportunities for humiliating herself" by "allowing herself to be unjustly rebuked" and "exercis[ing] charity in secret."[62]

But when this Catholic image of feminine submission does not stop her father's tirade, she calls the police. Henceforth Lucy discards her mother's and Saint Teresa's self-effacing form of feminine power.

Though her entire family is opposed to Lucy's confrontational form of power, she is increasingly convinced of not just the effectiveness but the virtue of her behaviour. She will not lie or compromise to protect others. Lucy understands her ability to see the worst in people as a virtue. Unlike her grandfather and her mother, she will not look the other way or make excuses for destructive actions.

However, Lucy's cynicism makes it impossible for her to have charity toward others. Her no-nonsense way attracts Roy Bassart, a young returning veteran, looking, whether he realizes it or not, for someone to tell him just what direction his life should take.

For her part, Lucy mistakenly sees him as the antithesis of her father. Roy has served in the military; her father had a medical waiver. Roy is looking for a girl with "a brain in her head"[63], not one with "thin little wrists and ankles."[64]

Roy is addicted to hydro cookies instead of whiskey. Yet he is as self-deceiving as Lucy and her father are. Although he waffles on whether he does indeed love Lucy, he insists she can "trust" him when he tries to undress her in his Car. He calls her his "angel," but accuses her of being a "c.t." when she refuses to have sex.[65] His shifting meanings, like her father's defensive accusations, make him extremely untrustworthy, and Lucy learns it the hard way. She cannot trust him to restrain himself, to keep her from becoming pregnant, or to marry her if she does. He coerces her into having sex and, predictably, she winds up pregnant during her first semester of college. She is not naïve; she is keenly aware of Roy's manipulations. It is her self-deceptions, rather naivete, that lead to her downfall.

Even as Lucy becomes more contemptuous of Roy, she enjoys being redefined as "Roy Bassart's girl" instead of her father's. Roy awakens in her a latent desire for social acceptance. She delights in being Roy's "Blondie" as his influential, outspoken Uncle Julian calls her. Though she plans to break up with Roy, she puts it off in favour of each new social event when she can bask in her new status.

Lucy also deceives herself when she recalls her first response to discovering she is pregnant. Though she later accuses Roy and her family of wanting to "Kill" the baby, she actively seeks an abortion as the only means by which she can escape her small town and her family. Her father, in his one moment of true effectiveness, offers to arrange an abortion for her, but her animus against him is stronger than her desire to escape her mother's life. She probes until she discovers that her father knows an abortionist because her mother has had an abortion. Appalled and outraged, she turns on her parents, "He degrades you Mother, and you let him! Always! All our lives!"[66] Suddenly, she persuades herself that abortion is no longer liberating, but degrading. She refuses the abortion and forces Roy to marry her. The novel's representation of Lucy shifts here.

This turns out to be a turning point. Hitherto Lucy has appeared as much a victim as a victimizer. But with this confrontation with and defeat of her father he goes on another long binge and eventually flees Liberty centre. She becomes increasingly tyrannical and self-absorbed. She loses the capacity to see herself or others in any other light except as static representations of male victimizers and female victims.

Roy's Uncle Julian is the novel's only character who actually comes up to Lucy's expectation of men; he admits to being a "beast," speaks incessantly of his "balls," and apparently has a pattern of hiring poor women at his Laundromats and making them his mistresses. He is the novel's only war hero and one of the most prosperous men in Liberty Center. Uncle Julian has the social and familial power of the patriarch and has no misgivings about wielding it to destroy his victims. Despite his lecherous ways, Lucy initially likes his direct, outspoken, blunt if vulgar manner. Here is a man who does not cover up unpleasant realities and who seems to like her, even single her out for praise, despite her family history. He initially seems to be the good patriarch Lucy desperately desires her own father to be. Soon she realizes that Uncle Julian sees her as another déclassé potential mistress. When he turns against her, he becomes the only man who can confront Lucy without wavering.

Roth stacks the deck by making Uncle Julian the protector of the hapless Roy and defenceless child Edward and by making Lucy irredeemably scornful. Lucy ridicules Roy's career ambitions and has no sympathy for his frustrations. She makes fun of him when he tells their young son stories of when he was in the service. She repeatedly and relentlessly berates and debunks him in Edward's presence, driving the child to flee from the room.

When Lucy learns that her father is in jail for embezzling, she is so enraged by her father's weakness and her family's compassion for him that she can barely contain her anger until getting home. She has not defeated her father; her mother and grandfather will forgive him and he will return. Instead of confiding in Roy, she turns her ire toward her father against him. She tears into her husband's body with such fervour that she feels her "organs will be torn loose", and Roy responds compassionately, even as he tries to protect the little boy. In this way, Lucy is depicted as such a monster of selfishness and Roy such a model of compassion that it becomes difficult to have any sympathy for Lucy's plight. Her foreshortened career, her family's shame, the oppressive gender dynamics of her community all seem to count for little against her pure destructiveness. As Roy tries to comfort and console her, she lashes out: "Oh, you're not a man, and you never will be, and you don't even care!"

She tries to hammer at his chest; first he pushes her hands down, then he protects himself with his forearms and elbows; then he just moves back, a step at a time.

> "Lucy, come on, now please we're not alone."
> But she ruthlessly and relentlessly chases him.
> "You're nothing! Less than nothing! Worse than nothing!"
> He grabs her two fists and utters:
> "Lucy. Get control. Stop, please."

And Lucy, in her madness speaks out:

> Get your hands off of me, Roy! Release me, Roy! Don't you dare attempt violence![67]

Lucy repeatedly uses her womanhood and motherhood to project herself as a victim and cast Roy, or anyone sympathetic to Roy, as a villain trying to deflower young girls, destroy babies, and undermine the sanctity of the family. If Roy obeys her, he is weak. If he doesn't he has fallen under the influence of others, especially his confrontational Uncle Julian and is again weak. If he defends himself, he is attacking her and is therefore a brute. If he doesn't defend himself, he is guilty of being unmanly. For Lucy, being a man is being a brute. So Roy has no positive identity to embrace. Because Lucy is so inconsistent and paradoxical as well as self-serving in her critique of patriarchy, she discredits and defies a feminist analysis of it.

In the final scene, Lucy returns to Liberty Center where Roy has taken Edward to escape her. Roy's Uncle Julian confronts her and physically intimidates her, but his wife, Irene, tries to defend Lucy.

Lucy is incapable of seeing women as potential allies, and she spurns Irene's sympathy just as she has misunderstood Irene's sympathetic position toward her throughout her marriage. Uncle Julian further alienates Lucy from the woman in the family by exposing her pose as "Saint Lucy":

> You busted his balls, and you funny now, let us see how funny it is going to strike you in the courtroom, because that is where I am dragging your ass, little mess when I get through with you, Saint Lucy.[68]

And who can blame Uncle Julian? Who doesn't want to checkmate Lucy and her self-serving delusions at this point? She spends the rest of the night calling Roy, his parents, and her own family, raving and raging about justice, motherhood, and her rights. Ultimately, her grandfather, the gentleman in love with Liberty Center's serene order, is joined by the police in their efforts to save Edward and Roy from Lucy's tantrums, which pose a veritable threat to peace and order. She flees in an ice storm and freezes to death.

Because Lucy is depicted in the last half of the novel as a "naturalist brute," a character type June Howard describes as "menacing and vulnerable Other incapable of acting as a self-conscious, Purposeful agent,"[69] she seems inexorably destined to meet a catastrophe, a tragic doom.

Roth himself calls Lucy's demise "Inescapable" and elaborates, "I simply didn't see how the disintegration of so enemy ridden and unforgivingly defiant, could lead, in that little town, to anything other than the madhouse or the grave."[70] Lucy's death is no accident, and she doesn't commit suicide in a fit of passion. She survives a day and a half in the snow before dying. It is a fantastic death, which is symbolically fitting but not probable. It leaves the characters in the novel, and likely many readers, feeling relieved.

Compared with Martha Reaganhart, who is drawn from a similar background, Lucy seems more a caricature than a character. She lacks the self-consciousness and capacity for feeling guilt that are the hallmarks of Roth's most finely drawn characters. Even Libby, who also descends into hysteria, has moments of clarity and repentance. Certainly, paranoid characters like Lucy can exist, but introducing Lucy at the moment when second-wave feminism emerged pitted Roth against early feminists. Lucy's fate would have been much different had she joined forces with her grandmother, who viewed Whitey and Myra in much the same way as Lucy did.

Similarly, Libby might have escaped the spiral of guilt and resentment that makes her and Paul so wretched had she confided in Paul's female colleagues rather than trying to charm and hobnob with his male counterparts. Roth's female characters seem trapped and acquiesce in undesirable compromises, in part, because Roth does not visualise the possibilities for female alliances they themselves probably would have entertained.

Thus Lucy Nelson presents a psychological study of a truculent, mercurial and furious adolescent who wants a decent life. She is presented as better than her world and is conscious of being so. She is constrained and arrayed against men who are deeply irritating types to many women. She is the protector of a passive, defenceless mother whose vulnerability drives her crazy. She happens to be raging and raving against several facets of middle class American life.

When She was Good deals with Lucy's frantic struggle to free herself from the terrible disappointment engendered in a daughter by an irresponsible father. It deals with her hatred of the father he was and her yearning for the father he couldn't be. Her husband is treated hostilely because he happens to be a big baby. This is a novel about a wounded daughter who has more than sufficient causes to be enraged with the men in her life. The dirty little secret is no longer sex; the dirty little secrets are contempt, hatred and rage. It's the tirade that's taboo. The nature of the anger is psychologically examined, as is the depth of the wound. So are the consequences of the scorn and anger for Lucy as for everyone else. In Roth, nearly all the women in the books are there to obstruct, or to help, or to console the male characters. There is the woman who cooks and consoles and is sane and calming, or the other kind of woman, the dangerous maniac, the obstructor. They occur as means of helping or obstructing Kapesh or Zukerman or Tarnopol. In these two critically neglected novels, Roth presents a painfully clear picture of woman's suffering in a patriarchal society, but offers no clear alternative to it.

Thus the two novels present the bruised battered psyche of a beleaguered female, her pathetic plight and tragic predicament.

Gabe Wallach wants to spend his whole life in giving pleasure to others and in the process he comes closer to the family of Paul and Libby. Although he tries his best to be morally sound yet he can't help kissing Libby in Paul's absence. Martha tries to possess all motherly qualities but she also yields to the carnal pleasure when she sleeps with Gabe and marries Sid. Lucy Nelson tries to reform the people around her but she herself gets pregnant before marriage. On the one hand, she tries to make her mother's life better but spoils her own because of her anger and short temper. Thus both the novels depict failed renunciation. They depict the psychology of repressed and driven characters. Roth has been charged that he does not extol virtues of courage, kindliness, responsibility. But in *When She was Good* the book begins with a significant sentence: it introduces the character of Willard Carroll, the grandfather in whose home the angry heroine is raised. "Not to be rich, not to be famous, not to be mighty, not even to be famous, but to be civilized—that was the dream of his life." The chapter then proceeds to enlarge Willard's idea of "civilization".

The novel reveals through a brief family history how he has been able to practice the virtues of courage, kindliness and responsibility. Only after Willard's way has been sufficiently explored does the focus of the novel turn in stages toward Lucy and her zeal for what she takes to be civilized life, what she understands courage to be and responsibility to mean and the place she assigns to kindliness in combat. The issue of authority over one's life is very much the crux of this novel. That a passion for freedom—chiefly from the bondage of heart-breaking past—plunges Lucy Nelson into a bondage more gruesome and ultimately insupportable is the pathetic and ugly irony which the novel reveals with telling effect.

References

1. Roth, Philip. *Letting Go,* New York: Random, 1962, pp.2-3.
2. Ibid., p.55.
3. Ibid., p.148.
4. Ibid., p.169.
5. Ibid., p.210.
6. Ibid., p.218.
7. Ibid., p.239.

8. Ibid., p.245.
9. Ibid., p.254.
10. Ibid., p.262.
11. Ibid., p.279.
12. Ibid.
13. Ibid.
14. Ibid., p.299.
15. Ibid., p.300.
16. Ibid., p.427.
17. Ibid., p.522.
18. Ibid., p.576.
19. Ibid., pp.2,3.
20. Ibid., p.94.
21. Ibid., p.95.
22. Ibid., p.97.
23. Ibid., p.94.
24. Ibid., p.98.
25. Ibid., p.97.
26. Ibid., p.141.
27. Ibid., p.94.
28. Ibid., p.97.
29. Ibid., p.123.
30. Ibid., p. 121.
31. Ibid., p.126.
32. Ibid.
33. Ibid., p.128.
34. Ibid., p.155.
35. Ibid., p.168.
36. Ibid.
37. Ibid., p.169.
38. Ibid., p.241.
39. Ibid., p.245.
40. Ibid., p.166.
41. Ibid., pp.270-271.
42. Ibid., p.387.
43. Ibid., p.576.
44. Quoted by Shymanik, Steve "Philip Roth—Welcome to the Canon". The New York Times: December 16, 2005.

45. Roth, Philip. *When She was Good,* New York: Random; 1967, p.22.
46. Ibid., p.52.
47. Ibid., p.83.
48. Ibid., p.141.
49. Ibid., p.166.
50. Ibid.
51. Ibid., p.206.
52. Ibid., p.211
53. Ibid., p.259.
54. Ibid., p.260.
55. Ibid., p.262.
56. Ibid., p.303.
57. Roth, Philip. *The Facts,* NewYork: Random, 1988, p.81.
58. Roth, Philip. *When She was Good,* op.cit., p. 277.
59. Ibid., p.17.
60. Ibid, p.18.
61. Ibid., p.19.
62. Ibid., p.80.
63. Ibid., p.95.
64. Ibid., p.17.
65. Ibid., p.106.
66. Ibid., p.185.
67. Ibid., p.262.
68. Ibid., pp. 277-278.
69. Ibid., p.104
70. Roth, Philip, *The Facts,* op.cut., pp.145-146.

2

Second Stage: Psychoanalytical Confession

Portnoy's Complaint which appeared two years after *When She was Good,* signifies a complete turnabout, "a break through" novel in which psychoanalysis makes its debut as both narrative setting and source of interpretations. Emotions that had formerly been held in check or isolated as symptoms are brought forward and articulated. It is a spectacularly Freudian novel, an uninhibited confession of masturbation, filial, impiety, failure in love, taboo violations of every minor sort and the presentation of guilt as the slapstick of the superego.

Portnoy's Complaint was Philip Roth's third novel. It is a story about a young man's search for freedom using forbidden sex as his way of escape. This book was found by many readers to be offensive and pornographic because of its protagonist's use of obscene language and sex scenes. The story records the intimate confessions of Alex Portnoy to his psychiatrist. Portnoy goes through his adolescent obsession with masturbation and his relationship with his over-possessive mother, Sophie.

Portnoy's Complaint refers to the damage done to him by the culture that has shaped him; although he is successful, his achievements are marred by a nagging sense of guilt. He finds himself on Dr. Speilvogel's couch, who tries to explore how and why he has become a sex maniac and moral obsessive in the hope of being cured. Instead Portnoy's narrative of past becomes the case history that serves as the evidential basis of a medical diagnosis. Speilvogel discovers Portnoy's complaint, and by doing so he has thereby authoritatively reduced Portnoy's experience into a category of neurosis. Speilvogel simply rewrites Portnoy's wild, comic ranting into a disorder in which strongly-felt ethical and altruistic impulses are perpetually warring with extreme sexual longings, often of perverse nature. Portnoy's approach to experience is often ironic and has the effect of a stand-up comedian's pattern.

A Jewish family and its values are held up to ridicule and, particularly, Roth's novel, *Portnoy's Complaint,* is the story of Alex Portnoy, a Jewish male with an oppressive, "Castrating" mother. As a boy, young Alex Portnoy nearly suffocates from parental expectations that he be the smartest, neatest and the best-behaved little boy in his school. His melodramatic mother, aspiring to impress gentile America with her perfect offspring, over-supervises him and turns minor infractions into major disappointments at times. For frustrating her, he is locked out of his home. Portnoy, in his adolescence, rebels against her mostly by indulging in acts of which she does not approve. Obscenity and masturbation become the primary ways in which he asserts his freedom.

As he grows older, these forms of rebellion persist. Often his transgression turns to guilt: "Why must the least deviation from respectable convention cause me such inner hell?...when I know better than the taboos!" Most of the times, however, he seems to find it surprisingly easy to transgress; the only obstacle to his freedom is his hesitation. After being treated to his first lobster dinner by his sister's boyfriend, Portnoy is tempted to masturbate on the darkened bus back to New Jersey with a gentile girl sitting beside him. The adult Portnoy, on second thoughts, speculates that when he was encouraged to violate the Jewish directory code by his mother, he was made vulnerable to taking sexual transgressions.

"The taboo so easily and simply broken, confidence may have been given to the whole slimy suicidal Dionysian side of my nature, the lesson may have been leached that to break law all you have to do is just go ahead and break it! Stop trembling and quaking and finding it unimaginable and beyond you: all you have to do is do it!". Not wanting to feel obedient and helpless also impels Portnoy to challenge the mainstream culture and this rebellion manifests itself sexually and revolves around his exclusive interest in Christian girls. If sex is exciting for Portnoy when it is secretive and "bad"–the antithesis of the moral goodness imbued in him by his parents–Sex with a "Shikse" is twice as arousing. It violates not only the Jewish community's expectations that he marries a Jew but also imposes his dirty will on the clear blond daughters of the gentle middle class; it asserts his arrival in the mainstream.

His speech is littered with obscenity and sexist language, and his relationship with women are self-serving. Women are merely objects through whom he might vent his anger and, as Irving Buchanan contends, "his sexuality is ... masturbatory sexuality employed to degrade, to revenge and to heap contempt on... women". Portnoy's impulse to degrade women is inextricably linked to his use of language. His obscenity reveals his sexual immaturity and pooh-poohs both the sex act he describes and the women he encounters. Indeed his reliance on "foul" language is meant to suggest a linguistic inadequacy that parallels his sexual inadequacy. As Robert Foray observes, the frustration born from Portnoy's "five hundred-word New Jersey vocabulary" is linked inextricably to the lack of sexual fulfilment that degenerates ultimately into impotence.

For all his shortcomings, Portnoy is an engaging figure in some respects. His narrative is amusing and the other characters in the novel seem extremely bland by comparison. As the book progresses, however, a more sinister dimension to Portnoy is revealed. For instance, his attempt near the end to force himself on the young Jewish woman, Naomi, is outrageous and unsettling. Portnoy's both social and verbal inadequacy is shown most powerfully at the close of the book with him, unreformed and impotent, shouting, "up societies ass". Finally, he abandons continent language altogether, terminating his narrative with howl.

Portnoy is an anti-hero; he is offered as an indictment of the self-obsessed male whose immaturity precludes meaningful relations with women. Ultimately, he is posited as morally and emotionally inferior to the females he meets. A dependency on obscenity is a compensation for the fact that his relationships are empty and meaningless.

Sex has become an obscenity because it is divorced from any kind of valid emotional life. Roth shows how 'foul' language becomes a kind of rhetoric compensation that struggles to fill the void at the heart of his characters' lives. Roth writes stories that are critical of their male protagonists and that offer implicit indictments of their language. They demonstrate, how men can be "unmanned"—rendered socially dysfunctional males—by their own sexist speech.

Gender politics is a crucial issue in contemporary American Jewish literature. One of the things that separate writers like Philip Roth from earlier American Jewish writers is the growing pressure to renegotiate relations between the sexes. A historical opposition between feminism and Judaism presents Roth with problems in so far as he wants to be both Jewish and a contemporary American. Roth's bad boy reputation with feminists is legendary. He wishes that feminist critics would discover that he dramatizes men's frailties rather than arguing for their superiority. He intends to show that men are "clay with aspirations". Roth uses anti-feminism to launch an attack on Judaism.

Finally, there is the transgressive quality of Portnoy's expressing his life in a "long complaint" or psychoanalytic confession which inadvertently and deliberately wounds and offends readers, who, like the author's parents, also over supervise their children. Roth's selection of the first person confessional monologue as the narrative form and viewpoint dramatizes his intention to unburden his psyche, despite the pain he'll cause to his parents, and the delight he'll provide to others like himself who are liberated, free-willing, and at odds with their religious and ethnic backgrounds. Roth repeatedly amazes, delights and shocks. At the peek of his masturbatory mischief, Portnoy tells us he has made use of a piece of liver before his mother prepared it.

After struggling for "several arduous year" with the "unfiery" style of *When She was Good,* Roth decided that "(i)t had been a long time between laughs" and that the needed to reignite his prose by writing "something freewheeling and funny."[1]

The genesis of Portnoy's complaint was long and complicated. It grew out of four unpublished pieces: a fiction called *The Jewboy* which, in Roth's words, "treated growing up in Newark as a species of folklore"; a play titled the nice jewish boy, which treated similar material more realistically; a scabrous scatological monologue in the form of a spoof lecture on the genitalia of various eminent men and women; and a "strongly autobiographical" novel with the working title 'Portrait of the Artist.'[2]

Incorporating elements of all these works, but within a framework (the psychoanalytic monologue) that enabled him legitimately, "to bring into my fiction the sort of intimate, shameful sexual detail (...) that in another fictional environment would have struck me as pornographic, exhibitionistic, and nothing but obscene," *Portnoy's Complaint* became an overnight publishing sensation and a bizarre cultural phenomenon, transforming Roth from a minor literary celebrity into the enfant terrible of American letters, the subject of media gossip, and chat show jokes.

It is difficult to summarize the plot of *Portnoy's Complaint,* because there isn't one (at least not in the traditional sense of the word). The novel consists of a long monologue (divided into six chapters, or sections) by Alexander Portnoy, apparently addressed to his psychoanalyst, Dr. Spielvogel. The first two sections, "The Most Unforgettable Character I've Ever Met." And "Whacking Off," vacillate between Portnoy's memories of childhood and adolescence, growing up in the predominantly Jewish neighbourhood of Weequahic, in Newark, New Jersey, and his mature reflections and recollections of his relationships with his overbearing mother and downtrodden father, representing Portnoy's adolescent discovery of masturbation as a king of rebellion from the suffocating family drama of his home life.

The third section of Portnoy's Complaint, "The Jewish Blues," elaborates and dwells on these themes of intergenerational conflict, focusing on the tension between the adolescent Portonoy's humanist secular convictions and the allegiance of his parents (and the community at large) to an idea of "the Jewish people". The fourth section, "Cunt Crazy," the longest of the novel, continues to mingle childhood memories with more recent history and Portnoy's retrospective interpretation of his past, but shifts the focus onto his sexuality, describing his compulsive adolescent masturbation in a series of hilarious vignettes.

The fifth section of Portnoy's Complaint, "The Most Prevalent form of Degradation in Erotic Life," concentrates on his adult sexual experiences with a succession of Gentile women, and the final section, "In Exile," revolves around Portnoy's encounter, in

Israel, with a feisty sabra (Israeli-born Jew) who resembles his mother in looks but whose contempt for "the culture of the Diaspora"—as personified by Portnoy—first infuriates and then emasculates him.

Portnoy's Complaint is in many ways a radical novel. Although its treatment of sexuality and use of obscenity might seem unexceptional and unexceptionable to a twenty-first century readership accustomed to erotic imagery in advertising, on television, and in the cinema (as well as in fiction and fine art), its candid, detailed discussion of orgasm was revolutionary in the late sixties, and its language was sufficiently and brutally explicit to ensure that it was banned from many public libraries in the United States. In form, too, the novel was innovative: instead of a conventional linear narrative, it proceeds through a series of "chunks of consciouess"; instead of a chronological plot, there are (apparently) random episodes, linked only by the associative movement of memory; instead of a sympathetic protagonist there is a neurotic, self-obsessed, self-dramatizing, possibly misogynistic, arguably misanthropic, compulsive masturbator; instead of dialogue there is monologue; instead of development there is stasis. In many ways, it resembles novels of stream of consciousness technique.

However, *Portnoy's Complaint* is also a highly literary novel in the great modernist tradition. Portnoy's long monologue is a (possibly spoken) version of the first-person stream of consciousness narration pioneered by wirters such as James Joyce and Virginia Woolf; his preoccupation with bodily functions is an extension of those exhibited by the narrators of Joyce's and D. H. Lawrence's fiction; his guilt and shame an echo of the morbid masochism of Franz Kafka; his comic neuroses inherited from the protagonists of Italo, Svevo and Gogol.

The particular form that Roth's novel takes, however, owes as much to Sigmund Freud as to any of Roth's literary predecessors. Roth was by no means the first American, or even the first Jewish American novelist, to draw on Freud's ideas. Whether positively, as in Henry Roth's *Call It Sleep* (1934), or negatively, as in the case of Jung's *Fear of Flying* (1973), the influence of Freud on postwar Jewish American Fiction is pervasive. Roth himself has already used psychoanalysis in his fiction in pervasive form. Before the publication of *Portnoy*, his first novel, *Letting Go,* features a lengthy description of Libby Herz's first session with her psychoanalyst, Dr. Lumin. The following year Roth published a short story, *The Psychoanalytic Express (1963),* in which the female protagonist, Ella Wittig, is in therapy with one Dr. Spielvogel (who was to reappear six years later as Portnoy's therapist). A year after the appearance of this story Saul Bellow, a writer whom Roth has always greatly admired (Roth's collection of essays, *Reading Myself and Others* is dedicated to him), referred implicitly and explicitly to Freud in his magnum opus, *Herzog (1964).* Apart from writing a letter to the founder of psychanalysis, Bellow's protagonist, Moses E. Herzog, begins the novel in a state of mental instability ("If I am out of my mind, it's all right with me, thought Moses Herzog"[3] is its famous opening line) and proceeds to recall, from a reclining position on a couch in his rural retreat in the Berkshires, the various events that contributed to his collapse. It is quite obvious that Roth's novel owes something to Bellow's, but the differences between them are as striking as the similarities.

Whereas *Herzog* is a third person narrative, focalized through its protagonist, *Portnoy's Complaint* is a first-person narrative, with no other voice to appear independently (i.e., not ventriloquized by Alex Portnoy himself) except that of his analyst in the final (punch) line of the novel: "Now vee may perhaps to begin. Yes?"[4]

Whereas Bellow takes from Freud the idea of a therapeutic confessional narrative, Roth actually frames his whole novel as a session (or perhaps the operating remakes or unspoken thoughts of the patients, prior to a session) of psychoanalysis. Moreover, Portnoy's attitude to Freud is profoundly ambivalent.

At times he seems to revere him: one of the chapters of the novel takes its title from one of Freud's essays ("The Most Prevalent Form of Degradation in Erotic Life") and features a detailed discussion of the theory articulated in the essay that:

> Certain men can only love women for whom they feel no sexual desire and can only experience sexual desire for women they cannot love...[5]

At other times, however, Portnoy comes close to blaming Freud for his predicament, accusing him of "trivializing complex human relationships and undermining human dignity."[6]

More than anything else, Portnoy uses Freudian ideas as a means of anticipating and deconstructing possible interpretations of his own behaviour. By explicitly drawing attention to the Freudian symbolism of many episodes in the novel, e.g., his mother threatening him with a knife when he won't finish his dinner; his late-descending testicle; breaking his leg while ice-skating in pursuit of the mythical girl of his dreams, whom he names Thereal Mccoy; his impotence when trying to rape Naomi, the Israeli soldier, Portnoy implicitly criticizes the tendency of psychoanalysis to incorporate all events into a phallocentric narrative.

Once Portnoy has preempted a Freudian reading of his psyche by presenting his narrative as a series of symbolic threats (like castration and emasculation) to his sexuality, such a reading loses its potency and immediately seems reductive and redundant. He is then able to present a counter narrative in which Freud is cast not as a sage or a shaman but as a "sadist (...) a quack and a lousy comedian."[7] This strategy—what spin doctors in the political context have called "getting in your retaliation first"—is not confined to the novel's treatment of psychoanalysis but extends to many other themes in the novel, most notably its representation of race and gender.

Apart from its obscenity, the aspect of *Portnoy's Complaint* that caused greatest controversy on its publication was its representation of Jewish identity. Roth had already received severe criticism from some sections of the Jewish American community for his satirical portraits of middle-class assimilated American Jewish boy in *Goodbye, Columbus* (particularly of the Patimkins in the title story of the collection). But this was as nothing compared to the storm provoked by the publication of *Portnoy's Complaint.* Besides being denounced by a series of indignant Rabbis, some of whom, as Irving Howe wryly remarked, "made a virtual career out of attacking his work", Roth also found himself vilified by many members of the Jewish American literary critical establishment as a self-hating Jew. Diana Trilling condemned what she saw as the novel's "grimly deterministic view of life."[8]

Disproportionate as the invective of Syrkin, Scholem, and Howe clearly was, it's not difficult to see why the book aroused such strong feeling. Portnoy's description of the strictures of his parents and their religion understandably outraged and enraged them. For example: "The hysteria and the superstition! The watch its and the be-carefuls (….) Oh, and the milchiks and the flaishks besides, all those meshuggeneh (crazy) rules and regulations on top of their own private craziness!"[9]

His portrait of Rabbi Warshow as a "Fat, pompous, impatient fraud, with an absolutely, grotesque superiority complex"[10], his invitation to "my people" to "stick your suffering heritage up your suffering ass"[11], his indignation at the "fucking Selfishness and Stupidity" of one Jewish mother (Mrs. Nimkin, whose son Ronalds commits suicide) and his accusation against all of them ("You Fucking Jewish Mothers are just too fucking much to bear!"[12] any one of these statements might have caused offence; cumulatively, they caused an furore. The identification of Roth with Portnoy underpinned much of the hostile criticism directed at the novel and its author.

The novel was often read as thinly veiled autobiography and Portnoy taken to be Roth's spokesman or surrogate. This viewpoint was the product both of naiveté (confessional novels are no necessarily any more autobiographical than science fiction or detective novels, they are simply another genre of fiction) and of selective reading.

Few of these critics noticed, or saw fit to mention, the fact that Roth has Naomi accuse Portnoy in the novel of being "nothing but a self hating Jew"[13], a charge given greater force by his sheer defeat in both physical and verbal conflict. Neither did they mention that there are moments of genuine tenderness in the novel, remembrances that are recalled not bitterly but nostalgically. When Portnoy recalls his mother describing the appearance of 'a real fall sky" to him when he was a young child, for example, he does so with "a rapturous, biting sense of loss."[14]

Moreover, the contempt for Jewish parochialism and dogma the *Portnoy* does exhibit is nothing as compared to his disdain for Christian ideology and iconography. As Portnoy himself puts it, "The Jews I despise for their narrow-mindedness, their self-righteousness (….) but when it comes to tawdriness and cheapness, to beliefs that would shame even a gorilla, you simply cannot top the goyim (non-Jews)."[15]

Although he berates his father for his "ignoran(ce) and barbari(sm)," when it comes to Christianity, Portnoy accepts his father's damning judgment: "you are never going to hear such a mishegoss (crazy lot) of mixed up crap and disgusting nonsense as the Christian religion in your entire life."[16] However, the novel implies that Jack Portnoy's views on Christianity are fuelled by resentment at the institutional anti semitism that severely limits his career prospects. Portnoy describes the insurance company which "exploited his father to the full" as "a billion dollar protestant outfit" whose president, with his crisp new England speech, "the sons in Harvard College and the daughters in finishing school," embodies all the smug privilege of a WASP establishment, part of a generation of American Jews for whom Jewishness seemed, if anything, more likely to facilitate than bar success. In spite of this, however, and in spite of his disapproval of the outrage, "the disgust inspired in my parents by the gentiles"[17] and his apparent attraction to Gentile women, Portnoy is actually more scathing about Christianity than he ever is about Judaism. Observing all the paraphernalia of Christmas, for example, he is moved to ask "How can they possible believe thesis shit?"[18]

Even when he seems to be most covetous of WASP characteristic, he turns out to be satirizing the very traits he is ostensibly professing to admire. As a boy, Portnoy is so awed by the sight of skating Gentile girls that his "circumcised Little dong is simply shriveled up with veneration"[19], and he dreams of dating one of those girls "whose older brothers are the engaging, good natured, confident, clean, swift and powerful halfbacks for the college football teams."[20] Yet as an adult he realises that "the secret to a shikse's heart (....) was not to pretend to be some hook-nosed variety of goy, as boring and vacuous as her own brother, but to be (...) whatever one was oneself (....) instead of doing some pathetic little Jewish imitation of one of those half dead, ice-cold shaygets pricks."[21] From an apparent object of envy "signified by the terms engaging, good natured, confident, clean, swift and powerful") the all American WASP college boy becomes the object of derision "(boring and vacuous (.....) half dead, ice cold shaygets pricks)." In fact, there is no real contradiction between the first description and the second: rather, the second set of terms makes clear that the first set, though apparently complimentary, actually constituted a coded indictment of their banality rather than a celebration of their prowess.

Just as in Jane Austen certain qualities, certain words, that would conventionally be regarded as terms of approbation are, in the context of her fiction, invariably signifiers of egoism and moral bankruptcy ("charm," "assurance," "ease," etc.), so in Philip Roth the word "good-natured," for example, is practically a synonym for "vacuous." Perhaps the finest, and funniest, example of this comes in the description of Portnoy's visit to the house of his first college girlfriend, Kay Campbell, for Thanksgiving. So painfully self-conscious is he (so anxious to ensure that he does not conform to any anti-semitic stereotypes that the Campbells might harbor) that "Whatever anybody say to me during my first twenty-four house in Iowa, I answer, 'Thank You'.[22] His (absurd) politeness is reciprocated and echoed by that of his hosts:

> Then there's an expression in English, "Good Morning," or so I have been told; the phrase has never been of any particular use to me. Why should it have been? At breakfast at home I am in fact known to the other boarders as "Mr. Sourball," and "The Crab." But suddenly, here in Iowa, in imitation of the local inhabitants, I am transformed into a veritable geyser of good mornings. That's all anybody around here knows how to say they feel the sunshine on their faces around, and it just sets off some sort of chemical reaction. Good morning! Good Morning! Good Morning! Sung to half a dozen different tunes! Next day all start asking each other if they had "a good night's sleep" (....) replies Mr. Campbell. And for the first time in my life I experience the full force of a simile (....) good morning, he says, and now it occurs to me that the word "morning" (....) refers specifically to the hours between eight A.M. and twelve noon.[23]

The passage begins as self-mockery (Portnoy's early morning irritability makes him the butt of the joke) but then modulates into mockery of the relentless good humour of the Campbells (good humour here, like good nature in the passage quoted above, connoting banality). Although it is funny, and a satirical reflection on his Jewish manners that Portnoy has never had occasion to use the phrase "good morning" prior to his visit to Iowa, it is even funnier, and a satirical reflection on the (Gentile) manners of the Campbells, that this is all they can think of saying to one another.

The comedy of the self-conscious Jew trying desperately not to offend his Gentile hosts becomes a parody of the platitudinous pleasantries repeated by the hosts and the tone of Portnoy's subsequent epiphanies ("for the first time (....) I experience the full force of a simile (....) now it occurs to me", etc.) is unmistakably ironic.

Sarah Abbot Maulsby, another of Portnoy's shikse, refuses to perform fellatio on him, Portnoy is convinced that this represents not simply a rejection of him personally but of his Jewishness.

"If I were some big blond goy in a pink riding suit and hundred dollar hunting boots, don't worry, she'd be down there eating me, of that I am sure!"[24]

The sexual aggression (sex as aggression, one might say) here is characteristic of Portnoy's relationships with women throughout the novel, and, like Roth's representation of Jews, his representation of women in the novel has been the subject of heated debate. On the face of it, there is much evidence in Portnoy's complaint to support the view that Roth is at best a sexist, at worst a misogynist.

Certainly, Portnoy's objectification of his girlfriends, as manifested most clearly in the nicknames he gives each one (Sarah Maulsby, as we have seen, becomes "The Pilgrim," Kay Campbell "The Pumpkin," and Mary Jane Reed "The Monkey"), is patronizing and demeaning. Portnoy's callous treatment of Mary Jane (leaving her in a suicidal state in a hotel in Athens, having engineered three in a bed scenario with a Roman prostitute), attempted rape of Naomi, and rejection of Kay and Sarah when they fail to sustain his sexual interest only seem to confirm this charge. Yet to condemn the novel in these terms is rather parochial, and possibly tendentious. First of all, Portnoy's contempt for women is arguably no greater than his contempt for men (and indeed perhaps milder than his contempt for himself). If Portnoy is a msogynist, then it might be argued that his misogyny is simply part of a larger misanthropy.

Porntoy's Complaint is a landmark novel, both in terms of Philip Roth's own career and in terms of the history of Jewish American fiction. Although Roth himself and his contemporaries, Saul Bellow and Bernard Malamud had been making inroads into the American literary critical establishment for more than a decade, no previous novel had put Jewish American fiction on the map in quite the way that "Portnoy's Complaint" did. And yet it did so by breaking the mould completely. Roth himself has attributed its popularity partly to the risque nature of the subject matter as he says: "That this shameful, solitary addiction (onanism) was described in graphic detail, and with gusto, must have done much to attract to the book an audience that previously had shown little interest in my writing and partly to the historical moment in which it was published. Without the distress and upheavals of the year 1968, coming as they did at the end of a decade that had been marked by blasphemous defiance of authority and loss of faith in public order. I doubt that a book like mine would have achieved such renown in 1969."[25]

Portnoy's Complaint represented a radical departure from the established tradition of Jewish American literarure not simply because it represented a sexually predatory Jew, a victimizer rather than a victim, but because it violated even more sacrosanct taboos. The second section of the novel, "The Jewish Blues," concludes with a conversation between the fourteen years old Portnoy and his sister, Hannah, in which she reminds him that if he had been born in Europe "you could have screamed all you wanted that your were not a jew, that you were a human being (....) and still you would have been taken away to be disposed of (by the Nazi)."[26]

In the final section of the novel, "In exile," Naomi tells Portnoy that it was the passivity and paranoia of Diaspora Jews—"Jews just like myself who had gone by the millions to the gas chambers without ever raising a hand against their persecutors"[27], as Portnoy puts it, that had enabled the Nazi genocide to take place. Whereas in the two previous decades, Bellow and Malamud had both published novels, *The Victim* (1947) and *The Assistant* (1957), respectively that dealt with anti-Semitism without any explicit reference to the events of the Second World War, Roth confronts two of the greatest sources of guilt in post-war Jewish life: the fact that American born Jews escaped, by accident of birth, the fate of their European brethren; and the fear that Jews might in some way have colluded with their persecutors by submitting without resistance to the systematic oppression that began with the enactment of the Nuremberg Law and ended with the death camps. Moreover, he implicitly rejects the implications of both these arguments that post war Jews have a moral duty to identify themselves with, and as, Jews as spurious justifications for the belligerence of Israel on the one hand and the defensiveness of American Jewry on the other. For all these reasons and because of its linguistic boldness and brio, *Portnoy's Complaint* revolutionized Jewish American fiction.

It also changed forever the course of Roth's career. Although Roth defended himself vigorously against the attacks of initial reviewers of the book, some of the criticism clearly stung him, particularly the volte-face performed by Irving Howe, formerly an admirer of Roth's, in his 1972 essay. For most of the 1970s Roth turned away from the explicit concern with Jewish identilty that had characterized *Portnoy's Complaint*, but with the publication of *The Ghost Writer* (1979) he began a remarkable sequence of novels that took as their subject the phenomenon of literary celebrity and notoriety in general, and in particular the predicament of a Jewish writer vilified by other Jews as a self-hating Jew. Although initially dismayed by aspects of both its popular and critical reception, arising from the fact that "a novel in the guise of confession [was (mis)read as] a confession in the guise of a novel,"[28] Roth went on to explore and exploit this confusion between reality and fantasy, fact and fiction. If *Portnoy's Complaint* was both the culmination of certain tradition of Jewish American fiction, and its death knell, it was a similarly pivotal moment in Roth's own career, firmly establishing him as one of the key figures in post-war American fiction and sowing the seeds for much of his later fiction.

Roth has been accused of creating distorted and demeaning portrayals of the Jewish American experience, and psyche and his work has also been assailed as tasteless and obscene. Ironically, two of his most accomplished books, *Goodbye, Columbus* and *Portnoy's Complaint*, have elicited the most hostile responses.

Roth has repeatedly asserted, however, that he views himself as neither a spokesperson nor an apologist for American Jews, but as an artist.

Portnoy's Complaint remains Roth's most controversial novel. Not surprisingly, it is this book which is most often cited when charges of anti-Semitism are brought against Roth. A compulsive masturbator and chronic whiner, Portnoy attributes the bulk of his difficulties to his background, and much of the novel consists of crude, slapstick versions of the Jewish experience. In addition, the book is unabashedly prurient, chronicling in explicit detail and uninhibited language the orgastic exploits of the protagonist, whose psychological problems are summarized in the ersatz encyclopaedia entry that prefaces the narrative:

> "Portnoy's Complaint" (Port noiz kem plant): A disorder in which strongly felt ethical and altruistic impulses are perpetually warring with extreme sexual longings, often of a perverse nature. Spielvogel says: Acts of exhibitionism, voyeurism, fetishism, auto eroticism and oral coitus are plentiful; as a consequence of the patient's "morality; " however, neither fantasy nor act issues in genuine sexual gratification, but rather in overriding feelings of shame and the dread of retribution, particularly in the form of castration."[29]

It is believed by Spielvogel that many of the symptoms can be traced to the bonds obtaining in the mother child relationship.

Perhaps most significantly, however, it reveals that beneath the surface of his extremely humorous work are concerns of a very serious nature. For all its hilariously irreverent comedy, the novel is presented as the record of a psychological "complaint." The narrative is a disjointed, stream of consciousness monologue delivered by analysed Portnoy on the couch of his listening psychiatrist, Dr. Spielvogel.

But the encyclopedia definition makes no reference to the fact that Portnoy ascribes his problems on his Jewishness and believes that he will achieve stability only by renouncing that heritage. He sees the Jewish cultural ethos as productive only of repression and neurotic self-abasement.

Porthoy is a character, not the image of Roth. *Portnoy's Complaint* depends for its very existence upon its author's perceptions of ethnicity. In this novel, however, the protagonist's ravings are for the most part entirely denunciatory of his heritage. And there are indications that Portnoy is, to some extent, a persona of Roth, that his strident denunciations constitute) (albeit in exaggerated form) a fictive expression of the author's feelings. Nevertheless, it would be wrong to interpret Portnoy's diatribes as totally reflective of Roth's attitudes, for he obviously intends

Portnoy as a psychological portrayal of an extremely unstable individual. Portnoy envisions himself as a typical Jewish male and repeatedly phrases his grievances in the first person plural, as in this passage: "Doctor Spielvogel, this is my life, my only life, and I'm living it in the middle of a Jewish Joke! I am the son in the Jewish Joke only it ain't no joke! Please, who crippled us like this? Who made us so morbid and hysterical and weak?"[30]

But Roth presents Portnoy neither as a representative Jew, nor as a representative man. Rather, Portnoy emerges not only as an uncommonly intelligent, perceptive and accomplished individual (he is New York City's Assistant Human Opportunity Commissioner under Mayor Lindsay), but also as an individual of uncommonly callous, self-obsessed, and disturbed psyche. Further, it is the sheer excessiveness of his situation most obviously exemplified by his prodigious feats of masturbation that makes his story worthy of book–length presentation.

In short, he is hardly the sort of character that Roth would be likely to choose as a self-projection. Roth has addressed this matter on several occasions, dismissing as naive and simplistic the too common practice of equating characters with their authors. The success of *Portnoy's Complaint* partially resulted from such misconstruction, and Roth has tried to correct such misconcoction spawned by *Portnoy's Complaint* and compounded largely out of the fantasies that it gave rise to because of its 'confessional' strategy.

It should be obvious that Alexander Portnoy is intended as a tragic figure; by the end of the novel he is thoroughly confused and desperate for any assistance that Spielvogel might be able to provide. He is, in sum, a very different person from the composed, self-assured, painstakingly rational individual who emerges in Roth's interviews and essays. Perhaps the temptation to view Portnoy as an authorial projection arises from a tendency to respond to the novel solely on the basis of its surface attractions: its antic humour, its witty reverence, and its seemingly "liberated" sexual candour. Despite his manic insouciance, however, Portnoy is a broken man.

Portnoy's psychological response to sexuality, and his correspondingly distorted dealings with women, illustrate most revealingly his basic inability to transcend the crippling limitations of an overriding self-centredness. In each of his affairs, Portnoy exploits the women. Even his habit of assigning depersonalizing titles to his lovers reveals that he views them not as individual human beings but simply as objects. Kay Campbell, Portnoy's college heartthrob, is called "The Pumpkin" not only because of her rotundity, but because to Portnoy she represents rural America, the agrarian midwest. Portnoy is fascinated by the gentile ambience of her home when he visits it for the Thanksgiving holiday, and initially feels that W.A.S.P. lifestyle is superior to his own. But the relationship disintegrates after she dismisses Portnoy's suggestion that she will convert to Judaism. That such an idea occurs to him so naturally reveals his basic confusion and the dichotomy of his psyche. He is at first attracted to Kay because she is not Jewish, but he ultimately rejects her for the same reason. This establishes a pattern that will remain constant in his other affairs as well.

Portnoy's adult relationship with the patrician Sarah Abbot Maulsby, a New Canaan Foxcroft Vassar alumma whom he calls "The Pilgrim,"is finally written off as "just something nice a son once did for his dad. A little vengeance on Mr. Lindabury for all those nights and Sundays Jack Portnoy spent collecting down in the colored district. A little bonus extracted from Boston & Northeastern, for all those years of service, and exploitation."[31] Again, what emerges is that Portnoy's desire for sexual conquest and his inability to love are linked to his Jewishness.

This aspect of Portnoy's situation is best illustrated by his tumultuous ten-month affair with Mary Jane Reed, whose wildly uninhibited sexual gusto earns her the appellation "The Monkey." The most fully rendered of 'Portnoy's lovers, she is a New York fashion model who has risen from "poor white" origins to captivate the sophisticated Commissioner Portnoy. Despite her pose of mean-spirited rural ignorance, in reality she is a rather intelligent and sensitive person, and is attracted to Portnoy because she sees in him the opportunity for a significant relationship. Her appeal for Portnoy, however, lies solely in her unbridled lasciviousness. She is the living embodiment of his adolescent sexual fantasies, "Thereal McCoy" incarnate, someone with whom to act out his wildest imaginings.

But he is unable to find happiness even with this "girl of his (erotic) dreams," precisely because he suddenly finds himself growing fond of her. After their idyllic weekend in Vermont during which the first stirrings of romantic love appears, Portnoy at once experiences doubts and misgivings.

After they talk of love, and Mary Jane rhapsodizes about marriage, Portnoy at once experiences doubts about marriage, He contrives to degrade the relationship in his own eyes. He induces her to participate in a ménage of trios with him and a prostitute, and then dismisses the whole affair as simply another sexual fling, devoid of any genuine feelings or abiding commitment.

To some extent, his problem can be seen as oedipal in nature. Sheldon Norman Grebstein has called the book "the most detailed account we have had of the tone and texture of the Jewish oedipal family experience." Portnoy is fairly obviously the victim of his mother's inadvertently overzealous and over-possessive (and over-seductive) affections. Consequently, he is unable to reconcile love and desire in later life because of his unconscious observance of the incest taboo. Sex becomes in his mind an evil and a means to subvert what he perceives as a too restrictive ethical system inculcated during his upbringing. In his attempt to free himself from the demanding rigours of the role of "nice Jewish boy," he turns first to excessive masturbation. Indeed, the innumerable madcap scenes chronicling his prodigious feats in this area of activity represent his frantic efforts of emancipation from the straitjacket of stereotyped Jewish priggishness.

Unfortunately for Portnoy, however, adult sexuality becomes simply an extension of this childhood compulsion. His sexual affairs with women serve much the same purpose as does his masturbation, becoming little more than a means of defying what he sees as a too restrictive cultural indoctrination. He tells Spielvogel that he wishes to "PUT THE ID BACK IN YID! Liberate this nice Jewish boy's libido"[32], for he naively believes that reticence and repression are exclusively Jewish phenomena:

> What else, I ask you, were all those prohibitive dietary rules and regulations all about to begin with, what else but to give us little Jewish children practice in being repressed? Practice, darling, practice, practice. Inhibition doesn't grow on trees, you know takes patience, and a hard working attentive little child to create in only a few years' time a really constrained and tight ass human being. Why else the two sets of dishes? Why else the kosher soap and salt? Why else, I ask you, but

> to remind us three times a day that life is boundaries and restrictions if it's anything, hunders of thousands of little rules laid down by none other than None Other...[33]

Although Portnoy's desire to lead a more spontaneous, uninhibited life is a worthy goal, the obsessive single-mindedness and ruthlessness with which he pursues sexual gratification as a means to that end renders his sex life ultimately unfulfilling and degraded. His objectification of his sex partners, further complicated by his oedipal confusions, results in neurosis.

Surely Portnoy's irrational behaviour makes him an "unreliable narrator." Hence all of his actions and statements are open to debate, and his denunciations of his ethnic background therefore lack credibility. As Patricia Meyer Spacks says in an excellent *Yale Review* essay, "Portnoy sees his own problems as products of his view. Indeed, they are invited to understand that the suffering and the comedy of Alexander Portnoy are the suffering and the comedy of modern man, who seeks and finds explanations for his plight but is unable to resolve it, whose understanding is as limited as his sense of possibility."[34] The essential difference between Portnoy's and Roth's opinions on Jewishness is a matter of focus and emphasis. The neurotic Portnoy, in typically egotistical and self-obsessed fashion, adopts a purely personal response, emitting a protracted diatribe that amounts to a renunciation of his ethnicity. But Roth's purpose in writing the novel was more broad ranging and certainly more constructive than that. In creating a Protagonist who has had particular experience of Jewish life, Roth presents a case that is extreme indeed; the book is finally about extremity, which, however, is believable. And in so doing, Roth is not himself renouncing the Jewish experience, but is merely criticizing what he believes it to have become in some cases. Portnoy, himself an exaggeration, rejects; Roth exaggerates to dissect.

Elsewhere, Roth's treatment of his characters' Jewishness is quite different. Often there is even a strong sense of ethnic pride, an almost celebratory quality that seems to validate his claim, "I have always been far more pleased by my good fortune in being born a Jew than my critics may begin to imagine." Works such as "I Always Wanted You to Admire My Fasting': Or Looking at Kafka," the "Salad Days" section of *My Life as a Man, The Breast, The Professor of Desire,* and others are obviously imbued with retrospective affection for the wholeheartedness of Jewish homelife, while earlier stories such as "Defender of the Faith" and "Eli, the Fanatic," despite the labels of anti-Semitism that have sometimes been applied to them, are clear-cut endorsements of the Jewish tradition.

As a Jewish American writer, Roth uses ethnicity as a framework or context within which to portray contemporary reality, and in his best works has done so with great skill.

Portnoy's Complaint (1969) is Philip Roth's fourth and still most popular novel with many of its salient characteristics, e.g., ribald, comedic, prose, themes of sexual desire and sexual frustration, a self-conscious literariness. Structurally, *Portnoy's Complaint* is a continuous monologue as narrated by its eponymous speaker, Alexander Portnoy, to his psychoanalyst, Dr. Spielvogel. This narration weaves effortlessly through time and describes scenes from each stage in Portnoy's life with every recollection in some way touching upon Portnoy's central dilemma—his inability to enjoy the fruits of his sexual escapades as his extreme libidinal urges force him to seek release in even more creative and, in his mind, degrading and shameful acts of eroticism. Roth is not subtle about defining this as the main theme of his book. On the first page of the novel one finds this clinical definition of "Portnoy's Complaint", as if, ripped from the pages of a manual on sexual dysfunction and its impact on the psyche of the sufferer: "Portnoy's Complaint": "A disorder in which strongly felt ethical and altruistic impulses are perpetually warring with extreme sexual longings, often of a perverse nature."[35]

Other topics touched on in the book include the assimilation experience of American Jews, their relationship to the Jews of Israel, and the pleasures and perils inherent in being the son of Jewish family.

Portnoy's Complaint, in addition to its purely literary status as a "comic masterpiece", is also emblematic of the time during which it was published. Most obviously, the book's sexual frankness was both a product of and an inspiration for the sexual revolution that was in full swing during the late 1960s.

And the book's narrative style, a huge departure from the stately, semi-Jamesian prose of Roth's earlier novels, has often been likened to the stand-up performances of the 60's comedian

Lenny Bruce. Portnoy is a great comic character who considers his mother the most unforgettable character he has met. He is his mother's favourite. He lives with his sister Hannah, and parents. His father is a clerk in insurance company and he often used to say:

> Alex, a man has got to have an umbrella for a rainy day. You don't have a wife and a child out in the rain without an umbrella![36]

His mother is a religious and sympathetic lady who lights candles for the dead, clears the weeds for the graves of her relatives. She sews, she knits, she darns, she irons. His mother used to frighten Alex with a knife when he was just six or seven year's old and his father would never stop her. He says to the doctor:

> Doctor, why, why, why oh why oh why does a mother pull a knife on her own son? I am six, seven years old, how do I know she really wouldn't use it?[37]

When he is not yet fourteen, he gets an incurable disease on his sexual organ. He has sexual craving from his adolescence. He spends much time in the bathroom masturbating.

Alex has affection for his mother. She was once a tall string bean of a girl whom the boys called 'Red' in high school. When Alex was nine and ten years old he had an absolute passion for her high school yearbook.

Sophie Ginsky, the boys call 'Red', She'll go far with her big brown eyes and her clever head. His mother is overconcerned about Alex. She irritates him by her question such as—"Why is your throat red? Do you have a headache you are not telling me about?" I am not going to allow you to go outside in this head and run around? His parents are filled with such a fearful sense of life. Alex says to Doctor:

> These people are incredible! These people are unbelievable. Doctor Spielvogel, this is my life, my only life, and I am living it in the middle of the Jewish joke! I am the son in the Jewish joke.[38]

He has inveterate sexual craving but feels frustrated sexually as he says:

> Why, alone on my bed in New York, why am I still hopelessly beating my meat? Doctor, what do you call this sickness I have? Is this the Jewish suffering I used to hear so much about? Bless me with manhood! Make me brave! Make me strong! Make me whole![39]

When he is just nine years old he suffers from impotency as he says: "There is a nine year old boy in New Jersey who is a boy in every way, except he can have babies."[40]

The mother image is always in his mind. The mother-shadow always follows him wherever he goes. He gets attracted to Christian females. One of them is Alice. He also has inferiority complex of being a Jew but he doesn't show it.

> "We were Jews—and we were not ashamed to say it!"[41]

Once his mother gets admitted in hospital because something is glowing in her uterus. The whole family gets disturbed but the mother has really a lot of affection for her son. She can even give him the food out of her mouth. She often asks, "Will you leave me, my baby boy, will you ever leave Mommy?"[42] She is an affectionate, domineering and possessive mother. She forbids him to eat lobster as she says: "There are plenty of good things to eat in the world, Alex, without eating anything like a lobster and running the risk of having paralyzed hands for the rest of your life."[43]

In New York, everybody starts questioning, when Alexander Portnoy is going to stop being selfish and give his parents, who are such wonderful people, grandchildren. Alex says that he cannot make his parents grandparents while everybody else has been marrying nice Jewish gir.. and having children and buying houses, while all the other sons have been carrying forward the family name.

But Alex is thirty-three years old and still he cannot control the fires in his being, the fevers in his brain, the desire continually burning within for the new, the wild, the unthought-of, the undreamt-of. But he can't marry because he simply will not enter into a contract to sleep with just one woman for the rest of his life.

He cannot control his urge for promiscuity and so he cannot remain bound to only one woman, i.e. his wife. He cannot face his wife's terrible tears who will suffer her loneliness and rejection. His parents are in a hurry to get their boy married because they say, "Who is there even to bring you a bowl of soup?"[44]

Now, he is thirty-three. He is the Assistant Commissioner for Human Opportunity for the city of New York! He graduates first in his law school class. At twenty-five, he was already special counsel to a Home Sub-Committee of the United States Congress. He is a highly respected man in his profession. He is conducting an investigation of unlawful discriminatory practices among the building traders in New York. Now he is going away from his family for a month. He wants to be free from the exile of living with his family. In fact, he does not want to give the information of his address in Europe to his family.

In New York, Alex gets involved in a sexual relationship with Monkey non-seriously but the girl starts loving him and later we find that she also tries to commit suicide. She has great expectation from Alex as she says:

> To you I'm just another her, any way! And all I am in your eyes is just a cunt—and a lesbian! And a whore! I want a child too! And a home! And a husband! I am not a lesbian! I am not a whore![45]

Alex knows his psychic urges very well. He cannot live and satisfy himself with one woman only. So when Monkey threatens to jump from the balcony unless he marries her, he leaves.

In Europe, he meets Shikses. He loves skating with Shikses. In fact, he never reveals his identity as a Jew to them nor does he reveal his real name as Portnoy which is an old French name, a corruption of Portenoir, meaning black door or gate. He also remembers a number of girls whom he knows and one of them is Thereal McCoy—Miss America—in her blue parka. Her parents are patient and dignified and her brother Billy knows how to take motors apart. Alex loves to be in McCoy's company. Meantime he keeps rememberin g Monkey who tried to injure herself by making a pass at her wrists with a razor on account of the way her current boyfriend treated her. She wants to marry but no one is seriously in love with her. So she has also to consult a psychiatrist.

Alex's case is very serious. Professionally, he has settled himself very well. He is a Jew who cares about the welfare of the poor of the city of New York. But he has also deep-rooted sexual desire and also frustration. He is a obsessed with cunt. He is a Jew, but he scorns Jews for their narrow-mindedness and their self-righteousness. He always dreamed to be baseball star. He has no faith in religion. Religion is the opiate of the people. He likes to be rather a communist in Russia than being a Jew in a synagogue. He believes in the rights of man regardless of race, religion or colour.

Monkey's reminiscences always keep on haunting and pricking his mind—how they spent time in Vermont away from New York; how they used to indulge in sex and lovemaking, how once she expressed her love for him.

"Oh, I think I love you, Alex, I really think I do, Oh, but a lot of good that's going to do me!"[46]

But Portnoy cannot marry her. He cannot bring a whore (Chippy) to his home. He has spent his whole adult life protecting the rights of the defencelss for five years. He was with the ACLU, fighting the good fights for practically nothing. Now he is Assistant Commissioner of Human Opportunity, preparing a special report on bias in the building trades. Such a step will harm her dignity as a public servant.

Monkey really loves him. She expresses her ardent love to him:

> "Alex! I open the door at night, I'm so dying to see you, thinking all day long about nothing but you." But Alex wanted to tell her, "May be then this is not a love affair. May be it's what's called a mistake. May be we should just go our different ways, with no hard feelings."[47]

But he cannot say so because she might commit suicide. She has tried to throw herself out the rear door of the taxi. Alex recalls the past days of Monkey (Mary Jane Read). He asks himself, "Why continue with this person? This brutalized woman! This coarse, tormented, self-loathing, bewildered, lost, identiless". How can he go on and on with someone whose reason, judgement and behaviour he cannot possibly appreciate and approve.

He has spent a lot of time with a number of girls—vivacious, lively, intelligent, self-respecting, self-assured and well behaved young women—social workers and research assistants, schoolteachers and copy readers, girls in whose company he never feels abject or ashamed.

Kay Campbell, his girlfriend at Antioch, is a more exemplary person. He calls her Pumpkin. She is a robust, genial, large-hearted, large-assed girl with a sweet baby face and yellow hair. She never raises her voice in an argument. He misses her. He adores her—barefooted Shikse. She invites him to her house and introduces him to her parents. He is called "a weekend guest"! 'a friend from school'. To each and every question he answers as 'Thank You'. She is a Jew. So he starts sniffing at her house due to the smell of Jewishness.

Kay writes poetry about having a baby and types term papers for extra money. They both love and like Dylan Thomas and Bertrand Russell. But later Alex realizes that it is only he who loves her, not vice versa. Then he returns to New Jersey that June wondering how he can ever have been so captivated by someone so ordinary and so fat. He feels disillusioned.

Another gentile heart-broken by him belongs to The Pilgrim, Sarah Abbott Maulsby—a tall, gentle, decorous twenty-two-years old, fresh from college and working as a receptionist in the office of the Senator from Connecticut. They meet and in the fall of 1959, Alex thinks, "Why didn't I marry that beautiful and adoring girl?" At that time Alex was 26 years old, impressive, cool, lucid, persistent. Suddenly, he thinks about Sarah—that there can never be any love in him for The Pilgrim. Intolerant of her frailties; jealous of her accomplishments; resentful of her family; he precludes every possibility of entertaining love for her.

One day his sexual advances are spurned by a young woman "with green eyes" because of his disease. He confesses to the doctor that he has no dream. He does not need dreams. The mother-image always haunts him, actually threatens him with the dreaded knife, who used to threaten him of castration. He also confesses to him that through fucking he will discover America, conquer America like Columbus, Captain Smith, General Washington and now Portnoy. As though his destiny is to seduce a girl from each of the forty-eight states.

His life is without latent content. He often remembers "Pumpkin" who resembles his mother—she was a real faultfinder, a professional critic of him. He wanted to lead his life with her. She was the kind of girl he aspired for—innocent, good-hearted, unsophisticated, un-fucked-up. He wanted her.

His final downfall comes with Naomi. She tells him the unpalatable truth that he has exposed the corruption of certain weak individuals but the system remains unshaken. The system remains intact because he himself is corrupted. He is only one of its policemen, a paid employee, an accomplice.

He gives vent to his feelings of love before Naomi and also tries to indulge in sexual intercourse with her which she resists but he forces her to yield to his carnal advances by sheer physical force. Disgusted she asks him to go back to his home and leave her alone.

So this time also he is left with memories of his perennial childhood. He suffers from guilt consciousness of what happened to Monkey. He made her sleep with whores. He thinks that she had already slept with a number of men. He has done the smallest thing only for fun, while other people harm each other for greed and hatred. But no suit is filed against them. In fact, Alex has disapproved of his own life. He seems to take some special pleasure, some pride in making himself the butt of his own peculiar sense of humour. He does not actually want to improve his life. Everything he says is somehow always twisted, to come out funny. In some little way or other everything is ironical or self-depreciating, self-mocking. He is nothing but a self-hating Jew.

The novel is a breakthrough, the harrowing narration of the insatiable thirst for promiscuous sex and the frustration of unfulfilled lust through the mouth of the hero himself. This is a very frank and candid representation of the hero. He knows his weakness and passion.

Our Gang and *The Great American* novels are "Portnoy" in another book. "Portnoy wasn't a character for me, he was an explosion and I wasn't finished exploding after Portnoy's Complaint. I was blowing up a lot of cold loyalties and inhibitions, literally as well as personal. This may be why so many Jews were incensed by *Portnoy's Complaint*. It wasn't that they'd never heard about kids masturbating before, or about Jewish family fighting. It was, rather, that if they couldn't even control someone like me anymore with all my respectable affiliations and credentials."[48]

Philip Roth lived in New York from 1962 until he moved to the country after *Portnoy's Complaint*. New York gave him *Portnoy's Complaint* in a way, when he was living and teaching in Iowa city and Princeton. He didn't ever feel so free as he did in New York, in the sixties, to indulge himself in comic performance. There were raucous evenings with his New York friends, there was uncensored shamelessness in his psychoanalysis of the city itself in the years after Kennedy's assassination. All this inspired him to try out a new voice, a fourth voice, a less page-bound voice than the voice of *Goodbye, Columbus,* or of *Letting Go* or of *When She was Good.*

So did the opposition to the war in Vietnam. There's always something behind a book to which it has no seeming connection, something invisible to the reader which has helped to release the writer's initial impulse. He was thinking about the rage and rebelliousness that were in the air, the vivid examples he saw around him of angry defiance and hysterical opposition. This gave him a few ideas for his act. So there was the ambience of defiance and non-conformism in New York, which Roth imbibed and which permeated the texture of *Portnoy's Complaint.* The novel articulates the spirit of defiance against inhibition and taboos in the realm of sex, against prudery and priggishness.

Philp Roth's *Portnoy's Complaint* discusses the potential value and meaning of sex education. Jews have a unique national character because of their special religious belief and historical development. However, behind the facade of morality and good manners and prudery, sexuality arising out of innate human instinct of fertility does annoy and upset the Jews. In *Portnoy's Complaint,* thirty-three years old Jewish American Portnoy is a prominent figure in press from childhood to adulthood. However, he has been tortured and tormented by sexuality since he was four. Things have been getting worse with time. His carnal travails and turmoils are beyond description. He is still single in his thirties. He starts from failing to outlive and outgrow the Oedipus complex. Then he undergoes the nagging stages of sex shows, then finding prostitutes for sex, then chasing cunt everywhere and finally suffering from sexual impotence. As a result, he needs to see a psychiatrist. The novel is intended to analyze Portnoy's symptoms of mental illness to find out a way to release his frustration and rage arising from inveterate, insatiable lust, thwarted lust through a discussion about the interplay and conflict between civilization and sexual satisfaction. Sigmund Freud's psychoanalysis theories are used to reinforce the possibility of its solution and to supply the solution with a strong theoretical basis. Thus a good model operation of sex education can be built to solve the universal problem of sexuality in a civilized society. It may be possible for Portnoy to pass the trail of the Oedipus complex, identify his father, cultivate masculinity and be able to make sacrifices for his family. He can finally get married and get rid of masturbation, endless sexual desire and sense of guilt.

Many critics say that Roth has used sex as an instrument of power and subjection, and achieved a desecration of pornography, and that he has recognized the obsessive character of sexual concerns and their enormous conditioning power. However, Roth does not agree to this estimate of his fiction.

To him, pornography is itself considered a verbal desecration of the acts by which men and women are supposed to consecrate their profound attachment to one another. He has not 'desecrated', rather defended its central obsession with the body as an erotic contraption at plaything—with orifices, secretions, friction, discharge and testicles of sex-tectonics—and then placed that obsession back into an utterly mundane family setting where, in use of power and subjection, it can be seen in its broad everyday aspect rather than through the lens of pornography. In fact, the comedy of *Portnoy's Complaint* arises largely out of the mishaps, wholly expressive of the individual. All his attempts to enter naked into the sacred realm of pornography are repeatedly foiled because, by his own definition, Alex Portnoy is a character in a Jewish joke—a genre, which, unlike pornography, pictures a wholly deconsecrated world: demystified, deromanticized, utterly de-deluded. Portnoy still cannot help but profane with his every word and gesture what the orthodox fuckist most reveres.

Some of the ideas that went into the book have been in Roth's mind ever since he began writing. For instance, the book proceeds by means of writing as "blocks of consciousness", chunks of material of varying shapes and sizes piled atop one another and held together by associations rather than chronology. Roth is very much attracted to prose that has the turns, vibrations, intonations and cadences, the spontaneity and ease of spoken language and at the same time that is solidly grounded on the page, weighted with irony, precision and ambiguity associated with a more traditional literary rhetoric.

So far as the obscenity is concerned, obscenity as a usable and valuable vocabulary and sexuality as a subject, have been available since Joyce, Henry Miller, and Lawrence. *Porthnoy's Compliant* is full of dirty words and dirty scenes but *When She was Good* had none. *When She was Good* is a story about small town Middle Westerns who more than willingly experience themselves as conventional and upright people and it is their own conventional and upright style of speech that he chose as his means of narration. As for obscenity, he was careful even when he had Roy Bassart, the young ex-G.I, in the novel, who was unable to utter more than the initial of that famous four letter word. So the problem demands style; correct presentation of the problem is the primary concern of Philip Roth.

Obscenity is not only a kind of language that is used in *Portnoy's Complaint,* it is very nearly the issue itself. The book is not full of dirty words because "that's the way people talk; that's one of the least persuasive reason for using the obscene in fiction. Besides, few people actually talk the way Portnoy does in this book this is a man speaking out of an over whelming obsession: he is obscene because he wants to be saved. An odd, may be mad, way to go about seeking his personal salvation, but none the less, the investigation of this passion, and of the combat that it precipitates with his conscience, is the quintessential theme of the novel.

Portnoy's pains arise out of his refusal to be bound any longer by taboos which, rightly or wrongly, he experiences as diminishing and unmanning. The joke on Portnoy is that for him breaking the taboo turns out to be as unmanning in the end as honouring it. So Roth is not simply after verisimilitude in this novel; rather he wants to raise obscenity to the level of a subject. That is why, at the conclusion of the novel, the Israeli girl whose body Portnoy has been wrestling for on the floor of his Haifa Hotel room says to him, with loathing:

> Tell me, please, why must you use that word all the time?[49]

So it is a case study, a psychological exploration.

Portnoy, full of complaint because of his sexual fake, is bent on tracking down the sources of his grievances. The same is the case with Lucy Nelson—wholly antithetical in cultural and moral orientation. She is in her imprisoning consuming passion and in the role she assumes of the enraged offspring. Though not necessarily "typical", Alexander Portnoy and Lucy Nelson, in their extreme resentment and disappointment, are like the legendary unhappy children out of two familiar American family myths.

In one book, it is the Jewish son railing against the seductive mother, in the other the Gentile daughter railing against the alcoholic father (equally loved, hated and feared). Ofcourse, Lucy Nelson is seen to destroy herself within an entirely different fictional matrix, but that would result, among other reasons, from the enormous difference between the two environments that inspire their rage as well as their shared sense of loss and nostalgia.

The theme of *Portnoy* was the throwing off of duty, its hero is determined, and indulges in futile attempts to free himself from responsibility and guilt. Portnoy complains to his parents, "These people are unbelievable!" "These two are the outstanding producers and packagers of guilt in our time!" "The very first distinction I learned....was not night and day or hot and cold, but goyishe and Jewish......Jew Jew Jew Jew Jew! It's coming out of my ears already, the saga of the suffering Jew! I happen also to be a human being!"[50]

Yet despite his railing against his parents—his depiction of that old sentimental favourite, the Jewish mother, as not only a downright guilt-giver but also a deft castrater, his caricature of her ever-popular silent as an artist, the Jewish father, as an upright insurance agent and eunuch—Portnoy is still so compulsively ensnarled in the web of his relationship to them that at one moment he whimpers imploringly: "At this last date! Doctor, what should I rid myself of, tell me, the hatred or the love?" Yet at almost the very next moment he blurts out in an impassioned way all his pent up anguish: "Doctor Spielvogel, this is my life, my only life and I am living it in the middle of a Jewish joke! I am the son in the Jewish joke—why, why are they screaming still, 'Watch out! Don't do it! Alex-no!' and why, alone on my bed in New York, why am I still hopelessly beating my meat?"[51]

As Portnoy matures—at least chronologically—he desperately wants to tear off his American-Jewish hair-shirt, to let go, to live a life without mother and father, a sex life free and unfettered, without guilt. However, if sexually stunted, psychologically doomed, Portnoy still makes a bravura run for it. His adventures and misadventures involve a penchant for unseemly masturbation, a fetish for untimely fellatio and even the staging of a mini-orgy in Rome.

He also manages to squeeze a succession of picturesque girlfriends whose nicknames are Jonsonian in their humour, e.g. The Pumpkin: a foil-bodied but flat chested middle-westerner, "The first of the Antioch nymphs to go barefoot to class," the Monkey, who turns out to be more like a sexual lioness.

But what finally drives Portnoy to the analyst's couch is a traumatic sojourn in the state of Israel: "Doctor, maybe other parents dream—with me, everything happens. I have a life without latent content. The dream thing happens! Doctor! I couldn't get it up in the state of Israel!"

And the novel ends at a beginning, with the straight man analyst speaking his own line: "So Now Vee may perhaps to begin. Yes?"[52]

Portnoy's Complaint explores the psychological plight of a mother-smothered Jewish man who released his anxieties in masturbation. Among the shameful things, Roth shows himself willing to explore the sly shame of immodesty; a man who can write about masturbation can write about self-pride. Though he often plays narrative games, Roth has the ease with his tricks to make his story lines appear both straightforward and obvious. The sheet anchor of drama is conflict. Roth might add, that conflict is the quintessence of argument. While reading his novels we become conscious of a man who at every stage of his life has been acutely aware of the large questions he was deciding, and the large questions that were being decided for him. The faith implicit in his secular doubts is just this: that all human relationships are plagued by arguments, whether these are between husband and wife, brother and brother, father and son, mistress and lover. These arguments shift over time, but every stage of life, every change of circumstance, can be relied on to produce them. And the job of the novelist is to listen to these questions and give a voice, if not an answer.

Philip Roth is a historian and a comic. He is a true American historian and the finest stand-up comic ever to lie down on the printed page. No group of his books makes for better vehicles for these two leading aspects of Roth than the strangely kindred trio with which Roth entered the Me Decade: *Our Gang* (1971), *The Breast* (1972), *and The Great American Novel* (1973).

In *Our Gang* Roth has through comic satire and caricature explored and debunked the tortuous and distorted psyche of unconscientious demagogues who play to the gallery for placating vote banks. *Our Gang* is a political satire that is far-fetched, jejune, unfair, logical, coarse and very funny. President Nixon was facing a clear and real danger; he had just discovered that under liberalized military procedures, the wives of servicemen were able to obtain abortions more easily than they would have under state regulations. He put a stop to that instantly. Roth's president complaints to his cabinet, when the boy scouts gather for a protest march on Washington with placards reading: "TRICK E. DIXON FAVORS SEXUAL INTERCOURSE, "What did I say? Let's look at the record. I said nothing! Absolutely nothing! I came out for the 'rights' of the unborn."[53]

One really feels for the President. The punishment seems excessive considering his more serious crimes. But this was a crime against language and Roth is a writer.

Our Gang begins with Tricky reassuring a citizen who is troubled lest Calley may have killed a pregnant woman, either inadvertently ("he assumed she was simply overweight," Tricky suggests) or advertently.

On the latter option Tricky hypothesizes, "This woman presented herself to lieutenant Cally for abortion with some kind of note, say that somebody had written for her in English and lieutenant Cally, let's say, in the heat and pressure of the moment, performed the abortion, during the course of which the woman died." Such a case would be "abortion on demand"[54] and Tricky admits he is prejudiced: "I will disqualify myself as a judge and pass the entire matter on to the Vice President."[55]

The last chapter, "Tricky in Hell" takes place after his assassination (a baffling one because there are many groups with motives—the boy scouts, the Danes with too many suspicion, ten of thousands of them in fact, converging on Washington, each with his or her confession, claiming credit with documentation and insisting on being arrested by the over worked police force). Tricky is running against Satan for the Presidency of Hell:

> My fellow fallen: Let me say at the outset that of course I agree with much of what Satan has said in his opening statement. I know that Satan feels as deeply as I do about what has to be done to make Wickedness all that it can be and should be in the creation.... And now let me say a word to those who point to my own record as President of the United States and contend that it is less than it could have been as regards suffering and anguish for all of the people regardless of race, creed or color.[56]

In between these termini, Roth has constructed a complete mini-novel coherent in its plot line and full of recognizable characters whose speech mannerisms are adroitly parodied. No doubt, the language is exaggerated, one-sided, fantastic. *Our Gang* is an exaggerated impersonation, a parody, of Nixon's style of discourse and thought. Roth says:

> "Satiric" probably isn't the right word here—I mean broadly comic in the style of Oleen and Johnson, the Marx brothers, the three stooges, Laurel and Hardy, Abbot and Costello, and the like.[57]

The novel is in fact a comic satire. Thus Roth has also been inspired to write this book out of frustration with the ways in which popular spokesman newspaper columnists, TV commentators, even congressmen and senates respond to Nixon.

Satire is a humorous attack upon men and institutions for the purpose of bringing about reform. That is a commendable response to malice. But to Philip Roth, writing satire is a literary, not a political act, however volcanic the reformist or even revolutionary passion goads th author.

Satire is moral rage transmuted into comic art as an elegy is grief transformed into poetic art. No elegy is expected to accomplish anything in the world. It's a means of organizing and ventilating sad, perplexing emotions. The desire to murder your enemy with blows is converted into the attempt to murder him with invective and insult, and is thus transmuted, sublimated, or socialized, in the art of satire.

Roth has used ludicrous manner in which Trick E. Dixon is disposed, he is found stuffed in a Baggie in the fetal position, so that he remembers those unborn for whose rights he speaks so eloquently throughout the book. He meets his end in a Baggie—this is a satiric retribution, a befitting nemesis.

And in the next chapter, he is alive and well, in hell, admittedly, but debating the pants off Satan, whom he's running against for Devil. Roth says:

> I submitted that last chapter on the comeback Trial" to suggest that you can't hold a Trick E. Dixon down, even by stuffing him into a Baggie and turning the twister seal.[58]

Back in 1966, Max Hayward edited and translated a chilling, depressing document that he called *On Trial*. It was the transcript of the Moscow trial of the Soviet writers Yuli Daniel and Andrei Sinyavsky who were given five and seven years sentences respectively in a forced labour camp for "slandering the state in their literary works. Juoye did not want to hear" about satire or jitneys or hyperbole or humour or the make believe aspect of literature. All he wanted to know was: "Why do you slander Lenin? Why do you slander the Russian people who suffered so in the war?"

He wanted to repeat a few elementary arguments about the nature of literature. The most rudimentary thing about literature is that words are not deeds. So Roth, by presenting the assassination of Tricky does not want the public to assassin Tricky. Rather his aim behind writing this book is that:

> All I can say to those who will fear for the President's life is that they would do better to lobby for a strong federal gun-control bill than to worry about the influence of "Our Gang" on potential assassins. It might be easier to get Attorney General Mitchell to push for a bill outlawing literature than for one making it impossible to buy a single through the mail for fifteen bucks, but the fact remains, more people are killed in this country every year by bullets than by satires.[59]

In the chapter "The Assassination of Tricky", Roth has ridiculed the discrepancy between official parties and the unpleasant truth. On the one hand, he has shown tens of thousands of people flocking to Washington to verify the news of the assassination of

Trick E. Dixon, and on the other, the television commentators who persist in describing these self-avowed killers as though they were the mourners who thronged to Washington after President Kennedy (or President Charisma, as he is called in the book) is killed. It really isn't Nixon and his friends who are being mocked in this chapter so much as the "Platitudinous" psyche of the media. Partly, the point is that Tricky, living or dead, in the White House or in the grave, is unworthy of such tribute, but the joke is that the chapter entitled "The Assassination of Tricky" is largely at the expense of network blindness. The implication is that the mass media are purveyors of the official version of reality and, for all their so-called criticism of the government can be counted on, when the chips are down, to cloud the issue and miss the point. Lastly, the chapter is concerned with the fine art of government lying, but then so is the entire book.

In *Our Gang*, the farcical style seems to work to becalm whatever anxiety might be allowed in the reader by a patricidal or regicidal fantasy made "real". However, simultaneous with the mischievous glee taken in the harmless, make-believe, sadistic fun, the reader probably can't help remembering that Presidents of the United States have been assassinated—and knowing that it is possible for President Nixon to be assassinated too. What is then most disturbing to the reader is that Roth has found himself enjoying a fantasy that he has known in reality to be appalling.

Our Gang is Philip Roth's ferocious political satire in the great tradition, brilliantly indignant response to the phenomenon of Richard M. Nixon and what appears to be his diseased and distorted psyche as an unscrupulous power hungry politician.

In the character of Trick E. Dixon, Roth shows us a man who outdoes the severest cynic, a peace-loving Quaker and believer in the sanctity of human life, who doesn't have qualms while killing unarmed women and children in self-defence. A consummate politician with a sense of honesty, he finds himself battling the boy scouts, declaring war on Pro-Pornography Denmark, all the time trusting in the basic indifference and nonchalance of the voting public.

Philp Roth has presented a caricature of Trick E. Dixon, who pretends to be generous and kind, and professes concern for the sanctity of human life, and is quite alive to defending the right of even unborn child.

> From personal and religious beliefs I consider abortions an unacceptable form of population control. Further form unrestricted abortion policies, or abortion on demand, I cannot square with my personal belief in the sanctity of human—life—including the life of the yet unborn. For, surely, the unborn have rights also, recognized in law, recognized even in principles expounded by the united nations.[60]

Tricky is the caricature of Richard Nixon in this novel. The novel is divided into six chapters. *Our Gang* is the gang of Trick E. Dixon and his friends. In the first chapter, Tricky comforts a troubled citizen who questions him about a Lieutenant Calley's killing twenty two Vietnamese civilians at My Lai. He always behaves as a politician. On the one hand, he reserves the rights of unborn child but, on other hand, he does not hesitate in killing others. But whatever he does, he does for self interest, for ating his position as a president.

> I am not going to interfere in the internal affairs of another country.[61]

But he does so. Outwardly, he tries to defend lieutenant Calley who killed Twenty-Two Vietnamese civilian's at My Lai.

> I in no way intend to interfere with the workings of the Vietnamese system of justice.[62]

The novelist presents the satire in a very humorous way. Citizen says:

> As I share your belief in the sanctity of human life—in as much as I feel as you do about the unborn child, I am seriously troubled by the possibility that lieutenant Calley may have committed an abortion, I hate to say this Mr. President, but I am seriously troubled when I think that one of those twenty-two Vietnamese civilians lieutenant Cally killed may have been a pregnant woman.[63]

Tricky E. Dixon answers that perhaps the lieutenant had no knowledge of that lady's pregnancy. And if she told him about pregnancy, the lieutenant could not understand the language, Vietnamese.

Tricky says perhaps it was abortion on demand. So he always tries to maintain his dignity, he tries to comfort that citizen by saying that:

> I will now be particularly careful to enquire whether there is so much as a single shred of evidence that one of those twenty-two in that ditch at My Lai was a pregnant woman. And if there is if I should find in the evidence against the lieutenant any thing what so ever that I can not square with my personal belief in the sanctity of human life, including the life of the yet unborn, I will disqualify myself as a judge and pass the entire matter on to the Vice-President.[64]

Tricky holds a press conference; he always tries to justify himself, he is not just talking about the rights of the foetus, he is talking about the microscopic embryos as well.

Mr. Respectful asks, "Why have you decided to devote yourself to this previously neglected issue of foetus rights?"

Tricky answers, "I will not tolerate injustice in a just society, not merely for the rich and the privileged, but the most powerless among us as well." Mr. Shrewd asks: "Mr. President, there are those who contend that you are guided in this matter solely by political considerations." But Tricky says that "I myself was once unborn, in the great state of California. I was an unborn Quaker, as a matter of fact. My wife was once unborn. My children were both unborn. But the bitter reality is that Dixon has turned to the issue of the unborn just for the sake of the votes... he always says that whatever he is doing is not only for our nation, but for all mankind. There are the Russians and the Chinese, who don't even allow adults to vote—I am always willing to listen and respond to an appeal from any minority group."[65]

He exaggerates the matter: "I only hope that all Americans will come as proud of our unborn as I am."[66]

He always indulges in self-justification and self-righteousness. He manages a conference because he is scared of the movement of boy scouts who called Tricky E. Dixon a sensualist. The boy scouts of America are screaming before the TV cameras that Trick E. Dixon favours sexual intercourse, favours fornication—between people!

Tricky says:

> And what about my wife—what is she going to think?
> What if she starts to believe it?
> What about my children? What about the Voters![67]

So votes were his paramount concern.

Then all the comrades of Tricky hatch a conspiracy against the boy scouts. They ask Tricky to go on television and say that he has had intercourse only once in his entire life. He goes to such an extent that he would declare in public that he is a homosexual. They go to the extent of killing and shooting the boy scouts. They are heartless beasts. Tricky calls himself cool, confident and decisive.

Then they make the list of five persons.

Hanoi

The Berrigans

The Black Panthers

Jane Fonda

Curt Flood

They exercise their vote to choose two persons who a to be blamed for killing. One is a baseball player—Curt Flood, born January 18, 1938 in Houstan, Taxas, Bats, who used to play under contract at a Salary of $110,000 a year to the Washington Senates on the morning of April 27, 1971. Flood is known to have purchased a ticket for Barcelona, he apparently disembarked in Lisbon—wearing a brown 'eather jacket, bell-bottomed trousers and sunglasses. The question arises: why did Mr. Curt Flood of the Washington baseball team find it necessary to leave the country in so precipitous and dramatic a fashion?

Then they surmise that Mr. Curt Flood must have fled to Copenhagen—a pro-pornography city. They want to justify their attack on the city. Then they think of the evidence and proof, which they would display before the public. In fact, they are identifying the issues on which they can play politics with the 72 elections.

The second one they choose is Jane Fonda, an actress.

"We shall meet to settle upon the exact nature of the crime. In the meantime, I will remain here in the locker room, in uniform"—says Tricky.[68]

Tricky appears on television with a 'message of national importance.'

He justifies his attack on Denmark and says: "It was true that I have effectively isolated Denmark from the rest of the world."[69]

As commander-in-chief, he orders the armed forces to discharge their responsibilities. But he is not ready to call it an invasion:

> Whatever reports you may have heard of an armed American invasion of Danish territory are categorically false and constitute a deliberate distortion of the facts.[70]

He speaks of the Liberation of the town of Ellsinore, the home of the fortress popularity known to tourists as "Hamlet's Castle". It is now occupied by American soldiers.

Roth has presented the matter in a very humorous tone. The guard an duty at Ellsinore is so taken by surprise that when roused from his bed by a knock at the gate, he comes to the door in his pajamas and opens it so wide that his brave mariners are able to overcome and secure the grounds in a matter of minutes.

The guard, who is the only foreign invader on the premises at that time, has been taken into custody following the liberation of Ellsinore. Tricky has sent a communiqué to the Pro-Pornography government in Copenhagen, making it absolutely clear that his action was in no way directed at the security interests of any nation, Denmark included.

He says that they wanted Copenhagen to surrender the fugitive Cult Flood—the man who fled this country on April 27, 1971, exactly one week before the day of the uprising of the boy scouts in Washington. Then he talks of a nexus between Curt Flood and the boy scouts.

> It was not to the dissolute, unprincipled and over indulged on our college campuses that Charles Curtis Flood turned with his plan of destroying America—but is the boy scouts of America, not only did Charles Curtis Flood tempt them to riot, and tamper with their morals, it was he alone who drove the boy scouts leading into the tragedy that occurred here yesterday in Washington, D.C.[71]

So he justified his killing only three of the boy scouts in order to maintain law and order. It means he allowed to kill only half a person a day. But he also expresses great sympathy for the families of the three boy scouts who were killed in Washington.

Then he shows their concealed weapons; first the bottle-opener, second is the lathe punch and the third one is "the screw driver". According to him, they concealed weapons upon their belts and carried them hundreds of miles across state line to the nation's capital. He also shows his generosity by taking the side of boy scouts and mainly accusing those who egged them on for instigating these riots:

> The cause of America's problems is not the boy scouts of America. But the men who incited them to this riot, he says closing his lecture; "Something is rotten in the State of Denmark.[72]

Thus in this chapter, Roth debunks Tricky's hollowness, his cunningness, craftiness and Machivellian approach. Tricky presents a link between his invasion on Denmark and Curtis Flood in order to make his skin safe and justify the invasion. He strictly behaves like a crafty and astute policitian. This novel is a breakthrough novel in his evolution as a novelist, in which he assails president Richard E. Nixon so sharply and openly.

Then Philip Roth ridicules the death of Tricky. The news spreads—the President of the United States is dead. Trick E. Dixon is dead.

Then conflicting stories continue to pour in concerning the death of the President. The Vice-President has flatly denies reports of the President's death. Unconfirmed reports from Walter Reed Hospital now indicate that the President was found dead at seven this morning. But nobody is ready to authenticate the news. They also get reports that he has been murdered by a boy scout while some say that the cause of death was drowning. He was found at 7.a.m., unclothed and bent into the foetal position, inside a large transparent baggie.

Many persons came forward to own responsibility of assassinating the President and furnish proof for the same. The eulogy over the baggie (As delivered live on National wide TV by the Reverend Billy Cup cake) runs as follows:

> He was not an ordinary leader.[73]

This is a left-handed compliment when the novelist says: He was not a leader in the ordinary sense of the word. In fact, he was a leader in the extraordinary sense of that word. He was absolutely ego-centred and his ego-centreity was unparalleled. There has never been another like him in history. There will never be another like him again. So Roth has provided us with many wonderful breakthroughs.

> The name was s simple one, my friends, the name was Tricky, Yes, to you to me, and to all Americans for generations to come, Tricky, he was and Tricky he shall be.[74]

Tricky considers himself the most vicious and meanest of all in hell.

> I have talked to sinners from all walks of life. I have eaten with degenerates and blasphemed with the impious. I have looked into the eyes of the depraved and the malicious. I have familiarized my self with viciousness and baseness of all kinds.[75]

Satan has been a constant source of inspiration to him from time immemorial. He confesses to Satan:

> I am just as sincere in my lying as he is in his.[76]

Tricky needs a new administration in hell, an administration with new horns, new half-truths, new horrors and new hypocrisies. He needs a new commitment to evil, new strategies and contrivances to make his dream of a totally fallen world a reality.

He confesses to all the evil persons or devils in hell: "I was able to maintain and perpetuate all that was evil in American life when I came to power."[77]

Even then he says that he was not so hideous on earth as he might be here in hell. He is relative newcomer to the Red Wickedness. Roth presents a very sharp and pungent satiric picture of Tricky saying:

> I am elected Devil, I intend to see evil triumph in the end; I intend to see that our children, and our children's children, need never know the terrible scourge or Righteousness and Peace.[78]

Philip Roth ends the novel on a note of revelation showing an angel coming down from heaven and shutting down the pit and sealing it so that Tricky can no longer deceive the nations. Roth most strongly felt political power as the fountainhead of coercion, corruption and degradation while he grew up in New Jersey during World War II. He was twelve when the war ended and during the first few years his first serious political allegiances began to take shape.

His entire clan—parents, aunts, uncles, cousins—were devout New Deal Democrats. He is proud to say that Richard Nixon was known as a crook in his kitchen some twenty-odd years before this wisdom dawned on the majority of Americans. He was in college during Joe McCarthy's heyday—when he began to identify political power with immoral coercion.

The Vietnam War years were the most "politicized" of Roth's life. He spent his days during this war writing fiction, but by being "politicized" he means something more telling than writing about politics or even taking direct political action. He means something akin to what ordinary citizens experience in countries like Czechoslovakia or Chile; a daily awareness of government as a coercive force.

Our Gang uses the "element of grotesque". Rather, it tries to objectify in a style of its own what is inherent in the moral character of a Richard Nixon. He, not the satire, is what is grotesque. There have been others as venal and lawless in American politics, but even a Joe McCarthy was more identifiable as a human clay than this guy is. The wonder of Nixon and contemporary America is that a man so transparently fraudulent leading the nation on the edge of disaster, could ever have won the confidence and approval of people who generally require at least a little something of the "human touch" in their leaders.

Our Gang is a real satire. In it, Philp Roth takes Nixon to task for what he saw as the gross and arrant incompatibility between Nixonian profession of the "sanctity of human life" and the indiscriminate and callous manner in which he sent young men to die in Vietnam and bring havoc there.

Roth's novel is written from the perspective of President Trick. E. Dixon, and is structured as a collection of transcripts from several presidential addresses, press conferences and newscasts.

In the novel, President Dixon wants to bring the right to vote to the unborn, despite the "fantastic mechanics" of doing so. When a reporter asks President Dixon how "embryos on the placenta, who haven't even developed nervous systems yet, let alone limbs," will go about casting their ballots, the president responds:

> Let me remind you that nothing in our constitution denies a man the right to vote just because he is physically handicapped.[79]

The novel explores and exposes the contemptible and satanic psyche of President Nixon, a hypocritical and Machiavellian demagogue.

The Breast is the story of a Jewish professor of comparative literature, David Kapesh, who turns into a huge female breast. The tale is told retrospectively as a first-person narrative in a confessional style that as we discover at the end of the novella, is supposedly Kapesh's hour-long lecture to an unnamed audience. Throughout the text the narrator, formerly a thirty-eight-year-old man of "stamina and appetite" but now a breast, is fed intravenously and remains immobile in a hammock in a private room at a hospital. He receives doctors, scientists from various disciplines, nurses who wash him, and visitors—his father, his wife Claire, and his colleague and old friend Arthur Schonbrunn, now the dean of arts and sciences at his university. He also engages in long conversations with his psychoanalyst, Dr. Klinger.

In *The Breast* (1972), the main character, David Kapesh, becomes 155 pound breast. Throughout the book we see Kapesh fighting with himself. Part of him wishes to give in to carnal desires, while the other part of him wants to be reasonable. He is schizophrenic, split personality torn between two conflicting loyalties, impaled on the horns of excruciating dilemma. In many ways this book has a lot in common with Kafka's novella *The Metamorphosis*. When Philip Roth published *The Breast* in 1972, the novella met with a flurry of notice. Some readers picked it up hoping to find Portnoy-like sexual outrageousness and they were not disappointed. Others predisposed to be offended, were likewise disposed to look no further, believing that Roth meant only to titillate. *The Breast* was clearly a work of its time in its explicit sexual references, and its readings were perhaps over-determined not only by the reputation of *Portnoy's Complaint* (1969) for unrestrained and taboo-breaking representations of sexuality but also by the ranting of *OUR GANG* (1971), the rather coarse political satire that immediately preceded the *Breast's* publication, and more broadly, by the novella's appearance on the American scene in the 1970s as part of a wave of transgresssive culture artefacts. One clue to the book's reception might be found in the puzzlement of a reviewer who asked "Why this conceit rather than another?" The answer to this question will show *The Breast* to be a book not just of its time but ahead of it. Roth anticipated recent investigations into psychic subjectivity and especially the masculine subject. *The Breast* deserves a second look because it challenges some of the most deeply juxtaposed oppositions—human versus non-human, masculine versus feminine, subject versus object, inside versus outside—that structure our thinking about our psyche by forcing a confrontation with the manifold meanings of the gendered body; by representing the very fleshliness of gendering. Roth makes a valuable contribution to thinking about the conventions of subjectivity.

Said Roth in 1977, "the *Breast* wasn't just about entrapment in the flesh and the horrors of desire, it was also inspired by some thinking I'd had to do about fame, notoriety, and scandal. When the idea for the book first came to me, I had myself only recently become an object of some curiosity, believed by some to be very much the sexual freak and grotesque." There could not a sequel to *The Breast;* Roth started one, but confessed, "writing about the brutal claustrophobic predicament wearied me and troubled me terribly, and the events themselves were pilling up with no interesting purpose that I could see."[80]

This rather defines *The Breast,* too. The breast is something he was working on between politics of *Our Gang* and the baseball of *The Great American Novel,* or, rather, something he was working on amidst politics and baseball, for *The Great American Novel* encompasses both, and all.

Philip Roth has concerned himself with men and women whose moorings have been cut and who are swept away from their native shores and out to sea, sometimes on a tide of their own righteousness or resentment. But in the *The Breast* Kapesh is definitely in a new and surprising relationship with his everyday self, his family and his friends. Lucy Nelson in *When she was Good*, Gabe wallach and Paul Herz in *Letting Go*, Alex Portnoy in *Portnoy's Complaint* all are living beyond their psychological and moral means. Kapesh's predicament is similar—with a difference: his unmooring can't be traced to psychological, social or historical causes. His longing to be at one again with his fellows and his old self is far more poignant and harrowing than Lucy Nelson's or Portnoy's. Those two characters, at the same time that they yearn for a more sociable and settled existence, are hell-bent on maintaining their isolation with all the rage and wildness in their arsenals. They are two very stubborn American children, locked in prototypical combat with the beloved enemy: the spirited Jewish boy pitted against his mother, the Cleopatra of the kitchen; the solemn Gentile girl pitted against her father. Kapesh strikes as far more heroic than either of these two: perhaps a man who turns into a breast is the first heroic character Roth has ever been able to portray. One difficulty in writing this kind of story is deciding what sort of claim to make on the reader's credulity: whether to invite him to accept the fantastic situation as taking place in the recognizable world or to ignore the realm of credibility and move into other imaginative make-believe realms of dream, hallucination, allegory, nonsense, play, self-consciousness, sadism and so on.

In *The Metamorphosis* Kafka asserts at the outset that the catastrophe is engulfing his hero in the very real, believable, mundane world of families, jobs, bosses, money and housekeepers. Kafka doesn't go more than a dozen sentences before he tells—"it was no dream". On the other hand, Gogol in *The Nose* is intermittently provocative and teasing about kovalev's misfortune. As Gogol says in the end, may be it's only a cock and bull story; then again, may be it is not.

But in *The Breast*, Philip Roth has presented the fantastic situation to be accepted as taking place in what we call the real world; at the same time Roth hopes to make the reality of the horror one of the issues of the story. "Is it really happening? Can I believe this?"—the question that Kafka settles on the very first page by asserting that the metamorphosis is "no dream". Whether it is or is not a dream a hallucination or a psychotic delusion, does not matter for Roth's hero Kapesh, or for Roth because he didn't choose to render the problem unproblematical by a wave of the author's magic wand.

The Nose and *The Metamorphosis*, are both cited by Kapesh in the story, part of his desperate struggle to make some sense of what has happened to him. It was fitting for a serious, dedicated professor of literature, that Kapesh was, to think of Gogol and Kafka when his own horrible transformation occurs.

Philip Roth was strongly influenced by a sit-down comic named Franz Kafka and a very funny bit he called *The Metamorphosis*. But it doesn't mean that he modelled his book after any work of Kafka or tried to write a Kafka-like novel. At the time Philip Roth was beginning to play with the ideas for what turned out to be *Portnoy's Complaint*, he was teaching a lot of Kafka in a course he gave once a week at the University of Pennsylvania.

Particularly after several arduous years spent on *When She was Good*, with its unfairly prose, its puritanical, haunted heroine, its unrelenting concern with banality, he was thinking to write something freewheeling and funny. It had been a long time between laughs. So he thought of writing *The Breast*.

A fiction is clear and straightforward about itself on the narrative level and opaque or difficult on the metaphorical level. The issue of *The Breast* is not opacity or transparency anyway—it is usability. What makes an image telling or even, meaningful is not how much meaning a writer can associate to it but the quality of the overall invention that it inspires, the freedom it gives the writer to explore his obsessions and his talent. A novelist does not persuade by what he is "trying to say" but by a sense of fictional authenticity he communicates, the sense of an imagination so relentless and thought-provoking that it is able to convert into its own non-convertible currency whatever the author has absorbed through reading, thinking and "raw experience". That's why Professor Kapesh writes that on the metaphorical level the fantasy remains rather opaque.

For Kapesh there is no way out of the monstrous situation, not even through literary interpretation. There is only the unrelenting education in his own misfortune. What he learns by the end is that, whatever else it is, it is the real thing; he is a breast, and must act accordingly.

Now what "accordingly" means is still another question, and the one Kapesh raises near the end of the story, with his daydream becoming his own one man or one-breast circus. Unlike Gregor

Samsa, who accepts his transformation into a beetle from the first sentence, Kapesh is continually challenging, questioning and defying his fate, and even after he consents to believe that he has actually become mammary gland, his mind is alive with alternative ways of being one.

Roth has presented psychic interplay between the sexual ecstasy that Kapesh discovers as breast and his spiritual pain, his excruciating sense of exile and aloneness, a psychological motif that is also central to *Portnoy's Complaint*, where the hero feels increasingly at odds with himself and his past the more sexually adventurous he becomes. It's the struggle to accommodate warring impulses and desires, the ethical and social yearnings on the one hand and the implacable, carnal cravings for the flesh and its pleasures on the other; the measured self vs. the insatiable self, the accommodating self vs. the ravenous self. Portnoy, for all his confusion and isolation, knows the world like the back of his own hand (to make the kind of joke that the book seems to inspire.) Unlike Portnoy, Kapesh is interested neither in making his misery entertaining, nor in tinging it with wild humour. If Portnoy could do that, it was because he had less territory to cover.

When David Kapesh awakes to find that he has metamorphosed into a six-foot mammary gland, the existential question of identity becomes painfully centred on his physical condition. His anatomy is his destiny; he is rewritten bodily as the other. All that remains recognizable of David Kapesh to the outside world is his voice. Roth's book uncovers Kapesh's desperate desire to find that the voice, which most clearly represents the subject as a sentient being to the world, can affirm the possibility of an irreducible self, a self that cannot be altered—morally, psychologically, ontologically—by accident or design. To understand Roth's choice of conceit, however—why a breast rather than some other thing or creature or body part and why a female body part—we should start with his choice of narrative form. The novella makes no attempt to disguise its indebtedness to Kafka's *The Metamorphosis*.

Like a latter-day Gregor Samsa, Professor David Kapesh wakes up one morning to find that he has been transformed. But while Kafka's protagonist turned into a giant beetle, the narrator of Philip Roth's richly conceived fantasy has become a 155-pound female breast. What follows is a deliriously funny yet touching exploration of the full psychological implications of Kapesh's metamorphosis, a daring, heretical book that brings us face to fact with the intrinsic strangeness of sex and subjectivity (or inner psyche).

The Breast is terrific... inventive, awesome and very funny. The trick which is the heart of the book is brilliant... and rich with meaning."[81] "Hilarious, serious, visionary, logical, sexual-philosophical; the ending amazes—the joke takes three steps beyond savagery and satire and turns into a sublimeness of pity. One knows when one is reading something that will permanently enter the culture."[82]

Kapesh calls his doctor Dr. Gordon when he finds abnormal symptoms. He feels agony for the next four hours. But his sexual cravings arouse again when he is transformed into a breast—a massive hormonal influx, an endocrinopathic catastrophe and/or a hermaphroditic explosion of chromosomes take place within his body between midnight and 4.a.m on February 18, 1971.

One morning he awakenes to feel something new happening, nothing like pain rather more like pleasure. He screams—"I've been burned! I was in a fire!"[83] Dr. Klinger always tells Kapesh that he is always stronger than he thought. But he replies, "I was never strong." Only determined Kapesh questions: "What Does It Mean? How could it have happened? In the entire history of the human race, why Professor Kapesh?"[84]

His father comes to meet him and talks about people. Claire comes and plays with his nipple if that is what he most desires. He had experimented with whores easily enough back in his twenties and he had also carried on a thrilling, overwrought affair with two young women. Arthur Schonbrunn comes and he is unable to speak and even laughe and later writes an apology letter. What happens next is that he refuses to believe that he has turned into a breast. He realizes that the whole thing is impossible. A man cannot turn into a breast other than in his own imagination.

He thinks that it is just a dream, a hallucination, a delusion—even a drug-induced state of mind. But the doctor says that it is none of these things. "It really happened to him. He is not insane. Insanity is no solution—neither imagined insanity nor the real thing."[85]

In this way, he is fooling none but himself. Kapesh considers himself a mental patient. "Better the banal than the apocalyptic,"

Prof. David Alan Kepesh says—the central character in Philip Roth's new novella, *The Breast*. For reasons not altogether clear to his doctors—"the assault of a volcanic secretion from the pituitary of 'mammogenic' fluid"—Kepesh has turned into an enormous breast, round at one end like a waterlemon, at the other end a nipple that can hear and talk and feel sexual stimulation but never reach orgasm, forever howling "more"! Perhaps it's a dream, Kapesh thinks, Perhaps madness. But the effect of transformation is real. So the professor rants and reasons, or tells banal jokes to himself and those who visit him. *The Breast*, though published five years before *The Professor of Desire*, anticipates the latter at this point and confirms Kapesh's fear of future transformation. Kapesh is now thirty-eight, his desire for Claire distressingly cooled, his father still alive.

"It began oddly", the book opens, and "it" turns out to be Kapesh's preposterous, Kafkaesque metamorphosis into a living, breathing speaking breast, "a mammary gland disconnected from any human form, a mammary gland such as could oniy appear, one would have thought, in a dream or a Dali painting."[86] A portion of "its" odd beginning is the brief return of Kapesh's physical desire for Claire; unfortunately, the "sheer tortuous pleasure" that he now finds in lovemaking only signals the transformation already occurring within his body.[87] We are given a pseudoclinical descripion of his change, categorized as "an endocrinopathic catastrophe" and "a heremaphorditic explosion of chromosomes,"[88] a description as plausible as the manifest implausibility of the situation will allow, plausible enough to meet Roth's aim of interrogating the relationship between fiction and reality. Claire and his father visit Kapesh in the hospital. Eventually he somewhat learns to accept his situation. The bulk of the tale consists of his self reflection on his plight with the aid of his psychoanalyst, Dr. Klinger. But en route to this acceptance, Kapesh struggles partially with two related facets of his transformation: its genesis and its reality.

He considers two theories of its genesis: the first his over-exuberance before Claire's breasts on a northeastern beach; the second his preoccupation with the fiction of Gogol and Kafka.

He entertains the second theory far longer and indeed never entirely rejects it. Though Klinger argues, quite sensibly, that many teachers teach Gogal and Kafka without the perusal of their fantastic texts disturbing the teacher's identity, Kapesh feels that his teaching of this pair may have been so passionate as to have effected a parodic incarnation: "So I took the leap. Made the word flesh. Don't you see, I have out-kafkaed-kafka." To Klinger's laughter at the notion, Kapesh asks, "Who is the greater artist, he who imagines the marvelous transformation, or he who marvelously transforms himself?"[89]

Milowitz suggests that Kapesh will either have to subvert Desire with professorial control or subvert 'Professor' with raw passions to live up to the title.[90]

Kapesh's loss of desire for Claire derives, paradoxically, from the happiness she brings him, because, according to Tolstoy's famous dictum, happy families are all alike and therefore lack drama. Kapesh's psyche is moulded by his wide reading of literature. So he needs to be unhappy, desires to desire, fears that happiness entails boredom and a lack of story. It is of immense psychological interest to see, as in the case of Kapesh, how does one explain and how does one proceed in the face of desires that are mutually exclusive, desires at once for stability and abandon, for Elisabeth and Birgitta, for true affection and emancipated manhood?

Technically at least, *The Breast* seems to me Roth's best book so far. The humour and pathos (it has fair amounts of both) come from his solid grasp of how life is, his firm knowledge of the importance of strength of character and the will to live. Or, as Kapesh calls them in his meetings with his psychiatrist, "S. of C., and the W. to L". He explains that these banal phrases are the therapeutic equivalent of his lame jokes. In these, his preposterous terms, we must keep to what is ordinary and familiar.

The trick, which is the heart of the book, is brilliant: to celebrate the ordinary, the silly, the banal, to create a grotesque and extraordinary banality—a huge detached breast with human consciousness and feeling. The trick is so good, so obvious and easy and yet so rich with meaning, it's a little hard to translate from what it is, a piece of art, into a reviewer's language.

Roth plays every possible game with his conceit. For instance, Kapesh mournfully and very touchingly compares his "real life" situation with the merely fictional situation of, among others, Kafka's Gregor Samsa, cockroach—a joke that gives Roth a chance to make fun of Freudian erotic and neurosis theories, to ape pompous and silly ideas of literary critics about "unique vision" and "genius" and to reconsider the whole theory of the non-realistic novel.

There are two secrets to pulling off such a literary trick, and Roth knows them.The first one is that in order to report the experience of a man turned to a breast the writer must by powerful imagination immerse himself in the situation.

The second secret is that one must, all the time one writes, be so steeped in the meaning of the central conceit (more a matter of feeling than of intellect) that nothing comes into the story just for the sake of laughter. Every event, every joke, must ambush the reader with reality while he laughs, and again Roth mostly pulls it off. Roth is no Gogol—a comparison he boldly and jokingly invites. But *The Breast* is terrific, inventive and sane and very funny, though filthy of course.

The critical reception of *The Breast* was not altogether flattering. However, unlike many other Roth's texts, the disapproval in this case was not based on allegations of anti-Semitism, sexism, or shallow character description, although that last reason is sometimes mentioned, but rather on an assumption that the text was merely comical and, therefore, of low value. For many, *The Breast* is flawed as a literary work, a text that proves how immature and whimsical a writer Roth was in the early 1970s. Sanford Pinsker, for instance, claims that *The Breast* can only be described as "masochistic."[91]

Irving Howe found that although *The Breast* is "well-enough written and reasonably ingenious, it is finally boring—tame, neither shocking nor outrageous and tasteless in both senses of the word."[92]

It is curious, nevertheless, that the themes of the writer-subject's transformation and the transformative relationship between fact and fiction that are so central to *The Breast* traverse Roth's later, more "serious" works including the Zuckerman trilogy, *The Counterlife,* and Louis Harap states that "Roth's obsession with sex and his satirical proclivities are fused in *The Breast.*"[93]

In *The Facts,* Roth returns to the theme of metamorphosis in his letters to his character Nathan Zuckerman and in Zuckerman's response to his author, which frame the main narrative. In the letter that opens the text, Roth explains that in this book he reversed his normal order of writing from facts to fiction, that is, he tells how he started writing "backward" from the already imagined and " as it were, desiccating it so as to restore my experience to the original, professionalized factuality."[94]

Roth or the character called Roth, no longer wants just to transform the past into writing but consciously to transform himself within the writing and, thus, make himself mor- "factual".

"I hadn't ever mapped out my life like this but rather as I've looked only at what could be transformed. Here, so as to fall former life, to retrieve my vitality, to transform myself into began rendering experience untransformed."[95]

Transformation may be read in that case as a kind of metatrope of writing that indicates not only the two-way movement intertwining fact and fiction in writing but also the (re) construction of the writing self in the text.

> My guess is that you've written metamorphoses of yourself so you no longer have any idea what you are or ever were. By now is a walking text.[96]

It is worthwhile to reread the critically neglected *The Breast* in terms of its highly self-reflexive use of the figure of metamorphosis. The driving force in the development of the story is the unexplainable nature of Kapesh's metamorphosis. For the most part, the narrative revolves around arguments concerning it: Kapesh's various explanations for his change; Dr. Klinger's rejections of those arguments, or Kapesh's doubts concerning them.

In the struggle to make sense of metamorphosis, Roth's text is explicitly connected, through direct references, allusions, and quotations, to a large body of literary or artistic texts. In subject matter, structure and themes the text utilizes previous literature and other texts, fuses precursor texts together and transforms them.

In *The Breast*, the transformed body creates a struggle with discursiveness. As Kapesh's body changes, his self-concept must also change. The two "crises" he records are dilemmas of the subject's self-concept: the first concerns the understanding of his new sexual body, and the second involves his psychic need to redefine his concepts of reality and of the self in that reality.

The reason for Kapesh's transformation remains an inexplicable "blind spot" in the text that initiates a ceaseless dynamic between the explanations of Kapesh and others and the ensuring rebuttals from Dr. Klinger or Kapesh himself. *The Breast* is not a story about the process of metamorphosis but abut explanations and protestations about being metamorphosed. The various arguments and counter-arguments proposed may be thought of as possible readings of the text, readings that anticipate the reader's role in deciding the meaning of text.

Kapesh launches the process of trying to find a cause for his metamorphosis by explaining that, before his transformation he was searching for reason (hypochondria, dye, cancer, resurgence of sexual desire) to explain the tingling in his groin, the discoloration of his penis, and his heightened sexual interest. He found all those explanations useless because what happened to him is basically unexplainable, "beyond understanding, beyond compassion, beyond comedy."[97]

However, before and immediately after his transformation, the uniqueness of his situation is not clear to him, and he spends his energies refuting his doctors' accounts and explanations of his change and their claim that he is a large breast. His denial is understandable on a practical level: he cannot see himself nor sense his body in the old way and thus must rely on the people around him. The first impression of his new body are troubling:

> When my "body" was touched, I didn't know what to make of it: was unexpectedly soothing, but far away, and reminded me of at a beach.[98]

The doctors offer various descriptions of his metamorphosis in pseudoscientific jargon: "a massive hormonal influx," "an endocrinopathic catastrophe," "a hermaphroditic explosion of chromosomes."[99] Kapesh, however, concludes that he must be a deaf and blind "quadruple amputee, "mutilated by the explosion of the boiler" "beneath the bedroom of my parlor-floor apartment."[100] Another explanation that he hints at but does not articulate directly is feelings of guilt from his lapsed sexual interest in his wife. Kapesh confesses: "We really did get on so easily[....] that it seemed to me something very like a disaster (little I knew about disaster) when out of the blue, I began to take no pleasure at all in our lovemaking."[101]

Another explanation given, but immediately rejected by the narrator, is Kapesh's infatuation with breasts, especially those of his wife Claire. Kapesh describes Claire's figure as "full-breasted," and remembers lying one day on the sand at the beach and suckling her breast, "that strange thing" as he calls it, like Poseidon or Zeus would be sucking a "soft globe, "until he turned green and Claire warned that the breast in his mouth would cut off his air."[102]

Kapesh follows that recollection with an ambiguous reflection on his present condition. On the one hand he explains his transformation by revealing that on the beach he actually wanted to be breasted. In a fantastic way, desire once put into words has become flesh: Kapesh has become the thing that he so badly wanted to be, or at least, wanted to have in his mouth, even to the point of endangering his well-being. On the other hand, the narrator challenges the wish-fulfilment theory, as he calls it even as he presents it. After all, the narrator is convinced, this text is not a fairy tale but a story about his life as he remembers it. The narrator addresses the reader and states that he does not include his text in that parti ular genre.

"But as this is decidedly not some fairy tale—not to me, dear reader—why should a wish like that have been the one to come true?"[103]

Kapesh finally rejects the reading of his story as a fantasy because his conception of reality "has style, "and is "grander than" a fulfilment of a wish. The short paragraph that follows and ends Kepesh's discussion on wish-fulfilment is truly paradoxical.

Kapesh's argument that the story of his transformation is not a fairy tale, because it happened in the reality of his life and because reality has style—whatever that means—is clearly self-contradictory. He claims that he knows what reality is, but his changing explanations and mental instability prove the opposite; in fact in the course of the story, Dr Klinger classifies many of his explanations as delusions.

The narrator's self-contradiction about the status of reality leads the reader to think that the explanation that Kapesh simultaneously rejects and considers might actually carry some truth in it. The narrator casts himself as an ironic, untrustworthy type. Kapesh appears blindly to believe in something in a "reality" that he does not quite grasp. Those self-reflexive, but ambiguous, discussions on the differences between a real story and a fairy tale, which the text effectively blurs, recur later when Kepesh believes that he has gone mad, but despite his imagined madness is able to differentiate between that which is real and that which is madness:

> Oh yes, I can feel the difference now, even as I talk I can sense the differences between the insane stuff and what's truly happened.[104]

Kapesh pretends to know the demarcations of reality. Yet he is deluded. The reader who would interpret Kapesh's notion of reality one way or another is duly warned.

The next phase in the dynamic of explanations and counter-explanations occurs about six months after his transformation and consists of Kapesh's "crisis of faith. "Probably the visit of his superior, Arthur Schonbrunn, causes that crisis in which Kapesh exhibits repressive behaviour and argues that he has not really turned into a breast. Through Schonbrunn, Kapesh faces his loss of social status in academics. The dean cannot help giggling, and finally openly laughing, when he sees his former colleague. The reaction is inappropriate from an intelligent and sensitive professor who has written a small book on Robert Musil—whose best known work, (The Man without Qualities 1930-43), corresponds, to some extent, with Kapesh's situation as a man who has lost almost his earlier identity. Again, as immediately after his transformation, Kapesh refuses to believe that he is a breast. He now argues that "a man cannot turn into a breast other than in his own imagination."[105] Therefore, he begins to think that he is still dreaming and then decides that he has gone mad. Dr. Klinger tries to convince him that he is not deluded but that he really is a breast.

Kapesh defends his new theory so strongly that, as the narrator explains in retrospect, he takes Dr. Klinger's words and systematically gives them their opposite meaning. Nevertheless, the doctor's rhetorical skills and psychoanalytical training weaken

Kapesh's arguments, and Kapesh must continually alter his own theory and produce new, more complicated and tortuous versions of it.

Kapesh thus appears to imagine that he is imagining. He cannot differentiate between reality and structures of imagination. According to Kapesh fictions of transformations and tales of grotesque bodies—he mentions Gogol's *The Nose* Kafka's *Verwandlung* and Swift's *Gulliver's Travels*—caused his change. He had often taught those books; indeed he had done so with conviction only a week before his own metamorphosis. If it was not simply the books themselves that caused his change, he surmises, it was the power of imagination in them or his own power as a reader to imagine these stories. Despite Dr. Klinger's warnings Kapesh convinces himself that those books made him fantasize his transformation and become oblivious of reality. He should just break out of his delusion and get back to teaching literature and not to try to live through it or let his subjectivity be constructed in it. He tells this newest theory to his father, explaining the central literary references, but Kapesh senior does not respond: he does not understand what his son means just as earlier he did not understand the value of his son's work as a professor of literature. The narrative continues to circle, entrap, and avoid David Kapesh's metamorphosed state.

In the last section of the text Kapesh returns to his arguments that literature produced his state. Again, the quintessential question is "hormones are hormones and art is art" and that they should be kept separate from each other. Kapesh still insists that books made him as he is now:

> I took the leap. Made the word flesh. Don't you see, I have out-Kafkaed Kafta.[106]

Kapesh's new tactic is to accept himself as a breast to obviate Dr. Klinger's criticism, but simultaneously, to continue to talk of himself as an art work, a product of artistic imagination. Kapesh asks: "who is the greater artist, he who imagines the marvelous transformation, or he who marvelously transforms himself?"[107] What he implies by that is that he himself is the greater artist for having been transformed into an art work. Finally, there is no complete explanation for Kapesh's change into a breast.

No reason is sufficient for the incredible change: neither Kapesh's impotency, his sexual fantasies, his mental disturbance, the nor fictionalizing, or the fictional overtaking of his world. Also for Kapesh himself his change remains a profoundly ambiguous event. In fact, it can be said that his metamorphosis is both a route of escape and a terrible accident. Kapesh concludes that he has both willed radical changes in his personality—because of his aging, fear of impotence, obsession with breasts, and other reasons that are further elaborated in the "sequel", *The professor of Desire*—and that what happened was an unpredictable catastrophe that made him a man without qualities. Because of his transformation Kapesh does not have to feel guilty about his impotence, or rather, his lack of desire for and sense of failure regarding Claire, nor does he need to leave her and have multiplied his sexual energy in other channels. In addition, the transformation into a breast, although it isolates him from the world, offers a recipe for the kind of *Portnoy's Complaint* that Kapesh has had about his life. In Roth's *Portnoy's Complaint*, Dr. Spielvogel, Alexander Portnoy's doctor, defines his patient's complaint as a disorder in which strongly-felt ethical and altruistic impulses are perpetually warring with extreme sexual longings, often of a perverse nature. Similarly, Kapesh has, as becomes clear later in *The Professor of Desire*, confronted the limitations put on his body and his fantasies by moral authority, social restraint, and thus obsession is ironically resolved.

In addition to psychoanalysis, a central problem for Kapesh is whether literature lies at the root of his transformation. What has happened to him reminds him so much of the metamorphosis stories he has read and taught. Therefore, Kapesh treats himself as a text.

In *The Breast*, the comical and the parodic are always tainted with other narrative modes. At several points in the narrative, the narrator predicts interpretations of himself as a comical character, interpretations that will somehow fall short of their subject. In the first part of the novella, in his description of his "incubation" period before the change, the narrator states that what happened to him is simply something that has never happened to anyone before. He anticipates the joke in his story as he claims that he too sees the joke in the outcome of his transformation, although enjoying it might be "another matter". If he laughs at himself, he says, it is always brief and bitter, although he ends the discussion by proposing that laughter may be something he just has to deal with: "But then maybe more laughs are what I have to look forward to, if the medical men are able to sustain life in me in this condition, and if I should continue to want them to."[108] The same problematic situation is evoked near the end of the story in his last dialogue with Dr. Klinger. Here Dr. Klinger comforts Kapesh:

> Of course the madmen and the morons will chatter anyway, you realize that you will never be taken on our own terms, regard you say. " " I 'll still be a joke." "A joke. A freak. If you induce the one to tell them, a charlatan too.[109]

It is difficult to affirm the ridiculousness in Kapesh's situation from both his own perspective and from that of the reader. On the one hand it is not necessary to take Kapesh's sensitivity at its face-value: the story and its main character may still be read as a joke; his seriousness may also be thought to be ironic. On the other hand, as the text includes several reflections on the comical effect of Kapesh's condition, It complicates the reading of Kapesh's character as a mere joke.

The comical aspect of *The Breast* may also be read against the tradition of metamorphosis stories where the ludicrous nature of an uncontrollable change is often emphasized.

David Kapesh seeks a mental transformation, because of his boredom or impotence or both, but instead he suffers an unexpected, comical, and ironic physical change. Gogol's *Nose* is a comment on Russian bureaucracy and its dishonest social climbers. The many possible readings of Kafka's *The Metamorphosis* range in their emphasis from philosophy and theology to psychological studies on the modern subject and estrangement.

The same fusion of the comical with the fantastic, the psychic, the tragic, or the moral occurs in *The Breast*. The comical may be more pervasive than in Kafka's text.The comical keeps blending with the tragic, with moral questioning, with the psychic questions concerning the status of reality, literature, and the psychological construction of one's subjectivity. Furthermore, the many literary or other references in the text may not be taken as mere substantiation for the subject matter in the text. Although *The Breast* proposes itself as a certain kind of story and in a way creates its own literary background through the allusions to Swift, Gogol, and Kafka, it simultaneously distances itself critically from those stories by commenting on them and joining them together in unprecedented ways. The comical in *The Breast* is caused not just by the form of Kapesh's extraordinary change but in parodic relation to other stories. It may stem from the self-aware association with, as well as the distancing from, previous metamorphosis stories that many Roth critics have lamented and not necessarily from its "pure comicality" or the way narrative tone irreconciliably sways between the comical, the fantastic, the ironic, and the tragic.

Swift's *Gulliver's Travels*, Gogol's *The Nose*, and Kafka's *Verwandlung* together with the Dostoyevsky references, the Shakespeare tapes that Kapesh listens to and the Rike quotation that ends the narrative engage the text in a metatextual polemic on intertexuality, the epistemological status of literature, and the relationship between the subject and texts. *The Breast* swerves from those precursor texts by commenting upon them and by joining them together. We see that parodic intertextuality mirrored when Kapesh, during his second nervous breakdown, uses his subversive rhetorical tactics turning every word into its opposite. Likewise, *The Breast* plays with multiple narrative modes, generic patterns, and story traditions. Through references to Swift, Gogol, and Kafka the text repeats and enforces the conventions of metamorphoses stories but also transforms them by combining those stories and engaging them in a metatextual polemic on representation and identity.

It is significant that Kapesh, in referring to the metamorphoses in Gogol and Kafka's stories consciously exploits the status of metamorphosis as a radical metaphor. The strategy becomes apparent as he poses the question of who is the greater artist: he who imagines the marvellous transformation or he who marvelously transforms himself?

The Swift, Gogol, Dostoevsky, Kafka, and Rilke subtexts are parodically related to each other in *THE BREAST* through metafictive commentary, including the problematization of metamorphosis as a metaphor, and through the figurative means of a synecdoche.

Swift's image of the giant breast, Gogol's figure of the headless torso, and Kafka's metamorphosis of a whole propose in this text a dynamic between a part and whole against which is reflected Kapesh's change into a body part. That metonymic or synecdochical dynamic also is made meaningful and comical in relation to Kapesh's effort to see his "whole" situation while he has become a body that is only a part of body.

The bodies of Swift's Gulliver, Gogol's Kovalyov, and Kafka's Gregor Samsa and their changes are central mental images for Kapesh when he tries to grasp what has happened to him. The first reference to Kafka is evoked when David Kapesh signs his family name as simply "K." in his response to colleague Arthur Schonbrunn. That is certainly a reference to Kafka: Kepesh will later mention Kafka's *The Metamorphosis* and, at a somewhat paranoid moment, ask Dr. Klinger whether he has realized that all their names begin with the letter K. Soon after the letter to Schonbrunn, and increasingly toward the end of the story, Kapesh imagines that the fiction of Swift, Gogol, and Kafka, which has long fascinated him and which he often taught in his classes, has finally taken over his imagination. From that point onward direct references to the three writers are frequent and recurrent. Kapesh also paraphrases the short stories of Gogol and Kafka for his father when he tries to convince him that his literature has made him mad.

What seems to be a common element especially in the stories of both Gogol and Roth is the narrator's efforts to comprehend his fate and his speculations on the possible reason for his change are central to the narrative. Gogol's main character Kovalyov, who has lost his nose, cannot believe at first what has happened or he thinks that it is only a dream or hallucination, a drunken vision. Later, he invents an explanation for the change that he thinks makes it totally conceivable. He is convinced that a certain officer's wife, Mrs. Podtotsina, must be behind his transformation because he has been neglecting her daughter, to whom the mother would like to see him married. He even writes a letter to her and accuses her of magic tricks. Roth's novella expands Kovalyov's imaginative paranoia in inventing explanations for Kapesh's change in his multiplying arguments and counterarguments which unravel the different layers at which his psyche is at play.

Other aspects that are common in the Gogol and Roth stories and on which Roth elaborates are the theme of castration and the wide public interest in the transformed body. Both characters are the talk of the town, and in Kapesh's case possibly the whole world is interested in him; both characters are ashamed of their bodily changes. If Kovalyov does not have his nose, he cannot have his former social self, he cannot pursue women, nor take part in any social events. In that respect, Roth's story out-ridicules Gogol's. Kapesh's physical change is so total that there seems to be no reason for his shame. In Roth's story there is no metaphor for a phallus, rather we witness the actual disappearance of a penis. Kepesh has "cooled down" sexually before his change, but after his metamorphosis his impotence is paradoxically cured as he loses his penis in the transformation. Here Roth's story out-ridicules Gogol's: Kapesh relocates his penis in his nipple, whereas Kovalyov's nose just returns to its place one day. Roth's text also simultaneously appropriates and turns around the synecdochical dynamic in Gogol's text: Kovalyov's part, his nose, becomes an image of whole (it disguises itself as a man) and again a part when it returns to Kovalyov's head; Kapesh as a breast is a whole man who has turned into a part of a body.

Like Kapesh, Gregor Samsa explains that his metamorphosis is not a dream. However, he does not ponder why he has changed; he accepts his fate in a disturbingly submissive manner with a spirit of resignation. He is also more severely cut off from the world than Kovayov or Kapesh as he cannot speak in his new form. But certain metafictive considerations and mirror structures in the narrative are common characteristics in these three stories—and are accentuated in Roth's work. In Gogol's story the narrator's voice comes to the surface at its end: he wonders how anything so fantastic and supernatural as Kovalyov's story could ever happen. The narrator even doubts his own story and his own reliability by asking how any writer could treat a subject like this. There is no value in such a story, he claims, although finally he professes that if the reader really considers it, he or she may realize that such things, although rare, may happen.

Gregor Samsa's metamorphosis is mirrored in *Verwandlung* in the picture of a woman that Samsa had recently cut out of an illustrated magazine and put into a "pretty gilt frame. "The picture depicts "a lady, with a fur cap o and a fur stole, whole of her forearm had vanished."[110] Before his transformation the picture and the fret-work of the picture frame had been Samsa's only source of amusement. After his transformation Gregor, now an insect is able to protect only the picture from his sister and mother who decide to move the furniture out of Gregor's room.

The framing of a mass-produced photograph is a symbol of Gregor's isolated and probably sexually frustrating bachelor life, hemmed in by his parents, and of his being constantly overworked and stressed, with no source of enjoyment outside the world of business and advertising. However, at the same time, it is also a mirror structure for his forthcoming metamorphosis and his metamorphosed body. Samsa's metamorphosis into an insect brings out the grotesque in this photograph, and vice versa: with her fur clothing, into which parts of her body vanish, the woman appears to be partly inhuman.

As a parallel to Kafka's use of the picture and its framing as a commentary, Roth's text is replete with literary and artistic allusions that comment on the story. Another line between Kafka and Roth may be Dostoevsky: Samsa's metamorphosis literalizes the narrator-main character's wish to turn into an insect in Dostoevsky's "Notes from Underground" Kapesh's change is a parodical transformation of Samsa's change. Dostoevsky's novel about the resident of a cellar recalls both Kafka and Roth's stories: by the physical restrictions put on the main character and by his relentless monologue or "confession" that proceeds through various self-contradictory statements and explanations as if, as Bakhtin stresses in his *Problems of Dostoyevsky's Poetics*, he anticipates someone's response. Also, Kapesh's ambiguous relationship with Claire repeats the traumatic bond between Dostoevsky's narrator and a prostitute called Liza.

An evident difference between the stories of Kafka, Roth, and Dostoevsky seems to be accentuated in the Breast. Gregor's relationship with his metamorphosed body is ultimately self-destructive, whereas Kapesh although suffering from a fierce mental crisis, always confirms his belief in life and ends his narrative, however ambiguous and ironic it may be, in a wish for everyone to proceed with his or her education. Dostoevsky's "anti-hero," whom the narrator calls a paradoxical human being, also keeps on living and narrating his story. But, perhaps more significantly, Kapesh's metamorphosed body "out-Kafkas" Kafka's story. He is a "mere" immobile organ; whereas Gregor Samsa still has tripartite body with a head, trunk and legs. The man-insect simile in Dostoevsky's tale and the literalized metaphor in Kafka's story thus become a synecdoche of a human in *The Breast.*

Embedded in the Swift subtext is another important figurative inversion that is based on a synecdochical move. The reference to Swift's *Gulliver's Travels* differs from the Gogol and Kafka connections in that Swift's book includes no actual cases of metamorphosis, and the main character's body does not change. Instead the protagonist's environment changes, causing his body and mental capacities to appear to be different. In the world's Gulliver visits, proportions and sizes differ, horses speak and can create their own well-functioning societies, people have overdeveloped aspects of mental capacities. Those and other fantastic elements create estranging effects and allow for Swift's biting satire. The second part of the book, the voyage to Brobdingnag, is the most important part in relation to *The Breast*. From that section the figure of the breast in Roth's story is most likely appropriated.

During his trip to Brobdingnag, Gulliver is seized by the natives, giants who are twelve times his size. To them Gulliver becomes a freak and a kind of pet. His life is constantly threatened by animals and insects of gigantic proportions, and by the jealous dwarf he encounters while staying with the nobility at the king's court. Of particular interest to us, is the appearance of a huge, disturbing breast. On Gulliver's arrival in Brobdingnag, he is brought to the house of the giant farmer whose baby mistakes Gulliver's head for a nipple or some other pacifier. The mother of the infant calms the restless and disappointed baby by nursing him, and Gulliver is sickened by the sight of her huge breast.

Gulliver, however, carefully observes the nursing mother from a close distance and gives the reader the exact measurements of the breast. The sight of the organ shocks Gulliver profoundly, but unfortunately he is confronted with many other giant breasts, some of them as disturbing as the first one.

Like David Kapesh and Gregor Samsa, Gulliver is taken to be something other than a true subject. He functions as various forms of an object; as a nipple, a pet, a status symbol, and a toy.

In Roth's novella Gulliver's predicament, his displacement as a nipple, is actualized by David Kapesh's transformation into a breast. Roth's story turns Swift's metaphor of a head that is like a nipple and the synecdochical play between the whole (Gulliver) and the part (nipple) into a radical process of change.

It is interesting that although the narrator asserts his optimism, his last evocation of Swift refers directly to the Brobdingnag episode, and is different from the previous allusions. Kapesh asks his listeners to reflect on the story and its main character.

Kapesh thus differentiates himself from Gulliver by proposing the possibility of pleasure in a deformed body and a "qualityless" state. Gulliver's adventures end in some kind of catastrophe or impasse that will force him back to his old form and reinforce the status quo of his old self, but the limits of Kapesh's identity in the "strange" land of opportunity, America, may be reformed in a way that is ironic but perhaps also satisfying.

This ironic, synecdochical dynamic is re-emphasized with Rilke and Rodin's figure of the headless torso inscribed at the end of the story. The cited text is the poem "Archaic Torso of Apollo" that Rilike, inspired by Rodin's sculpture, wrote in Paris in 1908. The entire poem is embedded in the novella and it is preceded by several ironic comments from Kapesh. Kapesh explains that as a literature professor he developed the habit of ending his lectures with something moving for the students "to carry from the uncontaminated classroom out into the fallen world of junk food and pop stars and dope."[111]

Roth's narrator also offers an ironic reading of Rilke's text by ambiguously stating that his life will illuminate the last lines of the poem in a new way. Kapesh wants to pinpoint the text's last phrase "You must change your life, "which Kapesh describes as "the poet's concluding admonition, which may not be so elevated a sentiment as appears at first glance."[112] Because of the critical framing of the sentence, "You must change your life" is a statement that simultaneously enables several readings-tragic, moral, comical, fantastic. In the poem a Rodin statue, the headless torso, seems to call for a change in the life of the poetic self. However, within the context of *The Breast* that piece of advice acquires a more comical and paradoxical meaning. The narrator changes his life mentally and psychologically and forges his subjectivity anew, and in that way he may be thought to be heeding Rilke's words. But those changes take place only after a radical change in his physicality, which is entirely out of his control. Kapesh literally must change his life. In the framing of the last line in the poem, he refers back to his own comical or tragic-comical state in which he lacks the agency to initiate the necessary changes. In the context of Kapesh's life the sentence functions as an ironic comment on his situation; and when it is seen against his vulnerable and erotic body, the ironic treatment of that imperative is also a comment on Rilke's elevated poetic style.

Can literature or art truly change one's life? And if it can, what if the change is something like what has happened to Kapesh? As Kapesh is a professor of literature and an adamant believer in the power of fiction, literature and life are closely interlinked in his mind. Yet, the problem of the relationship between fiction and reality, which is found throughout the text and is connected with much of the intertextual commentary, is also the problem of identity. The description of Kapesh's life as a breast and the discussion of Shakespeare, Swift, Gogol, and Kafta finally lead to a far-reaching ethical dialogue between Kapesh and his psychoanalyst that focuses on the intricate relationship between literature, reality and subjectivity.

Early in the tale the difference between reality, or verisimilitude, and fiction was evoked as the narrator rejected the reading of his story as a fairy tale. The same problem is elaborated during Kapesh's second crisis, again by his conviction that fiction has created his change, and also in the final discussion between Kapesh and Dr. Klinger. The very end of the text is profoundly ambiguous about the relationship and does not privilege one state over the other: only in Kapesh's imagination does he again take on his old role as professor of literature. Is he is now "ending a lecture" and citing poetry or is he truly speaking to an unnamed audience?

Another significant facet is added at the fag end of the story when Dr. Klinger advises Kapesh to keep in mind "our friend with the bread who sits on the throne."[113] By that Dr. Klinger means "Mr. Reality," or Freud, ar d his reality principle that Klinger believes Kapesh has neglected in his theory of the fictional source of his metamorphosis.

With reference to Freud's concept of the reality principle (as opposed to the pleasure principle), we return to psychoanalysis as an important subtext and allegory in *The Breast*. But, simultaneously, Kapesh's situation poses an epistemological question concerning books of fiction: what can be known through them? The narrator reflects on past stories of metamorphoses or deformations of the body, and he simultaneously tells a similar story of his metamorphosis and convinces himself that his life story derives from the earlier stories. Clearly, the narrative probes how literature may affect one's conception of reality and how it may take part in the formation of one's identity or one's psyche. The contrary positions of Kapesh and Dr. Klinger keep the discussion at play. Although he modifies his position at several points, Kapesh seems to believe that fiction may, and actually does, change one's life—almost as radically as a child's entrance into language may construct her or his subjectivity. His own life, he has convinced himself, is proof of that.

Dr. Klinger, on the other hand, opines that reality and fiction should be kept strictly separate: to do so enables one to avoid mental disturbances and other discomforts. In his mind, those two worlds have no points of convergence. For Dr. Klinger, the reality principle and common sense must be the structure for one's subjectivity and for one's relationship with society.

The Breast blurs the distinction between "reality" and fiction. Baumgarten and Gottfried have noticed that Kapesh does not just use literature to reflect on his situation, but in fact needs books as a kind of nourishment for his mind and body; that need can be likened to that of a baby who, dependent on nursing, needs a breast. Tellingly, Kapesh's relationship with literature changes when he is a breast. He states that he can now listen to a book and enjoy it or give himself over to the genius of the actor if he likes, whereas, when he was still a professor, he experienced literature as something unavoidably tainted by his "self-consciousness and all the responsibilities of serious discourse."[114] His new way of reading or listening to literature is also less concentrated. He explains that while listening:

> I invariably miss the meaning of an unfamiliar sound, or lose convoluted syntax, and then my mind begins to wander, and when again, little makes sense for lines on end.[115]

Kapesh listens to recordings of Shakespeare several hours every morning and again sometimes in the afternoon. He finds comfort in the symbolic order of language, in the literature that he listens to. He is marginalized out of the visual and secular orders of reality by his metamorphosis, but in literature he certainly finds a possibility of retaining some of his old social self. Literature has become a source of order and sustenance although its difference from "reality" appears ever more uncertain.

Kapesh's physical change obviously accentuates the sense of uncertainty about the status of reality. The new limitations put on—and to a certain degree the new possibilities found in—his sensory organs restructure his sense of reality and affect his capacity to verbalize his subjectivity and its relationship with the world. As he puts it, his old social self was that of "a professor of literature, a lover, a son, a friend, a neighbor, a customer, a client, and a citizen."[116]

Most of those determinates disappear once he is a breast. He still tries to study literature and write lectures, but he is no longer a professor. His sexuality has totally changed and he can no longer occupy the position of a neighbour, a customer or a client. Therefore, what happens after his metamorphosis is a radical change in the conceptualization of his occupational position, sexuality and ethnicity as well as the concept of morality and the change in his relationship vis-a-vis his parents and his wife.

With regard to his senses, David Kapesh's physical change is profound. In his new form he cannot see, smell, taste or move. Lack of sight obviously restricts his capacity to understand the exterior world. It makes Kapesh paranoid, doubtful about what he hears from the others. Although he certainly is under the surveillance of the doctors and scientists who visit him, his fears of being constantly observed, viewed and discussed in public and made into a sort of media event are not fully confirmed. Understandably he wonders:

> But how do I know anyone has ever left me alone, or that this is even a room?[117]

In a way, though, the fact that he could be ceaselessly watched finally does not matter. In his new body, without sight, he dwells in a world of his own. At the end of the story it appears that it is comforting to him to be always isolated at some level as he cannot see or sense in the same way as the people around him.

The complications that derive from the impossibility of seeing are further enhanced by other deficiencies. His hearing has weakened considerably: "at least it has seemed to me that I am able to make myself heard through my nipple, and, faintly, to hear through it what is going on around me."[118] Moreover, being armless and unable to move makes him utterly passive and dependent on other people. That may be an ironic slap at David Kapesh's earlier strong sense of himself as an individual who went so far as to live separately from his girlfriend to assert this independence.

Because he is capable of speaking and thinking, Kapesh's transformation still functions as a passage within the realm of language and literature. The change also takes place in the sphere of moral judgements; Kapesh can still discuss and listen to literature, and try to find new conceptions of morality through those discursive interactions.

His change forces him to redefine his sexuality, his family relationships and his culture, to negotiate a new position and moral imperative for him self in relation to others. His predominant struggle is with the forces that shape and attempt to impose limitations upon him. Before his change those forces were the moral imperatives set on him by his work, by marriage and sex, and by his roles as son, friend, neighbour, client and citizen. After his change his social ties seem to have loosened and his duties have lessened in important ways. Although the many social regulations that had caused him distress begin to lose meaning, his body now becomes a site of anxiety. Part of the problem is the limitations put on him and the question of his sexual identity. After all, his change, having transformed a man into part of a woman, questions socially defined gender roles. Further, he finds new sensual pleasures in his transformed body—eventually we see that his whole body becomes an erogenous field.

During Claire's first visit her touch arouses him unexpectedly, creating his first major crisis. From then on his erotic needs escalate, and he desires that his wife roll on him and make love to his nipple. Beyond the absurdity of those possibilities lies a very definite change: he must remain passive and immobile in his new sexual role. His pleasure appears to come "out of nothingness". His erotic body is thus an ironic version of the stereotypical female sexual role in which a woman attains gratification passively without orgasm.

A central issue in Kapesh's transformed sexuality is the problem of how to control erotic desire, a problem that arises in the form of homophobia. Soon after he becomes conscious following his transformation, he is aroused by the touches of a male nurse, and that distresses him greatly. He decides then that it must be a female nurse who washes him or his wife who rubs his nipple if he is going to get any physical pleasure from human contact. For him to be wholly satisfied, the bathing or other erotic acts must involve only himself and a woman; no other person may be present in the room. Despite those precautions, unsettling thoughts keep bothering him. After Claire has excited him with her touch during her first visit, he immediately speculates on the possibility of her turning into a male organ: "If Claire had become a penis[..]"[119]

Kapesh quickly brushes off the thought, calls it ridiculous and thus represses it. But he is obviously still horrified by the thought of homo- or bisexuality: he doubts if he would be capable of reciprocating the (apparently homosexual) devotion that Claire shows to him, when she is transformed into a large male member.

Further, the fact that Claire so obediently tries to please him is doubly unsettling to Kapesh because she had often rejected certain sexual adventures that he had suggested before his metamorphosis. Strangely, after his change, he actually traps her into a continuous "lesbian" affair with his female body.

Homophobia is crucial for Kapesh in the reconstitution of his gendered self and of a new moral imperative for his sexual body. His first "crisis, " which concerns his uncontrollable and overwhelming sexual needs, passes when he is closed with anesthetics, and the nurse is replaced. The disturbingly arousing touch of the new male nurse causes enough resistance in him to control the overwhelming erotic feelings he has felt. He concludes that inserting:

> My nipple into either the mouth or the anus of Mr. Brooks, the nurse, is something I just can't imagine with anything like to I would imagine my nipple in Claire, or even in Miss Clark (a nurse], though I realize that the conjunction of male mouth and nipple can hardly be described as a homosexual act.[120]

What Kapesh, in fact, realizes here is that one's sexual identity is not simply physical, but may be based finally on one's mental and psychic orientation. Homophobia, then, helps him negatively to relocate his maleness. He mentally and psychologically relocates his lost penis in nipple. He wants to penetrate a woman with his nipple; he wants to occupy an active role in a sexual act. In Lacanian terms Kapesh thus reconstitutes the phallic order, that is, he centers his subjectivity anew around the redefinition of his nipple. The symbolic mutilation of his sexual organ, his actual castration, thus permits him to find a new sense of masculinity, a new awareness of masculine psyche.

Through all the ironic reversals of sexual identity—in Kapesh and Claire's changing relationship, in the contradictions between Kapesh's psyche and his body, and in the definition of his maleness—the narrative creates a situation of sexual ambiguity. One's sexuality is not found to be simply physical or unconscious but appears to be based on one's conscious self, mental orientation and psychic proclivity as well.

In the case of *The Breast*, however, repression follows closely on the tail of transgression. The metamorphosed body of David Kapesh is given the right to be sexual although his sexual needs are thoroughly changed. His transformation gives him a new, castrated sexual identity which at first is out of his control and a source of great anxiety but which later he masters. He takes control over this situation in several ways: his mounting homophobia; the redefinition of his nipple as a male organ; his discussions with the psychoanalyst Dr. Kligner; his safe haven in literature. The symbolic order of language and literature helps him, like the monster Frankenstein, to overcome his feelings of being ludicrous or monstrous in the eyes of others.

A close refer nce point might also be Virginia Woolf's Orlando, which is concerned with a man's transformation into woman. The main character Orlando, however, does not maintain her old psychological masculinity as strictly as Kapesh. Although she still sometimes plays the man, she also starts to act according to the gender that culture has bound to her new body—thus disrupting, at many levels, the essentialist equation between biological sex and social gender. The new gender of Kapesh's body and its contradictory relationship with his male psyche (in Orlando the "gender" of the main character's psyche may be more ambiguous are essential) elements that link his metamorphosis to the problematics of psychic subjectivity and not merely to an intertextual comment within literature.

In a very general sense the Jewish schlemiel's predicament, or what Freud sees as the mixture of self-irony and self-pity in Jewish marriage-broker stories, applies to David Kapesh's situation. He failed in all of his relationships with women, including also in the end with his wife Claire, and then turned into a breast. To further emphasize the sense of tragicomedy in his life he is juxtaposed with the socially successful male types like his father, Dr. Klinger, and his peer Arthur Schonbrunn. Kapesh's parents, and mostly his father, represent Kapesh's Jewish ethnicity in the text: He American Jewish ethnic identity is first confirmed in relation to his father's visits.

Kapesh is puzzled by his father's unchanged social and familial behaviour in the presence of his changed son. He is also annoyed by his father's obvious preoccupation with petty gossip. One of the rumors his father relays evokes a source of the schlemiel tradition. Kapesh's father tells the story of an intercultural marriage—between an Egyptian and a Jew—with a tone of disapproval and dismay. Kapesh, who also is married to a non-Jew, reacts to that with slient rage: "But doesn't he [David's father] get what has happened? Doesn't the man understand that some things are more unusual even than a Jew marrying an Egyptian?"[121]

What is significant about this bit of gossip is the questioning of the acceptability of a Jewish-gentile marriage. By bringing up this dilemma Kapesh's father, or at least so Kapesh feels, is indirectly calling Kapesh's marriage into question and hinting that he is a schlemiel. It is also obvious that his father is so locked into his Jewishness that a Jew-gentile marriage is more bizarre to him than his transformation.

Similar anxiety in predominantly sexual relationships is present in various of Roth's books in which a Jewish man tries to come to terms with his restless desires concerning gentile women. *The Breast* is one of the stories in which the problem culminates. This inter-racial relationship dwelt in his various novels is of profound psychological interest. Thus *The Breast* has the crust of an outlandish fantasy and bizarre comedy, but beneath this crust lies the kernel of psychic exploration and psychological realism through tracing the manifold and myriad-faceted impact of this external transformation on the inner self and personality of its victim.

Philip Roth, who has lately seemed an author in search of a subject, turns to an old interest in his new novel. "Oh, to be a center fielder, a center fielder—and nothing more!" was the yearning cry of Alexander Portnoy—a son, a sexual creature and a human being, among other things. For thinking men, non-performers, sports offer a tempting glimpse of grace, of the merging of self into pure and formal function.

The Great American Novel is a book about baseball and its power as heroic and pastoral myth. In a novel within a novel, the protagonist, or narrator, of this ingenious story, the author one Word Smith, tells us the story of perhaps the greatest cover up in national history. The story, of course, is that of the third Major League, The Patriot League, that was dissolved in 1946 after a massive infiltration of communists threatened to destroy the integrity of the game.

In the apparent plot to destroy the American spirit; the communists tried to discredit and destroy the game of baseball, which was thought by many to be the true American religion. The story is told through the tale of the 90 years old author, Word Smith, affectionately known as 'Smitty'. More importantly, we see that the Patriot League was expunged not just from the history books, but also from the halls of Cooperstown today where no mention of the patriot league remains. There is no tribute to Luke Gofannon, the only man ever with a higher lifetime batting average than Ty Cobb, or any of the other immortals of that league.

The tale begins with an event that turned the Patriot League, and Major League baseball on its ear in 1933 when the first pitches in Major League history took seriously the fans cries and tried to "Kill the Umps". The Umpire involved was mike "The Mouth" Masterson who had just made a bad call that ended a perfect game for the rookie pitcher Gil Gamesh. Gamesh, a pitcher of Babylonian decent, had pitched a record six straight shutouts after entering the League and seemed destined for greatness. Following the muffed call he threw a fastball, estimated as a match for one of Ryan's best, into the throat of Masterson that crushed his larynx and nearly killed him. Gamesh was banished from the game for life.

Fast forward ten years, where one of the proudest franchises of the Patriot League "The Rupert-Mundys" finds themselves homeless, a victim of greedy owners and the war department's need for a port city staging area to ship soldiers and supplies to the war in Europe. The Mundys were at best a shadow of the great team they had once been; all of their belongings been sold off by the sons of the deceased owner Glorious Mundy who had loved the game.

During wartime finding decent players was an uphill taste and the sons of Glorious Mundy did not even try. They built a team of misfits, freaks, and whomever they could find cheaply. As a matter of fact, they cared so little that they felt the janitor in charge of the team when they went on vacation. For the sake of the money they could earn by leasing their stadium, the "Rupert" became baseball's only homeless franchise. So in 1943 the Mundys played 154 games, all on the road, managing to lose 120 of them. They were not a good baseball team—not even a halfway decent one. In 1943 they finished 50 games out of the running. It was the beginning of the end of the Patriot League. How would a team with a 14-years-old second baseman, a French-Canadian shortstop who spoke no English and had only played in Japan, a catcher with a wooden leg, a dwarf as a starting pitcher, and a first basemen who once led the prison league in hitting, but could only hit while drunk, have hoped to win? These were men who would have done almost anything to get away from the embarrassment of being a Mundy and some humiliated themselves to try to get that chance.

This book in many ways is their story and the story of how the Patriot League came to be infiltrated with communists. Even though League president General Oakheart tried hard to fight the scourge and testified before the house committee on un-American activities about the infiltration, it was the fans that spoke loudest by boycotting the Patriot League games following the uncovering of the plot. Even the cities that once housed the eight great teams were tainted and chose to rename themselves than be affiliated with the Patriot League teams who once bore their names.

Roth in truth has a lot of fun with this book: he poked fun at baseball, government, communism, capitalism and even at himself, with "Smitty's" testimony before the Un-American Activities Committee and the rejection letters for his manuscript. His mockery of Hemningway, Twain and many others seem just in line with his style.

The year1943 was a bad year in the Patriot League, which was the third major league. In the golden age its stars, Luke Gofannon, Mike Mazda, Smokey Woden and the rest had been the peers in skill and fame of Cobb, Ruth and Johnson; but decline followed and World War II drew off most of the able-bodied players. With Roth we follow the season of the worst team in the history of the game, the Mundys of Port Rupert, New Jersey, who lost even their stadium to the demands of the war effort.

The ballplayers of Roth's fable, though they bear the names of deities, are anything but images of perfection. The Mundys consist of 50-year-old veterans who have tottered out of retirement, a French-Canadian refuge from the Japanese League, adolescent boys, an alcoholic ex-con ("the Babe Rush of the Big House" when he played for sing-sing), a peg-legged catcher, a one-armed outfielder, a midget-relief pitcher and so on. Named for their founder, the legendary Glorious Mundy, they are the scarifies implicit in his credo ("baseball in this country's religion"), and their season of shame, relieved only by an 11-game winning streak powered by a secret diet of synthetic wheaties concocted by a teenage genius, culminated in a 31-0 loss to the pennant-winning Tri-City Tycoons on the final day of the season.

After this, the destruction of the Patriot League itself, in 1944, is anti-climax. Having literally seen the death of their old manager, the saintly Ulysses S. Fairsmith, they get as their new one the sinister Gil Gamesh, the only Baby lonian-American ever to make the big leagues, who was banned for life in 1933 for deliberately beaning an umpire. He returns from exile in Russia and persuades the League president that his teams have been infiltrated by Red agents. Gamesh is in fact a double agent, stirring up his wretched players against the oppressive "ideals" of capitalists' fair play, but the player who discovers his subversive perfidy, the gifted innocent Roland Agni, is assassinated in mid-game. The ensuing Dies Committee hearings and the imprisonment of 10 Mundys for contempt lead to the dissolution of the Patriot League and the expunging of its history from the records of the game. Thus the League is relegated to the limbo of oblivion. Even the League's cities—Asylum, Ohio; Terra Incognita, Wyoming; Kakoola, Wisconsin and the others—change their names to escape the disgrace. One of them, Port Rupert itself, evidently became Philip Roth's hometown, New York.

Roth's talent for the cruel and shameless comic extravaganza gives us marvellously raunchy vignettes of the sporting life, certainly, and he gleefully exploits our readiness to let baseball stand for America itself. But his determination to get in every joke he can think of about our past and present follies—patriotic paranoia, racism, sexual infantilism, the vulgarity of the media—finally is exhausting and self-defeating.

Nor does the book's other large dimension, that of literary parody and game-playing quite justify the effort expended in it. The narrator is a decent-minded but hopelessly logorrheic octogenarian sportswriter, Word Smith, condemned to an old-age home in Valhalla, New York, but still trying to redeem the suppressed story of the patriot league for history. "Call me Smitty", he begins his narrative and we soon see that not only Melville, but various other great American novelists—Hawthorne, Twain, Hemingway and company—are presences in his way of telling his tale.

Roth means something serious by this appeal to a fictional tradition of socially-alienated wisdom. "Truth is stranger than fiction, but stranger still are lies",. Smith contumaciously informs Congressman Dies (winning himself a year in Lewisburg). He also tells about the plight of the truth-knower isolated by mass disbelief and trying to combat large lies with small fictions is still worth thinking about. But Smith is mostly a bore and Roth allows him his literary jokes and his liberal verities with rather too much of the indulgence that marred *Our Gang* and *The Breast*.

And yet, if *The Great American Novel* thumbs its nose a little too insistently at the decorum of novel-writing and the frailer conventions of the national style, it remains respectful to the nostalgia most adult American males feel in baseball itself. If Roth's ball players are mostly stupid, incompetent, childish and morally retarded—just like the real ones, if Jim Bouton is to be believed—the game itself still glows with mythic possibility. Contemplating Chico Mecoatl, the sore-armed Mexican reliever who writes a little "Eeeep!" of pain every time he releases the ball, Roth reveals his own responsiveness to the elegiac lyricism, in the secret heart of every fan.

In baseball, we rediscover the pastoral world—sunlit and complex simplicity in the midst of urban distraction; but it is always pastoral in decline, on the verge of disappearing, doomed in the way that our own remembered childhood is doomed by the simple fact that it is ourselves, grown into wisdom and weariness, who do the remembering. It seems no accident that the good novels about baseball—Malamud's *The Natural*, Mark Harris's, *Bang the Drum Slowly*, Robert Coover's *The Universal Baseball Association* all focus on disaster, on death revealing itself even in Arcadia. *The Boys of Summer*, as Dylan Thomas and Roger Kahn remind us, are most moving in their ruin, which is also our ruin, individually and perhaps as Roth mockingly hints, nationally as well.

When he was a boy, baseball literally meant the world to Roth. He writes in *The Facts*, "My larger boyhood society cohered around the most inherently American phenomenon at hand—the game of baseball, whose mystique was encapsulated in three relatively inexpensive fetishes that you could have always have at your side in your room, not only while you did your homework but in bed while you slept, if you were a worshiper as primitive as I was at ten and eleven: they were a ball, a bat, and a glove."[122]

Roth's best writing is about "inherently American phenomena," particularly those he loves or hates; here, baseball and writing are what he loves, and gargantuan economic greed and political terrorism are what he hates. The combination makes for romping reading that still manages to resonate. In this novel the writer has dissected the American psyche, the natural psyche which adores and adulates Baseball.

Word Smith, also known as Smitty, is a very old man and longtime sportswriter (though blacklisted from publishing} living in the Valhalla Home for the Aged. Where else could a lover of baseball be suspended between life and death but Valhalla?

Smitty is fond of alliteration in his writing—which he's still undertaking at 87. Fond of alliteration is far too mild; Smitty's alliterations run so far out into left fields as to be over the wall and breaking windshields in the street. His doctor ("philistine physician") warns him that he must "give up alliteration if [he wants] to live to be four score and eight", but Smitty will die first.

What writer would you meet in Florida in March 1936, when you went down for spring training? Ernest Hemingway, of course. Ballplayers in the 1920s and 1930s hunted and fished and drank together in the midst of conditioning that looks downright easy by today's compulsive standards, and a mellow slate of friendly games.

Hemingway fits right into the world of the novel without the slightest stretch. And as Smitty delivers time to us, he is just as we've always imagined him; "when he was having a good day they didn't make them any more generous or sweet-tempered, but when he was having a bad day, well, he could be the biggest prick in all of literature."[123]

The Vassar waitress and diarist who comes fishing with Smitty and Hem is just a type, too, a little girl on the outside of a men's world (whether baseball, fishing, or American "literature," as Hem puts it) that has, and makes, no place for her. That she writes everything up in her diary sets her against Smitty, the "honest" unfiltered chronicler with his stream, or rather flood, of consciousness style; nameless "Vassar" is one of those self-involved diarists whose journals are more fiction than fact, written not for themselves but in the hope of being read later, fancying themselves Virginia Woolf but consigned while still alive to the dustbin of history. Hemingway's dismissal of the girl with one or two précis of all the great American novels she whimperingly offers for consideration are perceptive, as, of course, is Roth using ad competition. To describe *Moby Dick* as a "book about blubber, with a madman; thrown in for excitement," Huckleberry Finn as "a book by a fellow who is thinking how nice it would be to be a youngster again" with "your old James" as "polychromatic crap, honey! Five hundred words where one would do!," and Faulkner as "unreadable unless you're some God damn professor!" is to state things both frank and true.[124]

Moby-Dick, Smitty thinks, is closest of all these to winning the title, as he'd say in baseball terms—and indeed for Smitty what makes Moby chief contender is that it is all one long baseball analogy. "Who is Captain Ahab if not the unappeasable Dodger manager Durocher, or the steadfast Giant John Mcgraw? Who are Flask, Starbuck, and Stubb, Ahab's trio of First mates, if not the Tinker, Evers, and Chance of the Pequot's Crew?"[125]

And as *Moby-Dick* begins with men going down to the sea in ships, *The Great American Novel* concludes its prologue, and Smitty's critical, opinions on Melville and Moby, with the Rupert

Mundys similarly hitting the road. The rest of the novel is largely a flashback. You can never fault Roth for sequence; his idea of order always works. For Roth—the historian—the past and present are kin.

He doesn't go much in the future, perhaps because he, and we, and his characters simply aren't there yet. Maybe it's tempting fate, somehow, to go there. At any rate, Roth rarely does. As Gil Gamesh says, "I have seen the future, General, and it stinks."[126]

Chapter one, "Home Sweet Home," as all the chapters will, with a long discursive archaic beginning, common in fiction through the eighteenth century, outlines what is to come. Henry Fielding and Swift were both parodying this style in their first novels, and Roth uses these head notes to parody his own work, thereby making it funnier. It's always easiest to appreciate an author able to comment on and laugh at his own characters before we even see them—although when Roth does this, we sometimes wriggle under his imposing his own critical opinions on us before we've had time to so much as meet the people in question. That we know Gil Gamesh will be expelled from baseball, and that this is the chapter "in which Mike the Mouth becomes baseball's Lear and the nation's Fool" doesn't spoil the surprise for us, as *The Great American Novel* is big on characters, not plot.

Like any baseball game and any individual at bat, "Home Sweet Home" begins at home but doesn't stay there long. Port Rubber is not so sweet. It's a nasty New Jersey seaport increasingly industrialized, and run by raucous rapacity-personified in its mayor, Boss Stuvwxyz, who would object to consigning the ball club to Hell, so long as his pockets had been lined with gold!"[127] Stuvwxyz is just one of the gaggle of names in this novel that might have been concocted by Don Marquis's cockroach, Archy, throwing himself upon the typewriter keys, and to an equivalent comic effect. That the players are named after pagan gods and goddesses almost seems normal by the second chapter, so persuasive and pervasive is the tall tale itself.

The poor homeless Mundys endure an existential hell of perpetual road trip all through the middle innings of the novel. That the Mundys "had been chosen to become the homeless team of baseball" to "help save the world for democracy'" is pathetic, in the passivity of "had been chosen," and also ridiculously hyperbolic, as are many political decisions of far greater import, and involving many more people than a group of minor leaguers and their loyal fans, intended to "save the world for democracy."[128]

Both the passive tone—for all their actions, and they do certainly act up, the Mundys just keep having things happen to them—and the political framing provide the novel's plot, such as it is. That the whole political frame is as weird and wacky as that of The Manchurian Candidate only reminds us of times when un-American activities were seen in even the most American of arenas, and what could be more American than baseball? Do Communists really kill General Oakhart, "soldier, patriot, and President of the [Patriot] League," and his running mate Bob Yamm, the Reapers pinch-hitter and midget (yes, Eddie Geadel was once a major leaguer: Roth reminds us, again and again, that fiction, no matter how lavish in imagination, has no roots but reality)? Can the man who shows up as the Mundys' manager in the late innings, a Soviet spy and graduate of "the International Lenin School for Subversion, Hatred, Infiltration and Terror, known popularly as SHIT,"[129] really be Gil Gamesh, the "beautiful Babylonian boy" who blew his own career with one rising fastball to an umpire's blue bow tie? Can the Patriot League really have been so infiltrated by Communists that even the memory of the league must be erased, or can Gamesh really be so vindictive as to argue this convincingly and make it so?

Or is it an economic decision, something characteristically American, to pull the plug on the hapless league and use communism as an excuse? Will Chairman Mao publish Smitty's great American novel? By the end of the novel, a reader trying to sort out the plot is not only lost at sea but helplessly as awash as Ishmael's\clinging to the coffin: "then all collapsed and the great shroud of the sea rolled on as it rolled five thousand years ago."[130] Remember that fiction is definitely that which is not fact-based in realities, but unreal; as Smitty explains the Progression, "Truth is stranger than fiction, but stranger still are lies."[131]

The real joy and rhythm of *The Great American Novel* lies not in the political and economic plot, but in the vignettes of Smitty, the players themselves, and the time Roth spends on the field; whether describing the unsavory Baal family (Spit, Base, and their game-time and locker-room antics) or Roland Agni, the sacrificial lamb and beautiful young centre fielder, Roth is at his lyric and comic best. Centre field is an iconic position for millions of baseball players and fans, one of the few positions (other that pitching) to have songs written about it, rhapsodies devoted to it.

The player who plays there is alone in a wide, groomed stretch of green grass all by himself, while remaining a most critical part of the team; it is up to him to steal home runs in the longest part of the field, while also covering for his teammates on both sides, and up the middle too. This might have been difficult even for Agni to do had the Mundys remained at home, where the headstone of Glorious Mundy, Founder, occupies deep centre field, bearing the inscription. "He had something to do with changing Luke Goganon from a pitcher into a centre-fielder."[132]

Even Alex Portnoy loves centre field: "you can't imagine how truly glorious it is out there, so alone in all that space [...] standing without a care in the world in the sunshine, like my king of kings, the Lord my God, the Duke himself."[133]

Any contemporary look at *The Great American Novel* must close, though with the following fact. How sweet it is, that, in the major leagues of today, a pitcher named Gil Mesh has come to pass. He plays for Seattle, he is dark and lovely, and he has a live young arm. All he needs is a "Ga" in his name.

Philip Roth still watches baseball. And baseball still forms a microcosm or perhaps a macrocosm of American culture, as well as intersecting with politics. Baseball is inveterately embedded in the American psyche. In *The London Daily Telegraph*, back in 2002, he was quoted as saying, "What we've been witnessing since Spetember 11 is an orgy of national narcissism and a gratuitous victim mentality which is repugnant. (....) and that's not the end of it. Even now, its impossible to see a baseball match which isn't preceded by singing 'God Bless America' and invocations to the memory of 'our heroes.' You want to say: stop. That's enough."[134] From this statement two points are crystal clear: that Roth will never flinch or cease from speaking his mind in non-negotiable terms; and that he was, at least in 2002, watching the New York Yankees (as of spring 2004), "God Bless America" is still delivered, either live or through a Kate Smith recording, during every home game in the Bronx.

> Comedy for me has been the most likely way. I could do it no other way, though it did require time to work up

> confidence to talk my instinct for comedy seriously, to let it contend with my earnest sobriety and finally take change. It's not that I don't trust my uncomic side or that I don't' have one; it's that the uncomic side more or less resembles everyone else's and a novelists qualities have to have their own distinctive force. Through the expressive gradations of comedy I can best imagine what I known.[135]

What Roth knows enables him to use the vast and variable imagination in comic ways, and also in ways that run too deep for laughter, or tears. Michiko Kakutani, viewing "American Pastoral" for *The New York Times,* noted that, "Writing less in anger than in sorrow, Mr. Roth uses his sharp reportorial eyes not to satirize his characters but to flesh them out from within,"[136] and there is in this sort of satire a good generosity ultimately more comforting than caustic, and also a pleasure to read and reread, things, for which Roth is almost never given credit or, to paraphrase Rodney Dangerfield, for which he doesn't get respect.

The Great American Novel is great for being richly ribald, witty and important as well as movingly perceptive about what we have invested in fragile culture. But bad taste alone does not make successful art and the book is too long for its own energies to sustain, too committed to a kind of "black humour" whose charm has seen its day, too easy in its confidence that inventiveness can do the work of design, that the author can say anything at any time and make us swallow it.

But then I suppose that only Philip Roth could write one of the few books about sports in English and leave one feeling, after many pages of rich local pleasure, disappointed and exasperated, still waiting for what his immense talent long ago promised us. Roth uses sport metaphorically in many contexts.

For example, he has employed it negatively, suggesting preoccupation with games and, by extension, about the society at large. Roth does this most obviously in *Our Gang,* in which President Trick E. Dixon wears a football uniform while conferring with his advisors. The implication is that something vital has gone out of the national pastime, and out of the nation itself.

To sum up, Roth's long, experimental book *The Great American Novel,* ostensibly the story of the Ruppert Mundys, a fictitious

World War II era baseball team in the mythical Patriot League, chronicles the bizarre misadventures of this grotesque contingent of various named would-be ball players. Their collective and individual misfortunes reach nearly epic proportions: they suffer 120 loses in a single season, are dispossessed of their home stadium, and are eventually expunged from the annals of organized sport. The Mundys' madcap saga can be read in several ways.

Although Roth once again channels the action through a first person narraror, in this case a cantankerous, eighty-seven-year-old sportswriter named Word Smith, and although he again chooses Newark, New Jersey as the setting for his fiction, *The Great American Novel* bears very little resemblance to his earlier works. In the first place, "Smitty" (unlike, say Neil Klugman or Alexander Portnoy) functions not as a significant presence in the book, but simply as a literary device, a convenient means whereby the novel's larger thematic concerns are revealed to the reader. Indeed, characterization in *The Great American Novel* is subordinate to theme. In this respect especially, *The Great American Novel* represents a real departure for Roth in that it attempts to achieve its end not so much by narrating any one individual's misadventures for their own sake (although Smitty's personal vendetta against the powers that be provides a nominal context), but by adopting a broadly panoramic approach, a nearly Pynchonesque dispersion that enables him to debunk on several levels simultaneously. Despite the novel's manic texture, he is seeking to make in *The Great American Novel* a rather large, comprehensive, and ultimately serious statement. He has explained his use of the seemingly trivial, baseball centered setting:

> It was a matter of discovering in baseball a means to dramatize the struggle between the benign national myth of itself that a great power prefers to perpetuate, and the relentlessly insidious, very nearly demonic reality to admit to the discovery of thematic reverberations, of depth, of overtone, finally of meaning, would seem to contradict what I have said about wanting fundamentally to be unserious; and it does. Yet out of this opposition, or rather out of the attempt to maintain these contradictory impulses in a state of contentious equilibrium, the book evoked.... his [Smitty's]

> are not so unlike the sort of fantasies with which the national imagination began to be plagued during this last demythologizing decade of disorder, upheaval, assassination, and war.... Smitty is to my mind correct in aligning himself with Melville and Hawthorne, whom he calls "my precursors, my kinsmen."[137]

They too were in search of some encapsulating fiction, or legend, that would in its own oblique, charged and cryptic way, constitute the "truth" about the national the national disease.

For Roth, baseball serves as that "myth" or "legend," as he succeeds in exposing not only the "truth" about the Mundys, but something much broader, which Ben Siegel terms "the schism between professed idealism or good will and an underlying self seeking grossness or vulgarity."[138]

Since Roth is, in a sense, social historian, it is not surprising that he has used athletics so often in his fiction, for sport so largely influences the American ethos, outlook and psyche. Especially in recent years, "sport in American fiction has served as a focal point for the examination of social or personal values," and this authors' books are among the best examples. Thus in *The Great American Novel* Roth has explored and exposed the innate dichotomy that bedevils the national psyche of America, the schizophrenic tension between the layers of soaring idealism and cross hardboiled pragmatism and vulgarity.

References

1. Roth, Philip. *Reading Myself and Others* (New York: Vintage, 2001), p.22.
2. Roth, Philip. *Portnoy's Complaint,* New York: Random, 1969, p. 33-34.
3. Bellow, Saul. *Herzog*. Harmondsworth: Penguin, 1965, p.1.
4. Roth, Philip. *Portnoy's Complai t* op.cit., p.250.
5. Freud, Sigmund. *The Most Prevalent Form of Degradation in Erotic Life*. pp.96,113.
6. Roth, Philip. *Portnoy's Complaint* op.cit., p.242.
7. Ibid., p. 242.
8. Roth Philip. *Reading Myself and Others*. NewYork: Vintage, 2001, p.30.
9. Roth, Philip. *Portnoy's Complaint*. op.cit., p.35.

10. Ibid., p.69.
11. Ibid., p.72.
12. Ibid., p.113
13. Ibid., p. 241
14. Ibid., pp.28-29.
15. Ibid., p.154.
16. Ibid., p.40.
17. Ibid., p. 55.
18. Ibid., p.133.
19. Ibid.
20. Ibid.
21. Ibid., p.140.
22. Ibid., p.201.
23. Ibid., pp.201, 202.
24. Ibid., p.217.
25. Roth, Philip. *Reading Myself and Others*. op.cit., p.220-221.
26. Roth, Philip. *Portnoy's Complaint*. op.cit., p.73.
27. Ibid., p.241.
28. Roth, Philip. *Reading Myself and Others*. op.cit., p.218.
29. Spielvogel, O. "The Puzzled Penis," *Internationable Zeitschrift fur Psychoanalyse*, Vol. Xxiv p. 909.
30. Roth, Philip. *Portnoy's Complaint*. op.cit., pp.36, 37.
31. Ibid., pp.240-241.
32. Ibid., p.124.
33. Ibid., pp.79-80.
34. Patricia Meyer Spacks, "About Portnoy", *Yale Review* 58, no.4 (1969):623.
35. Spielvogel, O. op.cit., p. 909.
36. Roth, Philip. *Portnoy's Complaint*. op.cit., p.7.
37. Ibid., p.16.
38. Ibid., pp.36,37.
39. Ibid., p.37.
40. Ibid., p.39.
41. Ibid., p.56.
42. Ibid., p.68.
43. Ibid., p.94.
44. Ibid., p.110.
45. Ibid., p.190.

46. Ibid., p. 198.
47. Ibid., pp. 211-212.
48. Roth, Philip. *Reading Myself and Others*. op.cit., p.134.
49. Roth, Philip. *Portnoy's Complaint*.op.cit., p.270.
50. Ibid., pp.36,37.
51. Ibid.,
52. Ibid., p.274.
53. Roth, Philip. *Our Gang,* New York:Vintage, 1971, p.29-30.
54. Ibid., p.8.
55. Ibid., p.10.
56. Ibid., p.185.
57. Roth, Philip. *Reading Myself and Others,* NewYork:Vintage, 2001, p.40.
58. Ibid., p.47.
59. Ibid., p.48.
60. Roth, Philip. *Our Gang*. op.cit.,1971.
61. Ibid . p.4.
62. Ibid. p.4.
63. Ibid., p.5.
64. Ibid., p.10.
65. Ibid., p.21.
66. Ibid. p.21.
67. Ibid., p.31.
68. Ibid., p.81.
69. Ibid., p.85.
70. Ibid., p.88.
71. Ibid., p.104.
72. Ibid., p.119.
73. Ibid., P.177.
74. Ibid., p.183.
75. Ibid., p.187.
76. Ibid. p.187.
77. Ibid., p.191.
78. Ibid., p.200.
79. Ibid., p.21.
80. Davidson, Sara. "Talk with Philip Roth". *New York Times Book Review,* 18 September 1977: p.51.
81. Gardner, John. *Critical Perspectives*. Edited by Robert A. Morace and Kathryn VanSpanckeren.

82. Ozick,Cynthia. Three letters (signed16 June 1972, 19 June 1972, and 5 0ctober 1972) to Holt, Rinehart, and Winston. Unpublished. Ken Lopez Bookseller, Catalog 126:R-S, Item 319.
83. Roth, Philip. *The Breast*. New York: Holt, 1972, p.25.
84. Ibid., p.27.
85. Ibid., p.61.
86. Ibid., p.13.
87. Ibid., p.11.
88. Ibid., p.13.
89. Ibid., p.82.
90. Milowitz, Steven. *Philip Roth Considered: The Concentrationary Universe of the American Writer*. New York: Garland, 2000, p.138.
91. Pinsker, Sanford. *The Schlemiel as Metaphor: Studies in the Yiddish and American Jewish Novel*. Carbondale: Southern Illnois UP, 1971, pp.10-11.
92. Bloom, Harold. *The Anxiety of Influence: A Theory of Poetry*. Oxford: Oxford UP, 1973, p. 88.
93. Harap, Louis. *The Mainstream: The Jewish Presence in Twentieth Century American Literature. 1950s-1980s*. (Westport: CT: Greenwood, 1987), p. 143.
94. Roth, Philip. *The Facts: A Novelist's Autobiography*. New York: Farrar, Straus & Giroux, 1988, p.3.
95. Ibid., p.5.
96. Ibid., p.162.
97. Roth, Philip. *The Breast. A Philip Roth Reader*. London: Vintage, 1993, p. 449.
98. Ibid., p.451.
99. Ibid., p.449.
100. Ibid., p.452.
101. Ibid., p.448.
102. Ibid., p.460.
103. Ibid., pp.460-61.
104. Ibid., p.470.
105. Ibid., p.467.
106. Ibid., p.480.
107. Ibid.
108. Ibid., p.449.
109. Ibid., p.483.
110. Kafka, Franz. "Metamorphosis". *Metamorphosis and Other Stories*. 1916. New York: Penguin, 1984, p. 9.

111. Roth, Philip. *The Breast. A Philip Roth Reader* op.cit., p. 482.
112. Ibid., p.483.
113. Ibid.
114. Ibid., p.479.
115. Ibid., p.478.
116. Ibid., p.454.
117. Ibid.
118. Ibid., pp.450-51.
119. Ibid., p.458.
120. Ibid., p.464.
121. Ibid., p.457.
122. Roth, Philip. *The Facts*. New York: Farrar, 1988, p.32.
123. Roth, Philip. *The Great American Novel*. New York: Farrar, 1973, p.25.
124. Ibid., pp.28-31.
125. Ibid., p.43.
126. Ibid., p.347.
127. Ibid., p.51.
128. Ibid., p.49.
129. Ibid., p.347.
130. Melville, Herman. *Moby Dick: or, Whale*. Ed. Charles Feidelson, Jr. New York: Macmillan, 1964, p.723.
131. Ibid., p.392.
132. Ibid., p.83.
133. Roth, Philip. *Portnoy's Complaint*. op.cit., p.70.
134. Leith, Sam. "Philip Roth attacks 'orgy of narcissism' post sept 11." *Daily Telegraph*, 5 Oct. 2002:21. p.21.
135. Roth, Philip. "Interview with *The London Sunday Times*." Rpt. In *Reading Myself and Others*. New York: Vintage, 2001, pp.111-118.
136. Kakutani, Michiko. "A Postwar Paradise Shattered From Within." Rev. of American Pastoral, by Philip Roth. *New York Times*, 15 April 1997, late ed.: C11.
137. Roth, "On *The Great American Novel*," in *Reading Myself and Others*, 89-92.
138. Ben Siegel, "The Myths of Summer: Philip Roth's The Great American Novel," *Contemporary Literature* 17, no.2 (1976): 175-76.

3

Third Stage: Beyond Psychoanalysis

My Life as a Man deals with the operatically unhappy marriage of a successful young writer. It confirms that despite his superb gifts as a mimic, and hyperbolist Roth is only good at fantasticating materials from his own life and exploring the working of human psyche in trying circumstances. As a satirist of Nixon, he is clever but uninspired. As a satirist of middle class Jewish life in New York or the suburbs he is brilliant and wicked, endowed with a perfect ear and a cold eye. And faced with the traumas of family life and the conflicts of the mental and moral life in *Portnoy,* Roth can be not only funny but lyrical—emotion recollected in hysteria.

My Life as a Man is a kind of sequel to *Portnoy* in a different key, giving a "real life" account of what happened to the young writer when he fell into marriage and trouble in his mid-career. His autobiography is labeled a novel but Roth has never seemed closer to the obvious facts of his personal history. To heighten the feeling of veracity, he eschews the comic highs and lows of *Portnoy* for a more flat, almost essayistic, style. He calls this longest section of the book "My True Story" and precedes it with two—previously published stories—one very fine, the other tedious and unconvincing—that fictionalize the same material. *My Life as a Man* thus adds a third part (and a third style) to the personal trilogy begun with *Goodbye Columbus* and *Portnoy's Complaint.* Many earlier characters recur in different guises: Brenda Patimkin becomes Sharon Shatzky, daughter of Al "The Zipper King" Shatzky; Alex Portnoy's parents play recognizable parts as do that famous pampered boyhood and the sexual confusions that followed; even the cartoon like Dr. Spielvogel, who delivered the punch line of *Portnoy*—"Now Vee May perhaps to begin."[1]—keeps his word and returns under his own name to treat and reject Peter to five years of analysis. He considers Peter "Among the nation's top young narcissists in the arts", "and causes him anguish by writing him up in a psychiatric journal"—another tormentor, like the wife, like the tyrannical alimony judge who is described as "the Stalin of Divorce Court Communism": "From each according to his ability, to each according to her need."

Maureen Tarnopol who hooks Peter into wedlock and manoeuvres prodigiously to keep him there, is of course the chief tormentor; she plays the female-monster role assigned to the mother in *Portnoy's Complaint,* but here the hero can't muster a grain of love to qualify his sense of outrage. Maureen has the same dramaturgical genius as Sophie Portnoy, the same histrionic powers of manipulation, persistence and emasculation.

My Life as a Man is an unpolemical mirror image of its literature, a case-study of female rage and resentment as a contribution to the literature of inter-sexual victimization. As Roth's alter-ego tells us repeatedly, his awful marriage became an obsession that continued to haunt him after he left his wife and even after her accidental death. Unable to exorcise the demon through his work or even to describe it convincingly, though it dominates all his waking thoughts, Peter turns to direct autobiography in a desperate gesture of exorcism. Perhaps the "facts" will speak for themselves and provide relief where the imagination found itself blocked and thwarted.

This is unlikely prospect on the face of it. Whatever therapeutic value such a book has for its author, the literary problem remains. Autobiography requires as much human and technical control as fiction; the narrative structure here is even unusually intricate for Roth, but by barring both the wild manic fantasies of a Portnoy and the rich descriptive texture of his still earlier work, Roth knowingly puts his imagination in sling. The first story, "Salad Days," one of the best Roth has written, is so full of nuanced detail and warmth of feeling that it becomes an object lesson in the veracity of fiction, over "fact," while Peter's autobiography, for all its humour and brio, is basically one shrill extended cry of "Foul!" The author has no handle on his material; he is still too close to it; despite the analysis he's been unable to work it through.

When Peter reaches the point to telling how Maureen had tricked him into marriage, feigning pregnancy by buying a specimen of someone else's urine he admits that he has tried and failed for five years to get the story into his fiction.

Why Peter (or Roth) should feel that telling the story this way, presumably telling it straight, would be any more free of self-pity and that bald sense of victimization is a mystery to me. As in his other work, but more so here, Roth, makes an intense effort to transcend "art" and get down to unpleasant facts, work which consists mainly of unpalatable facts about other people. Roth's hero is typically obsessed by the difference between the world of his childhood, when he was his mother's young prince, and the fate that awaited him as an adult, especially at the hands of women.

> What made me so pathetic in dealing with Maureen in her wildest moments was that I simply could not believe that any body like her could exist in a world that had been advertised to me as Peter's oyster.

But Peter chooses such women, and partly because they are so much like his adoring, impossible mother. There are usually two sorts of women in Roth's hero's lives: bitchy, castrating women, who attract and destroy them, and doting sexual slaves who eventually bore them. Unable to combine love and sensuality his men read like textbook out of Freud's essay on "The Most Prevalent Form of Degradation in Erotic Life".

However painful this feeling of victimization can be for the man, for a writer it can be peculiarly poisonous if it prevents him from granting full reality to his characters, from getting any distance on the troubles and travails of his protagonist. The wife Maureen might as well be a creature from Mars: Peter and Roth haven't a clue about what makes her tick, or why he stays and collaborates with her. His point of view makes no sense, here it is non-existent. (In the "fictional" version we get in the second story. "Courting Disaster," the motivation is even more incredible.). Maureen swoops down on him like some calamity of nature, then simply clings with superhuman force. In both versions Roth cooks up a general explanation dealing with the premature seriousness of young people in the 1950's and with his hero's self-abnegating "literary" notation of marriage and morality but neither reason is plausible enough to account for the perverse, neurotic behaviour of this bizarre couple, whose antics utterly resist culture generalization.

At the root of the creative problem is the pervasive un-generosity that has always marked Roth's work. (His early Jewish critics were misguided; his quarrel was not with Jews but with people.) Even a satirist must love his characters a little, especially if he also loathes them. He must be drawn to them in an animating way, must need to give them life. He can't use novels simply to settle old scores. Roth's genius is all for surfaces—the telling descriptive detail, the absurd mannerism, the tics and turns of real speech, the ludicrous flaw of personality—rarely for human depths. He does have an affinity for people at their most frantic, pompous and ridiculous level, in part because he admires the sheer energy of human waste, but also because they confirm his own sense of superiority.

The fatal flaw of his protagonists, which Roth never sees, is their self righteousness, from Neil Klugman's smug dismissal of Brenda Patimkin, to Portnoy's dogged attempts to blame everyone but himself, to Peter Tarnopol's post-mortem revenge on his monster of a wife.

My Life as a Man is Roth's most blistering novel, a fiction within a fiction, a labyrinthine edifice of funny, mouthful and harrowing meditations on the fetal impose between a man and a woman. At its heart lies the marriage of Peter and Maureen Tarnopol, a gifted young writer and the woman who wants to be his muse but who instead is his nemesis. Their union is based on fraud and shored up by moral blackmail, but it is so professedly durable that long after Maureen's death, Peter is still trying and failing to write his way free of it. Out of desperate inventions and cauterizing trusts, acts of weakness, tender-heartedness and consternating cruelty Philip Roth creates a work worthy of Strindberg—a fierce tragedy of sexual need and blindness.

The novel is divided into two parts—"Useful Fictions" and "My True Story". "Useful Fictions" consists of two short stories about a character named Nathan Zuckerman (although he shares a name with the character that would inhabit many of Roth's later novels). The second part of the novel "My True Story" assumes the form of a first person memory by Peter Tarnopol, a Jewish writer who authored the two stories in the first section.

This novel is first of Roth's work that deals with the idea of the nexus between a writer's life and his work, a theme that Roth would intently focus on in many subsequent novels, particularly "Operation Shylock". In his autobiography, Roth reveals that much of the fictional Tornopol's life is based on his own experience. For example Roth's disastrous marriage to Margaret Martinson is portrayed through Tarnopol's traumatic relationship with Maureen. The first story "Salad Days" presents the life of a family. Mr. Zuckerman, who has a store, in the very beginning teaches his son Nathan (whom he calls Natie out of love) how to sign his name. The story is written in third person narration. The author gives us the details of their family and outdoor events. Once Nathan went out for fishing with his father and his uncle Philly where Nathan was thrashed with a belt for nearly taking his uncle's eye out while clowning around with hook.

His father had gone bankrupt in the years between the wars. Business crumbled but the household remained unaffected and the bona fides of the head of the house were questioned. His mother Betty did not lose her faith in her husband. There was a perfect understanding between the couple.

Sherman, their older son was coming out of the navy and young Nathan was entering high school. Business suddenly began to boom in the Camden Store and by 1949, the year Zuckerman entered college, a brand new "Mr. Z" Shoe store had opened out at the two million dollar... Nathan was asked to pay for his education himself when he was at the college." When he was nineteen years old, he fell in love with Betty Zuckerman as though she were not his mother but a famous actress who for some incredible reason also cooked his meals and kept his room in apple-pie order.

The mother had a strong bond with Sherman, the older son. One of the big surprises of Zuckerman's life was seeing the way his mother carried on after his brother Sherman entered the navy. She behaved like a young girl whose fiancé was marching off to die in the front lines. Nathan did everything he would possibly think of to cheer her up: helped with the dishes, talked nonstop even about a subject that ordinarily embarrassed him, his little girl friends. How awful her suffering was—also how odd. Sherman was also important for Nathan. As a small boy Nathan's attachment to Sherman had been so pronounced and so obvious that the other kids used to make jokes about it. But how could his mother miss Sherman so much, when he was still around and being nicer. Nathan was thirteen by this time and already an honour student at the high school.

Sherman was a jazz musician; he had already been assigned no special services because of his musical talent. When he came home on his first liberty after boot camp, he brought a bag full of dirty photographs to show to Nathan. And when, upon being discharged Sherman made directly for New York and found a job playing piano in a bar in Greenwich village. He was married to Sheila, a skinny-Jewish girl who talked in baby talk and worked as a dental technician somewhere. Nathan couldn't believe it, what had happened to his glamorous brother! He read a book called *Of Time and the River* that was to metamorphose not only his attitude toward Bass, but toward life itself. He did not continue his military training and this decision infuriated his father. His mother asked him to consult Sherman on this matter but he refused.

Now he met Caroline Benson who conducted the seminar. Alone with Bass's two other most displaced Jews, Zuckerman was the intellectual powerhouse of the seminar which assembled every Wednesday there in the afternoon until after six. Who was Nathan Zuckerman of Camden, New Jersey to turn his untitled back on the wisdom of Caroline Benson, educated in England? She had taught him to pronounce the 'l' in length and to aspirate the 'h' in 'whole'.

The afternoon in May of his senior year when he was invited to take tea with Caroline Benson in the English garden back of her house, he was asked to bring along with him the senior honours paper he had just completed. He read aloud to Miss Benson his thirty-page paper entitled "Subdued Hysteria: A Study of the undercurrent of Agony" in some *Novels of Virginia Woolf.* Miss. Benson expected him to continue his literary studies at either Oxford or at Cambridge. They did not embrace only because of Miss Benson's age, position and character. Zuckerman had been ready and willing, the urge in him to embrace and be embraced was all but overpowering. Now he got busy with fragility.

On telephone, he used to cry talking to his worried mother and father. He would find himself at the age of twenty-one as tearful and panic-stricken as he had been at four. Telephoning Sharon, the seventeen-year old daughter of Al the Zipper King Shatzky, would also reduce him to tears afterward. With her family she had recently moved into country club hills. On the outskirts of Camden, Sharon was called 'a perfect little lady' by Nathan's mother and 'a lovely-lovely child' by his father. Sharon was the daughter of Al and Minna. Zuckerman's father said that if Sharon had any questions about college life she should ask his son, who had been editor up at Bass of "the school paper". It had been the literary magazine that Zuckerman had edited and he answered Shatzky's questions about 'college life' without a trace of sarcasm or snobbishness. After all what business a student of English letters who had taken tea and sandwiches only a few weeks earlier in the garden of Caroline Benson have with the pampered middle-class daughter of Al "the Zipper King "Shatzky"?

By the time Zuckerman was about to graduate from MP school, Sharon was a freshman at Juliana Junior College. Every night she wrote him scandalous letter. She used to talk of cunt-and prick:

> Dearest-dearest all I Could think about while playing tennis in gym class was getting down on my hands and knees and crawling across the room toward your prick and then pressing your prick against my face I love it with your prick in my face just pressing your prick against my cheeks my lips my tongue my nose my eyes my ears wrapping your gorgeous prick in my hair.[2]

Sharon had sexual urges and her use of facile hyperbole, her style frequently jarred him. Nor was he pleased by her incorrect use of grammar: the absence of punctuation and capitalization in her obscene letters. He talks of Sharon's sensual adventurousness. The sense of adventure that surrounded their lovemaking was heightened further by the presence often of the four parents in some other part of the house. Best of all were "the shows". For Zuckerman's pleasure and at his instigation, Sharon would stand in the bathroom with the door open, performing for him as though she were on a stage, while he would be seated in the dark living room at the other end of the corridor. She whispered to him, "I want to be your whore."[3] While on the back terrace her mother told his mother how adorable Sharon looked in the winter coat they had bought for her that afternoon. Sharon hated her father because of that ugly name of her which he refused to do anything about.

Al and Minna's five-foot-nine-inch body girl was a tantalizing slave and an extraordinary lady but hardly a soul mate for someone who felt as he did about great writers and great books. The girl wept into the phone:

> I miss your prick so much. Oh, Nathan, "I am touching my cunt, I'm touching my cunt and making believe it's you.[4]

In tears, in terror, he went receding from the phone booth. There was only irrational guilt over Sharon and Nathan; it was only fear of punishment for buggering the daughter right under the father's nose. And then, after the light weeks of infantry training followed by eight more at MP school, he was assigned a job as a clerk-typist, where he intended to bring charges against Captain Clerk who held secret membership in the KKK. Pain would come to Zuckerman in time—in the form of estrangement, mortification; pain would enter his life soon enough not entirely without invitation; he would have to pay for the vanity and the ignorance, but above all for the contradictions: the stinging tongue and the tender hide, the spiritual aspirations and the carnal desires, the softy boyish needs and the manly, the magisterial ambitions.

The story of Zuckerman's suffering calls for an approach more serious than that which seems appropriate to the tale of his easeful salad days. Another story requires just another author.

The story "Courting Disaster" presents Nathan as a mature figure working as a professor in the University where Lydia comes as a student and now starts a life which Nathan finds suffocating because he cannot be supposed to behave perversely before his family and society. In this story we meet that Nathan who has left Sharon, and develops relations with Lydia and her daughter, Monica. Nathan is caught between his principles, his dignity, his appearance and his inner urges. He is trapped and torn between his sexual urges and social inhibitions and taboos. The reason is that he has incestuous relationship with his stepdaughter, Monica, with whom he cannot live at the Hyde Park and Monica is not ready to marry him. But the protagonist suffers from inner conflict in his mind because he was an ambitious writer and professor, he never expected such perversity in his life. So he is a split personality, a person bedeviled by schizophrenic and ambivalence.

The story is narrated in first person narration. He remembers Lydia Ketterer, a divorced woman, five years his senior and mother of ten years old girl who lives with Lydia's former husband and his second wife. Ketterer is the second man nearly to destroy her: the first, Lydia's father, had seduced her when she was twelve. Lydia has been taken to be raised in the home of two spinster aunts in Skokie until she runs off with Ketterer at the age of eighteen. Her life is bedevilled by punishment, humiliation, betrayal and defeat. To such a life,

Nathan is drawn in spite of his contrary familial background—suffocating, diphtheria, fevers, allergies. The whole family used to take care of him so much that he feels irritated. Nathan's sister, Sonia, suffers inexplicable marriages, twice to the sons of Sicilians: the first an embezzler and in the end a suicider; the second, honest in his business but otherwise "common as dirt". The author wonders:

> Why their two off springs should have wasted themselves as they did, why both children should have wed themselves to disaster, is difficult to understand. That my sister's first husband and my wife should both have taken their own lives would seem to suggest something about our common upbringing.[5]

Mr. Zuckerman is a bookkeeper because of his excellent memory. He is considered the local savant in our neighbourhood of hard-working first-generation Jews, and is the man most frequently consulted by people in trouble. In Nathan's sickness his father tries to amuse him by teaching him how to solve arithmetical puzzles.

Nathan remembers that Sonia's first husband Billy committed suicide in the very room of his in-laws, and the second husband was also the same foolish personality. Nathan wonders how his sister, a beautiful singer, could marry such stupids.

Lydia's story of incest influences Nathan. Her father seduces her: "You are all I have, Lydia, You are all Daddy has. I am married to a corpse."[6]

Lydia does not scream out because she is afraid that her screams would awaken her mother. She suffers too much; at eighteen, she elopes with Ketterer who tortures her physically. Lydia's cousin Bob also exposes him to her. She is shattered completely and consequently she has lunatic fits. She is sent to hospital and the custody of the child is given to Ketterer. Nathan is drawn to her story because of the way the tale is told. Lydia's easy, familiar, even cozy acceptance of misery, her droll acceptance of her own madness greatly enhances the story's appeal:

> Who would call Crazy a woman who spoke with such detachment of her history of craziness?[7]

Nathan says: "I met the woman with whom I was to ruin my life only a few months after arriving back in Chicago in the fall of 1956, following a premature discharge from the army."[8]

Nathan does not know the word 'failure'. He is a voracious reader and an indefatigable writer. He can read three books in a month and 36 in a year. "What confidence I had in those days! What willpower and energy! And what a devourer of schedules and routines!"[9]

He judges himself by the most exacting standards in those days. Owning his own library is his only materialistic ambition. In the midst of his contentment there is one difficulty, his headaches. In Chicago, a civilian again, he is examined by a neurologist who can offer no explanation for the headaches. He vomites during the headache not quite daring to move.

When he is twenty-four, a professor he teaches many young girls including Mrs. Slater who casts amorous looks at him. Then Lydia comes. She is twenty-nine and mother of a ten-year old. She has a job as an interviewer with a university-sponsored social science research project at two dollars an hour and she likes this job. Also at that time, she is the willing and grateful potent of a lay psychoanalyst, a woman named Rutherford.

Nathan teaches his students to be precise, accurate and measured, not totally imaginative. Within a month he has seduced Lydia against her inclination and against his own principles. They live together for almost six years, the first eighteen months as lovers and the following four years until her suicide, as husband and wife. He is drawn to Lydia not out of passion for Monica, not because she has suffered so much, but because she is too brave. During the first months of his love affair witl. Lydia, he continues to receive letters and telephone calls from Sharon Shatzky with whom he has concluded a passionate romance prior to his return to Chicago. When he begins to suffer from migraines, Mr. Shatzky grows fearful that if he does not intervene, his daughter might one day marry a man whom she would have to support for the rest of her life.

Nathan is an ambitious figure in his twenties; he cannot marry Sharon for whom he has no strong erotic attachment. Sharon weeps for him but it falls on deaf ears because now he loves Lydia. Every Sunday, Monica was delivered to the door by Eujene Ketterer whom Nathan hated.

Monica is a stupid, broken, illiterate child. She does not know her right hand from her left, will not read the clock; she is a developing child but used to arguing with Lydia. Lydia wants to teach her subtraction but she does not want to learn. She is a pampered child. Lydia commits suicide because of an adulterous relationship between Moonie (Monica) and Nathan. Lydia is 35 when she dies. He is just thirty and Moonie sixteen. After Ketterer's second divorce, he accepts the custody of Lydia's daughter. Under the guise of father and daughter, they touch and fondle one another's flesh. So he flees with Moonie to Italy after Lydia's death. They both love each other. In fact, whenever he goes out of the room, leaving her behind, she feels as if she has ceases to exist. She is no longer stupid or stubborn, though she is too often morose. When she is twenty-one, he decides to marry her; but she declines; she does not ever want to be a wife. Then they continue to live together in this unmarried state but:

> This is not the life I wanted and planned for! Was made for! By my own standards, my private life is a failure and a disgrace, neither decorous, nor sober and surely not responsible. I am full of shame and believe myself to be a scandalous figure. I can't imagine that I shall ever have the courage to return to live in Chicago or any where in America.[10]

Nathan wants to go back to his ailing father but he is panic-stricken; he suffers from the the panic of the escaped convict. He knows that nobody cares any longer that this twenty-four-year-old woman was once his own stepdaughter and that he took her virginity at sixteen and fondled her at 12. He knows that he has two alternatives: either he must leave her or return with her to America where they will live like two lovers. But he is too humiliated to do either.

"My True Story" is narrated by Peter Tarnopol who was born in Yonkers, New York, thirty-four years ago. He is educated in Public School there and graduates *summa cum laude* from Brown

University in 1954. He briefly attends graduate school and then serves for two years as an MP with U.S. Army, Germany, the setting for "A Jewish Father". Since then he has published only a handful of stories, devoting himself almost exclusively in the intervening years to his nightmarish marriage to the former Maureen Johnson of Elmira, New York.

In her lifetime, Mrs. Tarnopol is a barmaid, an abstract painter, a sculptress, a waitress, an actress, a short story writer, a liar and a psychopath. Married in 1959, the Tarnopols are legally separated in 1962 when Mrs. Tarnopol accuses the author, before Judge Milton Rosenzweig of the Supreme Court of the Country of New York, as "a well-known seducer of college girls". The marriage terminates in 1966 by Maureen's violent death. At the time of her demise she is unemployed and a patient in group therapy in Manhattan; she is receiving one hundred dollars a week in alimony.

From 1963 to 1966, Mr. Tarnopol conduct a love affair with Susan Seabury McCall, herself a young widow. Upon the conclusion of the affair, Mrs. McCall attempts unsuccessfully to kill herself and is currently living unhappily in Princeton, New Jersey, with a mother she cannot abide. Like Mr. Tarnopol Susan has no child. She wants to marry him and have children but Peter is frightened of remarrying.

From 1962 until 1967, Mr. Tarnopol is the patient of the psychoanalyst Dr. Otto Spielvogel of New York city, whose articles on creativity and neurosis have appeared in numerous journals, most notably the *American Forum for Psychoanalytic Studies* of which he is a contributing editor. Mr. Tarnopol is considered by Dr. Spielvogel to be among the nation's top young narcissists in the arts. Six months ago Mr. Tarnopol terminates his psychoanalytical engagement with Dr. Spielvogel and goes on leave from the university in order to take up temporary residence at the Quahsay Colony, a foundation supported retreat for writers, painters, sculptors and composers in rural Vermont. There he keeps mostly to himself, devoting nights as well as days to considering what has become of his life. He is confused, perturbed and incredulous much of the time, and on the subject of the late Mrs. Tarnopol, he continues to be a man possessed; he is haunted by the excruciating and harrowing reminiscences of his tortuous relationship with her.

Presently he is preparing to forsake the art of fiction for a while and embarks upon an autobiographical narrative, an endeavour which he approaches warily being uncertain about both its advisability and usefulness.

Peter remembers the June afternoon of 1962 when he first stepped into Dr. Spielvogel's office and began to weep into his hands, grieving for the loss of his strength, his confidence and his future. When he came East that June from Wisconsin to participate as a staff member in two-week writing work shop at Brooklyn College, he could not utter a single sentence; over a hundred students were present in the auditorium. He often recalls his quarrels with Maureen and feels crestfallen and dazed. His writing by this time is wholly at the mercy of his marital confusion and discord:

> Hopeless at my work and miserable in my marriage, with all the solid achievements of my early twenties gone up in smoke.[11]

Before his marriage to Maureen, his brother Morries, his sister Johnny and his parents try to persuade him not to marry that girl. But he does not listen to them, and suffers. His brother, Morris, is truly content with his wife and children. Joan has recently written inviting him to leave Quahsay and come out to California to stay with her and her family for as long as he likes. He dreams out loud in his analyst's office about becoming again that confident and triumphant college kid he once was at 20. He also writes to his sister about an Idaho woman, a stocky painter in her fifties who has been married five times because she does not want to die shrivelled up. He also writes:

> I am no more courageous at thirty four than I was a boy. I think the funeral was another trick—she's alive!" somehow or other, she will reappear!" Maureen's death is not true to life. And as time passes and I get older I find that they (Maureen's reminiscences) do with increasing frequency.[12]

He sends the copies of 'Salad Days' and 'Courting Disaster' to his sister, brother and Dr. Spielvogel. His sister, John rebukes him for hiding himself in the woods like a fugitive from justice. His stories are nothing but reflection of his state of mind—plagued by regret, constration and turmoil.

Back in 1960, John and Alvin gave a party for him at the house. He had become "The golden boy of America Literature" for "A Jewish Father". Maureen often broke out with Peter over his flirtations with young and beautiful girls, Maureen always over estimated herself. She wanted Peter to accept that she helped him in correcting spellings. Peter often calls her "egomaniac! Must you always be at the center of everything?"[13].

And Maureen says to him:

> Why do you punish me like this, why do you lust after every woman in this whole world, expect your own wife.[14]

He wants to live away from his wife but she does not leave him alone. In fact she becomes the cause of his nervous breakdown and trauma. He often thinks of the kind, thoughtful and pretty young girl, his twenty-year old student Karen Oakes who has left him. Maureen threaten to kill herself if Peter does not marry her. Under this, he has to marry her but three years later, he comes to know that his wife is a liar who told him that she was three months pregnant and got her urine tested which she bought from a pregnant Negro lady.

From 1963 to 1966, he hobnobs with Susan but cannot marry her for many reasons. He is not legally divorced because Maureen continues to refuse to grant him a divorce. But Susan wants to have a family before it was "too late". She is into her thirties and is frightened of two emotional breakdowns that she under goes, first in her freshman year at Wellesley, and then after her husband had been killed in a plane crash eleven months into their marriage and most recently when her father, whom she had doted upon has succumbed after suffering severe pain of bone cancer. She has become the patient of Dr. Golding.

Maureen has two marriages—Mezik, the brute who was the first husband, even Walker, the homosexual; she is also seduced by her father at 12. Peter can't muster courage to marry Susan despite his awareness that she will definitely prove to be a good wife and mother.

I no longer had the dairing or the heart or the confidence to marry again. Susan would have to find some man who was braver, or stronger or wiser or...[15]

Susan tries to kill herself six months after he has announced the affair as closed for good. In fact both suffered badly after taking leave. She has no contact with him for six weeks and attempts to kill herself but is saved and then both decide to live apart. Susan's mother tells Peter: "Peter like yourself and my daughter, experimenting with one another's genitals, up there is New York. They don't believe in marriage, with its risks, and its trials and its difficulties; only in sex, till it bores them."[16]

Both Susan and Peter are fellow sufferers. The broken shall succour and empathise with the broken. Susan is a good cook who knows how to cook French, Italian and Chinese specialties. Peter has never tasted food so delicious. He asks her to go back to college. Gradually both fall in love. In fact, it requires his doctor to get him to continue to take his medicine named Susan. Now he wants to leave her because he knows that she will commit suicide without him. And the doctor says:

> You think every woman in the world is going to kill herself over you?[17]

Peter remembers his enthusiasm in 1958, he used to read books and wanted to write them. He was highly impressed by Flaubert—"Be regular and orderly in your life like a bourgeois so that you may be violent and original in your work".

At the age of sixteen, an eleventh grader, Maureen runs away from her family' home in Elmira—a runaway, that gets him. He chooses an agent and subsequently signs a publisher's contract that provides him with a modest advance for the novel he is writing. Prior to Maureen, he comes in contact with the girl named Grete. He is fascinated by whatever she can tell him about her experience of the war. He is a dark Jew and she a blonde Aryan. With Maureen he used to have 10 or 15 quarrels per day. She asks him to leave writing because he is 'frightened' of competition from women.

He first meets Dr. Spielvogel the year Maureen and he are married—a tall, quiet decorous man, growing stout in his middle forties. His appearance, like Peter's, has changed for the worse in three years. He reminds him of Dr. Roger Chillingworth in Hawthorne's *Scarlet Letter*. Peter thinks that he cannot disclose to anyone what has happened between him and Maureen. But he is helpless. He sobs into tears before the doctor and tell him everything about Karen Oakes. He divulges his love for her. Karen goes home for spring vacation and never comes back. That's how overbearing and frightening a character he has become. After she fails to return from spring recess, he makes desperate phone calls to Racine practically daily. But she is the smartest girl in his class and has no intention of letting some overwrought creative writing teacher with a failed marriage and a stalled career ruin her life. She cannot save him from her wife and tells him that he will have to do it himself. Maureen chases him and then bursts out:

> If you forgive me for the urine, I'll forgive you for your mistress.[18]

He sobs, tears his clothes off and puts a Maureen's underwear; he pulls open her dresses and puts on a pair of her underpants. He also places his sperm on the top of the soap dish, on the bindings of boots in the library. Once he seals an envelope with it. He totally turns out to be a defenceless boy before Maureen.

> Even after she had confessed to committing the urine fraud, even then I couldn't get up and go! Why? Why should some one who had battled so determinedly all his life to be independent—his own child, his own adolescent his own men—why should some one with my devotion to 'seriousness' and 'maturity' knuckle under like defenseless little boy to his cornball Clytemnestra?[19]

He has been reduced in his marriage to a bewildered, helpless and hapless little boy. Spielvogel talks of his mother as "a phallic threatening figure."[20]

His dispute with Spielvogel breaks out over an article he has written for the *American Forum for Psychoanalytic Studies*. He gets that copy from his office and he finds that he is in that book.

A successful Italian-American poet in his forties entered into therapy became of anxiety states experienced as a result of his enormous ambivalence about leaving his wife. Leaving his semen on fixtures, towels, etc..., so completely legitimized was his anger; on another occasion, he dressed himself in nothing but his wife's underpants, brassier and stockings.[21]

So he quarrels with the doctor over it because it exhibits his personality in New York but the doctor does not feel sorry for it and he cannot leave the doctor because "it was Spielvogel who prevented me from leaving her whenever I became distressed about those dreams of marriage and family that I did not share."[22]

In the spring of 1966 Maureen telephones him that she wants to meet him at his apartment to talk about the divorce. She comes and wants to recite the short story she has written, "Dressing up in Mommy's clothes", and tells him that she will not grant him divorce. Then Peter beats her and later Maureen commits suicide. He goes to meet her in hospital where he meets Mr. Walker. She is really a liar and psychopath.

He goes to his apartment where he finds her diary and can opener. His father says "stop being out there on your own, please you have not listened to any body since you were four and a half years old and went off to conquer the world."[23]

In *My Life as a Man* and other novels of Roth, there is an important relationship between a character and his psychoanalyst. In *Letting Go*, Libby Herz, a frantic young woman in despair over her husband's increasing remoteness and gloom, spends a hapless hour with a analyst in Chicago.

Portnoy's Complaint is a novel cast in the form of an analytic monologue by a lust-consumed mother-addicted young Jewish bachelor. In *The Breast*, David Kapesh, an intelligent professor of imaginative literature who has turned overnight into a enormous female breast, engages in a daily dialectic with his former analyst about his new plight; and in *My Life as a Man*, Peter Tarnopol, a baffled writer and humiliated husband, suffers a breakdown following the debacle and collapse of a disastrous marriage, and during the long effort to make sense of what happened, struggles with his doctor over fundamental differences of opinion, a struggle that eventually destroys their genuine, thereupetic friendship.

All these characters, in agony and in tribulation, turn to doctors because they believe psychoanalysis may save them from total disintegration and devastation. Unhappy people define themselves as "ill" or agree to view themselves as "patients" and then visit psychoanalysts and get treatment. The condition between patient and analyst varies considerably from one book to the next.

Until *My Life as a Man*, the psychoanalyst in Roth's fiction has not been much of a character, in the conventional novelistic sense.

In *Portnoy's Complaint*, Dr.Spielvogel was nothing more a listener than for whom Portnoy re-enacted the drama, or vaudeville skit of his life, much like the priest discreetly hidden away in the confession box. Dr. Spielvogel is silent until the last mortifying detail has been extracted from the babbling sinner. Moreover, it is a highly stylized confession that this imaginary Dr. Spielvogei gets to hear and it bears as much resemblance to the drift and tone of what a real psychopathologist hears in his everyday life as a love sonnet does to the lambs and dactyls that lovers whisper into one another's ears in motel rooms and over the phone. In fact in *Portnoy's Complaint*, the writer wants to use a stratagem that would permit him to bring into his fiction the sort of intimate, shameful sexual detail and coarse, abusive sexual language that has largely been beside the pale of his first three books. In *Portnoy's Complaint*, he does not set out to write a book about an analysis, but utilizes the permissive conventions of the patient-analyst situation.

In *The Breast*, another analyst appears, this time one who speaks and does so more or less in the voice of enlightened common sense. Dr. Klinger favours the cadences and vocabulary of psychotherapeutic demystification. The difficulty is that the affliction confronting him—Kapesh's transformation into a human-size mammary gland—is bottomlessly mysterious and horrifying. Then in the course of a day, a doctor in Klinger's line of work dutifully hears out half a dozen patients who, if they do not consider themselves to be breasts, imagine with some degree of conviction that they are testicles or vaginas or bellies or brains or buttocks or nose or two left feet or all thumbs or all heart or all eyes, or what have you. "I am a prick! She's a cunt! My partner is an asshole!"

David Kapesh manages to maintain a tenuous hold, not only on his sanity which is just the half of it for this former literature professor—but on his moral dignity. Dr. Spielvogel who turns up as the analyst in *My Life as a Man*, has no such luck with his patient—nor does the patient (Peter Tarnopol) with his doctor. In the end there is no meeting of minds or capitulation on either side to the other's sense of reality. And not because Spielvogel is a fool and a tyrant—he is neither the All-knowing Analyst out of patient fairy tales, nor is he the Big Bad idiot analyst out of anti-Freudian folklore or because Tarnopol lacks sympathy for the man as also for his method. If Tarnopol cannot agree to see himself as

Spielvogel sees him, it is partly because Tarnopol cannot for any length of time see himself as Tarnopol either. Tarnopol the patient finally rejects Spielvogel's version of him and his world as so much fiction; but as a novelist who takes himself and his personal life as his subject, so too does he reject his own fictions as so much fiction.

How Portnoy conceives of Portnoy is not much of an issue in that book. Portnoy knows precisely how to present himself; a good part of his complaint is that his sense of himself, his past and his ridiculous destiny is so fixed. In *The Breast,* Kapesh must be educated to understand what he is, and very much against the grain of his own defiant hopefulness. But for Tarnopol the presentation or description of himself is what is most problematical and what remains unresolved. Tarnopol's attempt to realize himself with the right words—as earlier in life he attempted realizing himself through the right deeds—is what's at the heart of the book and when the novel is considered in its entirety, it is understood as Tarnopol's struggle to achieve a description.

"Bizarre projections" arising out of ordinary human relations were the main concern of Roth in *My Life as a Man,* a novel that might have been called "Don't Do With Me What You Will". One of the prominent themes in his writing seems to be the hero's recognition of a certain loss in his life, along with regret for the loss, and finally an ironic "acceptance" of this regret considering the young girl in *Goodbye Columbus* and her twin in *My Life as a Man,* both of whom are eventually rejected. But the loss might have broader emotional and psychological implications as well—that is, the beautiful too—young girls must have represented qualities that were also transpersonal. In *My Life as a Man* as Tarnopol's Dina Dornbusch, the "rich, pretty, protected, smart, sexy, adoring, young, vibrant, clever confident ambitious" Sarah Lawrence girl he gives up because she's not what the young literary fellow, in his romantic ambitiousness, recognizes as a "woman"—by which he means a knocked-around on-her-own volatile, combative handful like Maureen. Furthermore Dina Dornbusch is herself reconstituted and reappraised by Tarnopol, in the two short stories preceding his own autobiographical narrative ("The Useful Fictions"). First in "Salad Days", she appears as the licentious, childish, slavish, nice suburban Jewish girl whom he buggers under her family ping-pong table, and then in "Courting Disaster", as the altogether attractive, astute academically ambitious college senior who tells Professor Zuckerman, after he has several relations with her—to take up with his own brand of "damaged" woman—that under all his "Flamboyant" "maturity" he is just a crazy little boy.

Both these characters are called Sharon Shatzky and together stand in relation to Dina Dornbusch as fictional distillations do to their models in the unwritten world. These Sharons are what can happen to a Dina when a Tarnopol sets her free from his life to play the role such a woman does in his personal mythology. This mythology, this legend of the self is a kind of idealized architect's drawing for what one may have constructed or is yet to construct. In this way, a Tarnopol's fiction is his idea of fate. Of course, Tarnopol is relentlessly kicking himself for his mistake, but it is just those kicks that reveal to him how strongly determined by character, how characteristically Tarnopolian that mistake was. He is his mistake and his mistake is him.

"This me who is me being me and none other!"[24]

The last line of *My Life as a Man* is meant to point out a harsher attitude toward the self. It is Bellow, in his last two pain-filled novels, who has sounded the theme of "loss... regret for the loss and ....ironic" acceptance "of the regret" as he did early at the conclusion to "Seize the Day". If there is an ironic acceptance of anything at the conclusion of *My Life as a Man*, it is of the 'determined self'.

An angry frustration, a deeply vexing sense of characterological enslavement, is strongly embedded in that ironic acceptance. It is the ironic acceptance of the loss that follows that struggle that Roth has presented as a theme of *My Life as a Man*. From a perusal of his novels, it is clear that the form most congenial to Roth was the novel of narcissism, just as his strongest gift was for the tragicomedy of paronoia, and in *Portnoy's Complaint* he was able to coordinate form and theme to extraordinary effect.

Spielvogel, who is cutely resurrected from *Portnoy's Complaint*, considers him to be "among the nation's top young narcissists in the arts" and diagnoses his troubles as seeming "narcissistic self-dramatization".

My Life as a Man, in short, is a totally "solipsistic" novel which may well make it a perfect expression of the times. It's appropriate setting is the psychiatrist's office where, as was literally the case in *Portnoy's Complaint*, the only sound is the sound of the narrator's voice. Throughout this monologue Tarnopol speculates continually about the relationship between his own life and that of his fictional alter-ego, expresses bafflement and bewilderment at the complexity of the problem and seems to be trying to create the impression that his (and Roth's) novel is really about the effort of the novelist to define and explore the connection between life and art. The writing of *My Life as a Man* would thus become for Roth not only a search but a record of the search for the novel's meaning. The novel's theme is to be discovered in Tarnopol's struggle to make fictional use of the materials of his life. Throughout the novel Tarnopol is repeatedly accused of fanatical preoccupation with his guilt, his Jewishness, his marriage and his ego, his promises, excessive sensitivity to the social conditions in which the creative imagination is obliged to function; there was undoubtedly no other decision he would have made. Almost all the people in Tarnopol's life—his relatives, mistresses, students, wife—write him letters about the stories and they all pay attention to shortcomings which Roth has had ample opportunity to discover his own writings possess. He has sent his brother Morris copies of the two stories which comprise the Zukerman narrative and Morris responds in part as follows: "What is it with you Jewish writers..."

Roth divides his narrative into two sections: the first purporting to be a fictional account written by a young novelist named Peter Tarnopol of the adventures of a young novelist. There is actually no discernible difference between Tarnopol and Roth just as there is no discernible reason why Tarnopol rather than Roth should be acting as a narrator. There is, furthermore, no evidence that Tarnopol is intended to function as an untrustworthy narrator, whose unreliability is corroborated by his errors of perception and extravagant responses.

The life-art relationship is given dramatic objectification in the novel's two-part structure, with its finale as the story about divorce. Tarnopol might as well have devoted the entire novel to the story of his own life or Roth might have devoted it to that of his own life. For a writer of Roth's particular talent and temperament there is only one reliable measure of credibility, i.e., what the self feels and thinks and only one compelling interest, namely, what the self experiences: in Roth's case, how events and people, especially women have assaulted and impaired his sanity, thwarted or provoked his sexuality and outraged his sense of moral virtue.

My Life as a Man is an ironic refraction of domestic crisis through competing points of view given by diverse persons like Maureen, Peter, Mo (Peter's brother), and Dr. Spielvogel, which are never resolved but merely added up. Thus the presentation of competing perspectives elevates the novel beyond mere psychoanalysis which makes it more complex than *Portnoy*, which views the theme from the sole angle of psychoanalysis and uses the jargon of Freud and other psychoanalyists. *Portnoy's Complaint* was a literary hand grenade perfectly suited to the explosive decade that produced it. A comic, hyperbolic howl of protest against oppressive authority—in this case, by a "nice Jewish boy" repressed and stressed by the expectations of the striving immigrant culture in which he was raised—the novel limned its protagonist's sexual obsession with a profane fluency that obscured an under current of pain. It was a huge breakthrough for Roth. "Something cracked open" while he was working on it, he recalls:

> I remember the exuberance of the writing I remember myself being surprised by the subject, and, of course, being surprised that it could be made into a literary subject.[25]

Portnoy sold more than 400,000 hardcover copies. More important it transformed Roth's public image from serious-minded literary craftsman to dirty-minded mass-culture phenomenon. He had to learn to cope with high contempt ("The cruelest thing any one can do with *Portnoy's Complaint* is to read it twice", wrote Irving Howe in a commentary).

Alexander Portnoy is hostile, oversexed, and "seething" with guilt. His libido simply will not behave. On the analyst's Couch, he performed a stand-up routine that doubles as an anti-bildungsroman. An equal opportunity offender, Portnoy rails against his father, Jews, blacks, women, WASPs. He also relishes his own selt-hatred by deploying "vaudevillian" humour ("a man's cartilage is his fate"). At stake for the sympathetic reader are larger questions about religion and morality. Opposed to decency and dignity, Portnoy exhibits the kind of attitude only an assimilated immigrant can offer.

The 1969 novel is best known for Portnoy's onanistic exploits and his explosive anger toward his mother, but therein Roth offers the notion of love as anger or why else would his anti hero spend so much time on the couch?

When She was Good is about a young woman's brutal disappointment in the weaknesses and failings of her father and her husband, and the raging desire in her to make them better men. It's about extreme moral ambitiousness and its pitfall, so in its own way is *Letting Go,* though in that novel, it's the two male heroes who sadly discover the limitations of their power and their virtue. Tarnopol in *My Life as a Man* gets an education on that subject as well. *My Life as a Man* is a bitter commentary on the theme of female power and male subservience which is the recurrent theme and refrain of Roth's fictional corpus from the very beginning.

Whether it is Neil Klugman in *Goodbye Columbus,* Gabe Wallach in *Letting Go,* Alaxender Portnoy in *Portnoy's Complaint,* Peter Tarnopol in *My Life as a Man,* David Kapesh in *The Professor of Desire,* bright, sensitive and painfully self-conscious, these protected children of lower middle class Jews are torn between duty and desire, boyish needs and manly aspirations, family loyalties and aesthetic obligations. They suffer onslaughts from inscrutable women, overbearing parents and their own guilt-ridden consciences.

References

1. Roth, Philip. *Portnoy's Complaint.* NewYork: Random, 1969), p.274.
2. Roth, Philip. *My Life as a Man.* New York: Holt, 1974, p.23.
3. Ibid., p.26.
4. Ibid., p.28.
5. Ibid., p.35.
6. Ibid., p.40.
7. Ibid., p.46.
8. Ibid.
9. Ibid., p.47.

10. Ibid., p.84.
11. Ibid., p.105.
12. Ibid., p.112.
13. Ibid., p.120.
14. Ibid., p.121.
15. Ibid., p.137.
16. Ibid., p.149.
17. Ibid., p.166.
18. Ibid., p.209.
19. Ibid., p.213.
20. Ibid., p.218.
21. Ibid., p.239.
22. Ibid., p.260.
23. Ibid., p.329.
24. Ibid., p.330.
25. Some Quotes by Roth by Bob Thompson, Washington, Nov 12, 2006.

4

Last Stage: Psychoanalytically Convalescent

The Professor of Desire is a novel of convalescence, which celebrates erotic and emotional recuperation. Its hero David Kapesh undergoes the same dismal marital conflict and deep self-doubt which plague Paul Herz of *Letting Go* and Peter Tarnopol of *My Life as a Man*. Only Kapesh survives, at least in this novel, emerging from divorce sufficiently unscathed to take a chance on love.

The Professor of Desire is the story of David Kapesh, an adventurous man of intelligence and feeling who wades his way through a world of sensual possibilities, trying to find both pleasure and dignity. The novel follows David Kapesh from the domesticity of childhood into the vast wilderness of erotic possibility, from a ménage a trios in London to the throes of loneliness in New York. Roth creates a supremely intelligent affecting, and often hilarious novel about the dilemma of pleasure: where we seek it; why we flee it; how we struggle to strike a truce between dignity and desire.

Can the provisions of sexual desire ultimately lead to happiness? The professor in Philip Roth's *The Professor of Desire,* David Kapesh, explores that question and its implications in this witty and erudite novel that begins, quite literally, with hilarious display of "bathroom" humour and ends with the pathos of a man reflecting on the ramifications of his personal history.

David Kapesh has only two things on his mind: women and literature. When he wins a Fulbright fellowship to study in London, Kapesh indulges himself in the erotic possibilities of his life while trying to keep his academic status at a high standard. During his adventures, he meets Helen, who eventually becomes his wife. Yet, despite everything they share in the sexual arena, there is not enough common ground in the rest of their life to provide a balance. So their wedded life ends in divorce and debacle.

The event sends Kapesh into a period of depression and self-reflection. His job as professor of comparative literature is the art of substance on which his sanity hinges. He puts his energy into his work and it is there, after a period of reasonable stability, that he is introduced to Claire.

It is in tracing the development of David and Claire's relationship that Roth really begins to shine. Poised between the bookends of Kapesh literary heroes—Kafka and Chekhov, David and Claire play out a drama that dances among the shadows of both writers in its quest for the happy light of a common sun. The result is that *The Professor of Desire* moves from the shelf of mere entertainment to a philosophical rendering of the dilemmas encountered as love and lust do battle in a war of the heart.

The Professor of Desire is a 1977 novel by Philip Roth. It features the youth, the college years and the academic career of Professor David Kapesh. And besides that, his sexual desires.

David is insecure in his emotionality. As a child, he grows up at the hotel his parents are managing, and he is also influenced by the queer artist Herbie Bratasky, who, thanks to his ingenuity in imitating sounds of fasts, defecation and toilet flushing, is credited with "mustering the whole Wagner scale of fecal storm and Stress". Herbie used to send pornographic mail to a nine-year-old child. David says:

> Does Bratasky really fail to understand how decent people feel about such things? Doesn't he know that even sending a letter like this he is probably breaking a law and making of me an accomplice?[1]

When David was eighteen, and a freshman at Syracuse, he also gave stage mimicry. He loved acting on the stage. But when he is twenty, he searches for his own self:

> At twenty I must stop impersonating others and become myself, or at least begin to impei onate the self I believe I ought now to be.[2]

He devotes himself to European literature and languages. His mother has been the flawless legal secretary ever to work for the firm of Mr. Clark. When he later attends a college he shares his bachelor pad room with a lazy, often masturbating, dodging fellow student, named Louis Jelinek, who in fact is his Kierkegaard mentor. Louis rents a room in a private house in town rather than live in the college dormitory. At first, he seems to accept the odd facts about his colleague—imagines him to be profoundly in touch with reality more than he is. Later, David is shocked when he is told by others that he has deviated from 80 many social norms. He is cross-questioned by police.

David often focuses on the breasts and butts of female co-students, but fails to accomplish any successful date.

> I observe the breasts beneath her blouse push softly into her folded arms. How I wish I were those arms![3]

He often annoys girls by telling them that they had gorgeous bodily properties: "Your ass is sensational. Your ass is marvelous."[4]

So between the yearnings and the myriad objects of desire, his world interposes its arguments and obstructions. Kapesh, with Fullbright grant in his pocket goes to London, where he learns to know two sexually interested Swedish girls, Birgitta and Elisabeth. Elisabeth has taken a year off to improve her English and is living with Birgitta, another Swede, who had left the university of Uppsala two years earlier to improve her English. Elisabeth falls in love with him and he goes to bed with two of them only because he wants her to do perverse things with him in the room. So David indulges in sexual activities in his twenties.

He finds Birgitta sane, clever, courageous, self-possessed and wildly lascivious." He hankes after such a woman. So in London, he fails to do any earnest advance in studying Nordic saga and Arthurian legends.

Back in America, he moves to California, where he gets acquainted with Helen, a woman dreaming of opening a store of her own. She has had a history of promiscuity when she, in her early twenties, lived in Hong Kong and other places in Asia. She had run off with a journalist twice her age to Hong Kong where he was already living with a wife and three children. Just six months prior to when she meets Kapesh—she had given up everyone and everything before—she already has been in fifty passionate affairs. Her lover has begun to talk about arranging for his wife to be killed in an 'accident'.

He marries Helen Baird, after nearly three full years beset with doubting, hoping, wanting and fearing. But Helen does not feel loved by Mr. Kapesh. She refuses to do household duties because he only gives her sexual attention but is unable to feel and express emotion and passion for her. He submits to that "fact" and ends up doing all the work a household entails beside teaching literature classes and writing papers on Anton Chekhov. In fact, fatherly emotions in him sprout when he sees a girl from Beverly Hills in his class. He wants to adopt her.

Then on a Saturday morning Helen goes to Hong Kong but gets herself in jail because Jimmy files a case of smuggling against her Cockyne but David manages to get her released.

But at the final stage, Kapesh separates from Helen and goes to New York to deliver lectures in literature but his emotional side is not refined yet. He takes endless session with a psychoanalyst (Frederick Klinger), a hearty, round-faced fellow, full of life, who smokes cigars incessantly throughout the sessions. He confesses to his psychoanalyst that he was a fearless sort of boy back in his early thirties. Then he says:

> And you want to be once again in your thirties.[5]

He always craves for old potency. Dr. Klinger tells him that he would rather be a primp than an associate Professor. When he feels lonesome, his parents arrive to live with him. His mother dies of cancer. David is also annoyed by a homosexualist who comes to ring the doorbell. Even he uses his literature class (which he later calls 'Desire 341' after the course number) to contrast his own desires and experiences with those which are displayed in works like Gustave Flaubert's *Madam Bovary*—he even persuades the students to discuss his own love life.

On a visit to Prague, the birthplace of the equally sexually unexperienced Franz Kafka, he dreams of visiting the still-living prostitute of Kafka and he insists on seeing her crotch. In the novel, there is a couple, Arthur and Deborah, who serve as a foil. Although Arthur's early life had been involved with a wildly neurotic and destructive woman, now he has overcome that situation after his interaction with Deborah.

Ralph Baumgarten is a Vizzy poet—unmarried—who writes perverse poems and is very casual about sex. But Deborah and Arthur despise Ralph for his perversity, and look down upon him as a murderous, unconscientious womanizer. Even Deborah says that Bauingarten has become David Kapesh's "alter ego" acting out fantasies of aggression against women.

David Kapesh often misses Helen and repents. He also shows her photographs to Ralph. He thinks that his relationship with no woman can be harmonious but after the summer, when he returns East he meets a young twenty-four-year-old woman, Claire Ovington, who has earned a degree from Cornell in experimental psychology, and a master's from Columbia in education. She is surprisingly innocent and guileless about the personal side of her life. She seems to embody innocence and dedication. David trusts her and then his sessions with Klinger end.

Claire and Kapesh fly to the north of Italy where they spend happy times. During this last year he has been teaching the Kafka course at the university. He was given the name and telephone number of an American spending the year teaching in Prague. Then there is the little country village where his sister had spent a year managing a farm and where he had gone to stay with her during a spell of illness. The inner conflict of Kapesh brings him to Kafka as he says:

> With sexual despair, with vows of chastity that seem somehow to have been taken by me behind my back and which I lived with against my will. Either I turned against my flesh, or it turned against me.[6]

He also goes to Franz Kafka's grave. He also visits the living whore of Kafka. Then one day Helen comes to meet him with her husband who saved her from her illness. After the break-up with Kapesh, she was extremely ill and then Lowery came in her life and married her and now she is pregnant. She also feels sorry for what had happened in the past between her and Kapesh.

Claire feels uneasy due to the arrival of Helen but then she recovers and confesses to Kapesh that she has aborted the child of Kapesh because she does not want to saddle Kapesh with a sense of responsibility. Rather she wants Kapesh to be contented with her and her ways. The father of Kapesh and his friend Mr. Barbatnik (Friend) come to spend a weekend with them and she attends them cheerfully and cordially.

So we find that at the end of the novel, Kapesh comes out of his emotional conflict and trauma, and lives in contentment with

Claire. They are in love. So ultimately Roth's hero, David Kapesh, has recovered from his intense inner conflict between pleasure and dignity. So this is the novel of convalescence.

Philip Roth's tenth book *The Professor of Desire* is a thoughtful, even gentle, stylistically elegant novel about the paradox of male desire, that lacerating sexual passion which may lead to happiness but cannot endure. The effect of the book is more that of discourse than that of fiction, a high-level discourse adorned with wit, with rhetorical devices—new and ancient—and with its piquant illustrations. Its form is that of a monologue, rather than first-person storytelling, for the scenes are more often adumbrated than dramatized, the characters more often indicated than developed. This method, designed to involve the reader intellectually rather than sensationally, is, of course perfectly intentional.

Professor Kapesh begins by sharing with us—or with Lit. 341—his recollections of a preposterous boyhood idol, Herbie Bratasky, "social director, bandleader, crooner, comic and M.C. of my family's mountainside resort hotel." Herbie's most memorable achievements are in mimicry; he is able to imitate vocally all the sounds made in bathroom, except for the unrolling of the toilet paper, and, driven, by ambition, is working on that feat when last encountered. His admiration for Herbie, Kapesh tells us, led him to aspire first to be an entertainer, then a serious actor, but the intensity with which he begins to develop himself is split—the seriousness into studying literature, the intensity into pursuing objects of lust. Intellectual development proceeds, personal development is blocked. Though Kapesh has a reputation as a great seducer in college it is only because he is always trying and chasing; he is more devoted to the game than being effective at it, often offending by frankness, for he is the perpetual victim of young women who both demanded honest declarations and found them unacceptable. This changes only when he goes to study in England and manages to involve himself with two representatives of the current legend of promiscuity and beauty, i.e., Swedish women.

This legend changes ethnicity now and then, being sometimes Spanish, French, English, Jewish or southern. This kaleidoscopic ethnic range released Kapesh's block more effectively than the first of the women concerned. Elisabeth, trying valiantly to measure down to the expected level of dissoluteness, becomes suicidal because what she really wants are a conventional home and husband. Birgitta, however, her roommate, is at last Kapesh's match in being eager to try everything and invent more. It is indicative of the restraint with which Philip Roth has composed. *The Professor of Desire* that the fulfilment with Kapesh of Birgitta's wildest sexual fantasy is not reported at the time it occurs, in London, when the reader might have had a voyeuristic wallow—or felt revulsion, for that matter—but long afterwards, in retrospect. Kapesh is by now in Venice with Claire, the woman with whom happiness will banish passion and whose sexual range, while deep, is narrow:

> Yes, sitting across from Claire... I am remembering... the sight of Birgitta kneeling before me while... Elisabeth, wearing her pink woolen robe, and reclining on the bed, looks on the frozen fascinations at the naked masturbator and his half-clothed suppliant.[7]

It is, as promised, an open account but goes no further. Conversation between Kapesh and the analyst is one of several departures which, for the sake of relief, the author permits himself from the lecturer's mode, and is used both for narration and reflection, a contemporary equivalent perhaps, as it has often seemed in other works, of the old epistolary.

Not long afterward, Mr. Roth does an actual epistolary sequence for us, and late in the book, yet another departure in another comedy routine. This last is introduced as a dream Kapesh has about an old woman who has become a literary tourist attraction, having once been Kafka's whore.

We are not, of course, meant to read this as a realist's attempts to reproduce a character's dream, but to recognize in it a comedian's convention, a current rhetorical device, just as we recognize and enjoy the use of many of the classical conventions—parallel sentence structure, periodic, metonymies, zeugmas, aphorisms, epigrams.

Even some of the dialogue, and particularly the crucial exchanges between Kapesh and the women he cares about, is made carefully artificial, for it is more important to the author to set forth clearly the ideas and descriptions of emotions that are being exchanged than to make the realist's attempt at reproducing human speech.

It is thus, in certain ways, quite an abstract novel, and even the world of David Kapesh, its inhabitants restricted to Jewish men and gentile women, is, if not precisely abstract, certainly arbitrary. But perhaps the classic device, that of literary allusion, is on the author's side in place of irony, as it often is throughout the book. For Kapesh compares his rage to that of Gogol's Kovalyov, a madman who loses his nose. See Kapesh as unhinged on the subject of his lost passion, and the problem of irony disappears.

The Professor of Desire includes some memorable tender passages about David Kapesh's parents, in particular those dealing with the mother's death and the father's old age. Generally, Jewish parents have been depicted as objects of satiric criticism. So it is refreshing to find them treated here as objects of simple affection.

As a widower, Kapesh's father becomes friends with another old man, Mr. Barbatnik, a concentration camp survivor whose role it is to declare that one may become something more than a man: a human being. These finer elements perhaps direct us to the conclusion that family affection is what civilized people need for mutual defence against the barbarities of loneliness and death, making desire no more than a brutish mechanism that initiates affection and is then to be discarded.

The Professor of Desire is a fine display of literary skills, a challenging brief novel, moving when it needs to be, an erudite examination of the troglodyte within us. In *The Professor of Desire (1977),* Philip Roth finally brings to some measure of completion Kapesh's struggle with the various incompatible, scarcely governable drives that both divide him and compose his very identity.

David Kapesh is in many ways another Alexander Portnoy, filled with and defined by desires that take resolutely sexual forms but that encompass even more fundamental relations and frustrations. "Between the yearnings and the myriad objects of desire," Kapesh states, "my world interposes its arguments and obstructions."[8]

Kapesh s capacity to feel the world as an obstacle to his desires, while at exactly the same time it both occasions and grounds those desires, indicates the degree to which desire's paradox afflicts and dominates him despite his application of considerable intellectual effort to the problem. His epithet is, after all, "The Professor of Desire," a title that refers to his career as a teacher of the great works on the struggles and maelstrom of human passion, including *Anna Karenina* and *Madame Bovary*. By the end of *The Professor of Desire* (the first of the three books according to Kapesh's life line), he laments an ebbing desire for someone he knows to be all he could ever need.

In this seemingly insoluble conflict between what he knows and what he craves for and in his imperfect ability to bridle his passions, Kapesh comes to symbolize the person divided within, one who feels cheated by a world fit more to arouse than to satisfy longing. Having studied the passions in the classroom and in his personal life, Kapesh, *The Professor of Desire*, can conclude only tragically, ironically that "you might as well know nothing!"[9]

The Professor of Desire opens with Kapesh recounting his earliest experiences, and it is not accidental that his first world, the novel's first word, is "temptation," for the tutelage of entertainer Herbie Bratasky in imitating the sounds of the toilet constitutes Kapesh's first movement away from this nine-year-old Kapesh, "awestruck" before Bratasky's "toots" and "tattoos," to Kapesh at eighteen, now a freshman at Syracuse University. His interest in acting and his rebellion against a medical career lead him to European literature, where he finds additional models of behaviour.

After the fashion of Lord Byron, Kapesh intends to be "studious by day, dissolute by night," and in the manner of Sir Richard Steele, he purposes to become "a rake among scholars, a scholar among rakes."[10] He soon embarks upon this new life when, just off the boat for a fellowship year in London, he encounters a whore in Shepherd Market. Yet it is in a three-way relationship with two Swedish girls, Elisabeth Elverskog and Birgitta Svanstrom, that his apprenticeship in dissolution truly begins. A night during which he and Birgitta coerce Elisabeth into stating and then enacting her most secret desire leads to her attempt at suicide and subsequent return to Sweden.

During this same scene Kapesh discovers his own capacity for cruelty and egocentrism "I know that I could do anything, and that I want to, and that I will !"[11] and discovers in Birgitta a partner in crime, as it were. Yet even as he and Birgitta tour the continent seeking new thrills, Kapesh also imagines a tranquil existence with Elisabeth and continues to write to her:

> There is Elisabeth's unfathomable and wonderful love and there is Birgitta's unfathomable and wonderful daring, and whichever I want I can have. Now isn't that unfathomable! Either the furnace or the hearth![12]

When an incident in a Parisian bar reawakens Kapash to his academic responsibilities, he drives Birgitta away with the claim that they will never be able to enjoy "ordinary" sex together, having "upped the ante" so far.[13] To his claim that he must go back to America without her, she retorts that he is just "a boy," unable to come to terms with his undeniable nature.[14]

The images of furnace and hearth come to structure the remainder of the novel as well, occupied as it is with Kapesh's fiery relationship with Helen Baird and his subsequent, more domestic relationship with Claire Ovington. Kapesh meets Helen as he is finishing a graduate degree in comparative literature at Stanford University; they marry (ominously) as he is working to publish his thesis on romantic disillusionment. Kapesh cannot compensate for Helen's memories of her previous life in the Far East, where she was the mistress of a powerful man, nor can he let go of his contempt for her vanity and for those memories. Helen flees to the East to search out her former lover, who rebuffs and frames her, and Kapesh travels to retrieve her from jail. As they rehearse their mutual recriminations on the return flight, and as Kapesh struggles to grade his students' papers on Chekhov, he finally breaks down at one pupil's conclusion that "we are granted only fragmentary happiness"[15] to balance the pain born of our struggle to gain knowledge in a world built on disillusionment and the fear of death.

With the aid of a new teaching position, a course of psychotherapy, and the friendship of the irreverent, chauvinistic poet Ralph Baumgarten and despite the death of his mother from cancer Kapesh manages to rebuild his life from the rubble of his divorce from Helen.

At this point he meets Claire, who is more than he can hope for: beautiful, calm, determined, possessing a "translucent mix of sober social aplomb and domestic enthusiasms and youthful susceptibility," not to mention "those breasts, those breasts."[16] They travel together to Venice, where Kapesh must struggle to suppress the lascivious memory of Birgitta. Yet Kapesh marshals himself, refuses to indulge his nostalgia, and concentrates instead on his good fortune. They travel from Venice to Vienna to see Freud's house, then on to Prague, Kafka's city. They visit Kafka's grave and other tourist sites, and one evening in the hotel lobby, inspired by Kafka's "Report to an Academy," Kapesh begins to write an introduction for an upcoming course in the literature of erotic desire, an introduction in which he argues the importance of the interpreter's own desires in constructing a referential relationship with literature. He later dreams that a Czech guide takes him to visit Kafka's whore, who asks if he would like to inspect her vagina; despite this inspection, Kapesh does not learn the secret of Kafka's desire.

Back in the States, Kapesh and Claire rent a summer house together, and though he senses his passion subsiding, Kapesh intends to embrace and accept that change. They then receive a surprise visit from Helen and her new husband, and Helen's revelation that she is pregnant provokes Clair's confession of an abortion.

After this visit, Kapesh and Claire receive his father and his father's friend Mr. Barbatnik, a Holocaust survivor. As the novel closes, the poignancy of Barbatnik's history, Kapesh's baseless concerns about his father's health, and his fear that his passion for Claire will soon die conspire to cast a pall over the future. He imagines himself another Gogol, searching desperately for his lost desire, a desire that has always seemed to demand either total, destructive allegiance or active, unmanning suppression. Following a night of distressing dreams, Kepesh seeks Clair's breast, which he sucks "in a desperate frenzy," pitting happiness and hope against his "fear of transformations yet to come."[17]

In *The Professor of Desire* Claire Ovington is "sane", "calm" and "consoling" with whom Kapesh establishes a tender liaison some years after the break-up of his marriage. This doesn't stand or fall on the fact that Claire Ovington is calm and sane but on what it is to have a mate—and why it is one would want to mate—who possesses these and other returns in abundance. She is also vulnerable to jealousy when Kapesh's ex-wife turns up uninvited and she carries with her certain sadness about her family background. She helps him and he helps her.

They are in love; she is there because Kapesh has fallen in love with a sane, calm and consoling woman after having been unhappily married to a difficult, recalcitrant and exciting woman he was unable to tackle. The irony of Kapesh's situation is that having found the calm and consoling woman he can live with, a woman of numerous qualities, he then finds his desire for her perversely seeping away, and realizes that unless this involuntary domination of passion can be arrested, he'll become ratiocinated from the best thing in his life. His emotional involvement with this serene, composed and assuaging lady, far from deepening and abiding, threatens to dwindle, and abate. Recovering from the turbulent phase of violent and fervid passion (with Helen) he fails to find enduring anchor in the equanimity and profundity of emotional attachment with Claire which he finds slowly but steadily diminishing and depleting. Thus his convalescence or recovery from thr trauma and vortex of passion remains incomplete and unconvincing. David undergoes the same dismal marital conflict and deep self-doubt which plague Paul Herz of *Letting Go* and Peter Tarnopol of *My Life as a Man.* Only Kapesh survives, at least in this novel, emerging from divorce sufficiently unscathed to take a chance on love. However, Roth's presentation of his recovery is not sufficiently convincing. Kapesh himself, with his Kafkesque nightmares and incubuses, can hardly believe his luck or render it credible to us.

This novel also indicates Roth's limitations as a novelist whose forte is the delineation of a character embroiled in a crisis constantly held back, a character doomed to aggression, despair, irony, misgivings, doubts and nascent panic. His characterization of Kapesh is not of a very high order like that of Patimkin (*Goodbye, Columbus*), Alex Portnoy (*Portnoy's Complaint*) and Peter Tarnopol (*My Life as a Man*), because the novelist has a penchant for the delineation of catastrophe, crisis and fiasco. However, this novel remains a tale of psychic convalescence, which celebrates and delineates erotic and emotional recuperation from the travails and turbulence of marital bleak and gruelling marital discord and excruciating self-doubt. The psyche of Kapesh outlives the blows and buffets of marital conflict which culminates in divorce, and reemerges from this spell of trials and tribulations sufficiently unmauled, phoenix-like, to embark anew, however diffidently, on the adventure of love (with Claire).

References

1. Roth, Philip. *The Professor of Desire*. New York: Farrar, 1977, p.9.
2. Ibid., p.12.
3. Ibid., p.22.
4. Ibid., p.23.
5. Ibid., p.99.
6. Ibid., p.171.
7. Bourjaily, Vance. *The Professor of Desire. The New York Times*: September 17, 1972.
8. Roth, Philip. *The Professor of Desire*. op.cit., p.26.
9. Ibid., p.262.
10. Ibid., p.17.
11. Ibid., pp.37-.38.
12. Ibid., p.47.
13. Ibid., p.48.
14. Ibid., p.50.
15. Ibid., p.94.
16. Ibid., pp.151-152.
17. Ibid., p.263.

5

Theoretical Perspectives

Roth has published his collected essays on literature and culture in *Reading Myself and Others.* These display his critical acumen as a perceptive and perspicacious interpreter of the complex and paradoxical emotional dynamics of modern lives and Jewish novels, including his own.

Roth was still in his twenties when *Goodbye Columbus* made him famous in 1959. Ten years later, after *Portnoy's Complaint,* he became a national public figure, the most notorious writer in the country except Mailer. Since then he has searched restlessly for something new to do, to break out of his apparent bondage and the results have not been good. Everyone knows that he can write beautifully and that he can be very funny, but the writing has become self-regarding and the humour has degenerated into giggles. Of course he may well have great productive years ahead, but at this point he has suffered badly from demands made on him, by himself and others, to think of himself as a major talent when what he has to work with is an excellent minor genius.

Now comes *Reading Myself and Others,* Roth's first work of non-fiction, a collection of essays and interviews that confirms all gloomy suspicions. Since *Portnoy's Complaint,* Roth has often been called on to account for his life and career, to justify and explain his role as an apparently scandalous Jew, to explain why he has written each thing the way he's done. Inevitably, the result is self-consciousness and self-regard—"the question of moral sovereignty, as it is examined in *Letting Go, Portnoy's Complaint* and *The Breast.* Roth treats himself as an object, an accomplished fact, a figure about to be entombed. He even becomes the central figure in an allegory in which sheer playfulness and deadly seriousness are his closest friends; it is with them that he takes those walks in the country at the end of the day.

The problem, remains though, and what has gone wrong with Roth is not just the result of there being no tradition of the minor novel in America. A number of other circumstances, most of them well beyond Roth's control, seem to have been conspiring against him when *Goodbye Columbus* appeared, Roth's elders, mostly Jews themselves, were able to hail him as the most recent of what must have seemed an inexhaustible Jewish postwar novelistic talent; he was different from Bellow and Malamud, but in ways that could do everyone credit. In the succeeding decade or more, however, no one has come along to take Roth's place as the youngest in the pantheon, though of course many young Jewish writers have appeared. As a result, Roth seemed to get more attention, more nagging and somewhat paternal attention—What is he doing? What will he become?—than is perhaps good for anyone. *Letting Go, When She Was Good,* Roth's grindingly realistic and mostly Midwest fictions, seemed not to satisfy, because in them he was not seriously influenced by external pressures.

Then came *Portnoy's Complaint,* at the climax of what Roth calls the demythologizing sixties and *Portnoy* did a lot of demythologizing, as Roth brilliantly suggests in "Imagining Jews". The novel scandalized and became a bestseller because he was imagining a Jew wanting and doing those things that "traditionally" Jews had imagined only the goyim doing; he was even accused of being anti-semitic.

The trouble is not that Roth had become a bad boy, but that he had put himself in a position where he didn't know what to do next. No point in repeating *Portnoy's Complaint,* no way to get back to the grim patient realism of his two previous novels. Surely there must be some-thing that can be done with the humour, because *Portnoy's Complaint,* whatever else, is both funny and fun in many places. But what?

Roth was now famous, the subject of gossip columnists as well as of literary critics and Hadassah gatherings; furthermore, Johnson and Nixon seemed to have managed to turn America into everyone's subject. Without much in the way of tradition to guide him, without much more that could be made of his, native-material, with only the uncertain figure of Kafka to act as a patron saint, wealthy yet personally retiring, Roth has bobbled, plunged, made one mistake after another.

Everything has become too stylized and too long. Instead of the four page, "The President Addresses the Nation", which is good and reprinted here, we have *Our Gang* where the joke is bloated into a book. Instead of the good book about baseball which Roth might have written, we get the truly silly *The Great American Novel* where instead of baseball we have America turned into pretentious force.

But unlike Mailer or Pynchon, Roth is not really very happy a performer, showman, public figure, rhetorician. He is too private a person, too lyrical, perhaps too much, still a Good Jew, for that *My Life as a Man* tries to get back, as if in realization of all this, and so, though it is a book mostly swamped in self-justification, there are some passages in it that are moving and lyrical, signs enough that of course Roth can still write. But the rest is all forced, writing projects that seem thought up, abstractions, things that have to be bludgeoned into existence by style. He may one day recover but as of now everything good he has written is derived from life he had led or known before he became a writer, childhood stuff, growing-up stuff, starting out in life stuff. That material seems to be gone now, and fame and underserved infamy have taken care of the rest. His present companions, as he says, are Sheer Playfulness and Deadly Seriousness; in such pure form, these can hardly be anyone's best friends; worse still, they become practically enemies when they are one's only friends.

Roth's novels present his preoccupation with the relationship between the written and unwritten world. He finds it more useful than the distinction between imagination and reality or art and life. *Reading Myself and Others* is divided into two parts: Part one is about Roth as a reader and read. This section consists mainly of interviews in which he describes what has generated his work, the means employed from book to book; Part 2 is made up of selected articles and essays to give a talk, to oppose an adversary, to introduce a writer, to mark an event.

When Philip Roth graduated, he was by and large a good, responsible, well-behaved boy, controlled by the social regulations of the self-conscious; his close adolescent companions were clever, respectful Jewish boys like himself. So for as his relationship with his parents is concerned, he did not try to disappoint his father and mother not out of fear but out of a broken heart.

Philip Roth enjoys solitude the way some people enjoy parties. It gives him an enormous sense of personal freedom and an exquisitely sense of being alive, and it provides him with the quiet and the breathing space he needs to get his imagination going and his work done. He takes no pleasure at all in being a creature of fantasy in the minds of those who don't know him.

For the solitude, he has lived mostly in the country for the last five years. Almost the whole of his life in public takes place in a classroom—he taught one semester of each year. He began to earn his living teaching full time in 1956 and now he is living on his writing income. He has also written about women, with some of whom he identified strongly and imagined himself into while he was working as he himself admits. In *Letting Go,* Martha Reganhart and Libby Herz; in *When She Was Good,* Lucy Nelson and her mother; and in *My Life as a Man,* Maureen Tarnopol and Susan McCall, Lydia Ketterer and Sharon Shatzkys. However much or little he is able to extend his imagination to "comprehend… life as a woman" is demonstrated in those books.

In *Letting Go,* where he began to write about female vulnerability, and to see this vulnerability not only as it determined the lives of the women—who felt it frequently at the center of their being—but the men to whom they looked for love and support, the women became characters his imagination could take hold of and enlarge upon. How this vulnerability shapes their relations with men is really at the heart of his novels. A major theme treated by Roth is the difficulty of close interpersonal dealings, especially between parents and children. Of course, this subject has been of perennial concern for novelists, but in the work of this author it is absolutely central. He views family relationships as extremely problematic and essentially frustrating but acknowledges their importance in human affairs and returns to them repeatedly as a subject for fiction.

Perhaps the most significant assumption shared by Roth is that in all relationships the individual ideas of family solidarity and reinforcement of personal identity through strong familial bonds appear to have lost their viability. Nowhere is this more bleakly apparent than in his most recent books. For example, the protagonist of Roth's *Zuckerman Unbound* exists in a familial void; childless and twice divorced, he has been spurned by his brother and cursed by his dying father. In "The Anatomy Lesson", he has been divorced a third time, is depressed about his estrangement from his brother, and is mourning his recently deceased mother. Roth seems to be suggesting that in the fragmented modern world we are left almost entirely to our own devices, cut off from even the most basic sources of communion. Much of his work constitutes a lament for these lost wellsprings of security, solace, and strength. His protagonists' confusions are rendered all the more vexing by the loss of vital personal ties and the concomitant sense of guilt and unworthiness that such a rupture engenders. He says:

> Portnoy, full of complaint because of his sexual fate, is bent on tracking down the source of his grievances...Well, so too with my heroine, Lucy Nelson. Wholly antithetic in cultural and moral orientation, she is, in her imprisoning passion and in the role she assumes of the enraged offspring, very much his soul mate.[1]

In Roth's novels, this predicament is dramatically obvious. While Portnoy, for example, blames this on his Jewishness, in so doing he denies his parents and in fact openly castigates them, especially, the mother, throughout his rambling diatribe. This renunciation is not without its price. As a consequence, Portnoy experiences extreme self-hatred, fueled largely by mixed feelings of love and hatred toward his parents, feelings that he can neither exorcise nor accept. Similarly, Neil Klugman of *Goodbye, Columbus,* in rejecting the old world Jewishness of Newark, also rejects his surrogate parents, Aunt Gladys and Uncle Max. Like Portnoy, he feels the wrench. Both characters frequently reveal deep affection for their families, even while criticizing them. Portnoy's poignant cry "This is my mother and father I'm talking about"[2] has much in common with Neil's wistful references to his aunt and uncle, sharing a Mounds bar in the cindery darkness of their alley, on beach chairs.

This theme runs throughout Roth's canon, receiving its most sombre treatment in the "Zuckerman" novels. In *The Ghost Writer,* Young Nathan Zuckerman has written a short story that has incurred his father's wrath, and the fledgling author seeks a surrogate father in the person of E. I. Lonoff, an established writer. Yet Zuckerman's fantasized marriage to Anne Frank reveals the intensity of his subconscious desire for family sanction. As mentioned above, in *Zuckerman Unbound,* the protagonist now a well known writer himself is cursed by his father from the latter's deathbed, leaving Zuckerman "no longer any man's son." thereby ending the novel on a profoundly negative note. And these fundamental disruptions continue to haunt Zuckerman in "The Anatomy Lesson". Conversely, Roth's most uplifting treatment of the father-son theme occurs in *The Professor of Desire.*

David Kapesh and his father enjoy a warm, mutually tolerant friendship which, although not without its conflicts, ultimately constitutes a source of fulfilment for both men. But the Kapeshes are the exception; in virtually every other instance in Roth's fiction, father and son are at loggerheads.

Letting Go chronicles several tears in the lives of five confused and unhappy people: Gabe Wallach, a young academic whose successful graduate career leads to a university professorship; Wallach's father, a prosperous dentist and recent widower; Paul Herz, a harassed colleague of Gabe; Libby; Herz's sickly, neurotic wife; and Martha Regenhart, a struggling divorcee with whom Gabe has an affair. But such capsule descriptions of the principals fail to convey the complexity of their many entanglements.

The various dilemmas of Gabe Wallach and company are but imperfectly resolved, for the causes of these people's problems are rooted in universal human conflicts: tensions between lovers, between husbands and wives, and, of course, between parents and children. All of sometime narrator Gabe Wallach's dealings are attempts to fathom the ambivalences of mutual responsibility, to discover an answer to the elemental questions posed by Hillel: "If I am not for myself, who will be? If I am only for myself, what am I?"[3]

This basic tension surfaces early in the novel in Gabe's impossible relationship with his father. The disconsolate elder Wallach does not fully understand his son, and suffers greatly from the sense of strained artificiality that thwarts their attempts at communication. Nevertheless, like most of Roth's other Jewish fathers, he is an endearing character. Self-sacrificing and right thinking, Dr. Wallach is a strong, virile, decent man who is not without sensitivity and wisdom. His too protective meddling in Gabe's affairs is the result only of his love for his son. Yet Gabe greatly resents what he interprets as his father's attempts to control his life.

Sons in Roth's books are typical Kapesh's father (Like Dr. Wallach, a recent widower) becomes an embodiment of tragicomic parental intensity, finally prompting Kapesh to remark wonderingly to himself, "Until death do us part the tremendous closeness and the tremendous distance between my father and myself will— continue in the same perplexing proportions as have existed all our lives."[4] Roth's portrayals not only of actual fathers, but also of elder men generally tend to be uniformly approving even if his young protagonists do not always see their elders that way. Often, for example, a character's uncle or elder brother acts as a surrogate father—Paul Herz's Uncle Jerry in *Letting Go*, Tarnopol's brother More in *My Life as a Man* and is presented in a favorable light, offering advice and guidance to his confused junior.

Roth's depiction of Dr. Wallach in *Letting Go* is consistent, then, with his tendency to portray father fingures warmly. Like Jack Portnoy and Abe Kepesh, Dr. Wallach well-meaningly beleaguers his son, harassing Gabe with long distance telephone calls to Iowa, where Gabe is a graduate student in literature.

> Two or three evenings a week my father and I had the same phone conversation, pointless on the surface, pleading beneath. The old man stood being familiyess all day, what with having his patients' mouths to look in to; it was alone with his avocado and lettuce dinner that he broke down. When he called his voice shook; when he hung up or when I did his vibrato passed directly in to the few meager objects in the room— — The trouble with the phone calls, in fact, was that all the time I felt it necessary to the preservation of my life and sanity to resist the old man, I understood how it was for him sitting in that huge Victorian living room all alone.[5]

Gabe's relationship with his father continues in this way even after he accepts a position at the University of Chicago. And although he confesses at one point, " I had been missing my father as much as he had been missing me[6], the necessity of living one's own life, of "letting go" of family ties, presents ir econcilable problems. As a consequence, even their time spent together during his holiday visit to New York is characterized by mutual discomfort. An atmosphere of strained artificiality is sharply evoked in his description of a tennis match at the West Side Athletic Club:

> We two Wallach men, my father and I, stood in place on the tennis court, pushing dull lifeless shorts back and forth at one another. Each of us had been trying for over an hour not

> to inconvenience his opponent by so much as a foot. For four days now, life off the court as well as on had consisted of just this sort of polite emotionless volleying.[7]

Of course, the discomfort of the relationship is caused by love, and this is what makes the situation so difficult. Both men are stymied by the intricacies of the paternal and filial bonds. At one point, after Gabe grants his father's request to examine his teeth, he experiences a lot uncharacteristic surge of affection for his father: "Then his face appeared above my own. I could have pulled him down and kissed him. But would he understand that I was not prepared to surrender my life to his? He was a wholehearted man, and such people are hard to kiss half-heartedly."[8]

Likewise, Dr. Wallach is aware of Gabe's needs:

> All sons. All sons leave their fathers. Of course. He considered himself a student of psychology and he was not native about certain facts of life. Just the other day on the beach he had had an interesting discussion about parental problems with Abe Cole—He had told Abe— that unhappy as he been when his son had off for good, he had known in his heart that a boy does not become a man living in his father's house—he believed that he said children grow up and go away. That was one of life's laws to which he and his son could not expect to be made exceptions. Nevertheless—there are certain circumstances, are there not? Special predicaments people wind up in that are not of their own choosing and the both child and parent have to recognize and make accommodations for? If only his son—had had an ounce of patience with him; if only he himself had displayed an ounce of control[9]

Yet there can be no total reconciliation. The father is finally able to relinquish his grip on Gabe only after he himself has remarried. Ironically, Gabe then resents his stepmother, at least partly because he is jealous of the attention that father lavishes upon her. *Letting Go* seems to suggest that conflict is inevitable in close interpersonal relationships and that human dealings are intrinsically and unavoidably enigmatic, especially within the family circle.

In *When She was Good,* the book's midwestern ambience and its female protagonist make it a most unrepresentative production. Yet *When She was Good* is in many ways a probing exploration of family tensions. Comparing this work to *Portnoy's Complaint,* Roth has observed that an alert reader familiar with both books might find in them a similar preoccupation with the warfare between parents and children. Likening protagonist Lucy Nelson to Portnoy, Roth has termed her "in her imprisoning passion and in the role she assumes of the enraged offspring, very much his soul mate."[10]

Lucy shares with Portnoy, and with Roth's other male protagonists, a tendency to assess life by illusory criteria. Roth's Lucy finds that the naively optimistic instances of her existence fall far short of the naively optimistic versions of American life that she has absorbed specifically; Lucy disapproves of her family. Although they are in fact a rather lacklustre contingent,— her father is a drinker, her mother is Weakly self-abnegating, and her young husband is somewhat immature and directionless,—they are by no means contemptible. Yet Lucy, having totally subscribed to the popular, mythical ideal of the "perfect" family, will settle for nothingless, and her outraged self-righteousness toward her family's shortcomings is as self-defeating as it is strident.

Like everyone else symbolically (and ironically) named Liberty Centre, Lucy has been subliminally conditioned from birth to imagine as normal the sort of domestic bliss pictured by Norman Rockwell on the covers of the old *Saturday Evening Post.* Unlike most other people, however, Lucy really believes in his form of the American Dream, and fails to recognize it for the idealized inflation that it actually is. Like Portnoy, Lucy not only takes herself quite seriously, but places unrealistically stringent demands on those around her as well. When her family fails to measure up, she rages. In her dealings with the men in her life her grandfather, her father, her uncle, her husband, she is particularly exacting: "She idealises the masculine role to the extent of ruining it." Wanting men to be "Protectors and defenders, heroes and weaklings, cheaters and liars" without realizing that her own violent demands on authority have made authority impossible. Even her grandfather must repeat "I am not God", while he tries and fails to convince her that he cannot totally control other people or their problems. And this, of course, is directly related to the novel's indictment of the destructive consequences of our culture's "furious insistence on the family as a unit," our communal belief that "the system must continue" at all costs.

As Jones and Nance point out, Lucy is the tragic victim of a social milieu—based on the patriarchal concept of the male as protector—in a family in which the males who purport to protect are powerless to do so.

The parallels to *Portnoy's Complaint* are obvious, as revealed by this passage from the opening section of that novel:

> We are on the big dirt field back of my school. He sets his collection book on the ground, and steps up to the plate in his coat and his brown fedora. He wears square steel rimmed spectacles, and his hair (Which now I wear) is a wild bush the color and texture of steel wool; and those teeth, which sit all night long in a glass in the bath room smiling at the toilet bowl, now smile out at me, his beloved, his flesh and his blood, the little boy upon whose head no rain shall ever fall. "Okay, Big Shot Ballplayer," he says, and grasps my new regulation bat somewhere near the middle and to my astonishment, with his left hand where his right hand should be. I am suddenly overcome with such sadness: I want to tell him, Hey your hands are wrong, but am unable to, for fear I might begin to cry or he might! "Come on, Big Short, throw the ball," he calls, and so I do and of course discover that on top of all the other things I am just beginning to suspect about my father, he isn't "King Kong" Charlie Keller either.[11]

Roth seems to imply that many of modern Americans' ills stem from a collective tendency to exalt the family out of all proportion to its actual powers as a social institution. Too much family, too much "love," Roth suggests, is as destructive as too little.

This idea appears in *Portnoy's Complaint* and elsewhere in Roth's fiction, but it is the major thesis of *When She was Good*. Here it takes on an additional dimension, too, for Lucy's simplistic, overly literal habits of mind apply not just to her family dealings, but generally to her whole outlook on life. Roth did not intend Lucy as a totally representative case, he says, but he believes that hers is a not uncommon personality: "it has always seemed to me that though we are, to be sure, not a nation of Lucy Nelsons, there is a strong American inclination to respond to life like a Lucy Nelson an inclination to reduce the complexities and mysteries of living to the most simple minded and childish issues of right and wrong."[12]

The large issue of personal moral responsibility and guilt is of great interest to Philip Roth, featuring centrally in practically everything he has written. It is integral to the themes of ethnic identity and family interactions but it finds expression in another area of shared emphasis as well: love and marriage.

He is largely concerned with human sexuality and its attendant complexities, specifically as manifested in romantic relationships. He deals with the contrary demands of the self versus one's obligations to others, and his characters are frequently beset by feelings of inadequacy and guilt because of their failure to understand or balance this basic opposition.

In Roth's earliest works (the *Goodbye, Columbus* novella and short stories) and in his most recent (the "Zuckerman" novels), the love marriage theme is obviously crucial. The mutually exploitive "summer romance" between Neil Klugman and Brenda Patimkin in the *Goodbye, Columbus* novella serves as a context wherin Roth explores several larger themes. But the principals' sexual relationship becomes an important consideration in its own right, permitting Roth to comment trenchantly upon the destructive consequences of romantic self-delusion. Two of the five *Goodbye, Columbus* short stories focus on married characters whose difficulties are directly related to their unsatisfactory marital relationships: the aging title character in "Epstein" is marred in the final throes of a disappointing union, and the marriage depiced in "Eli, the Fanatic" contributes heavily to the protagonist's problems. In "The Ghost Writers", young Nathan Zuckerman is shocked by the acrimonious discord of his mentor's homelife, while the mature "Nathan of Zuckerman Unbound" and "The Anatomy Lesson" has himself experienced a series of unsuccessful marriages and romances. As we have seen, such predicaments feature prominently in Roth's other works as well, particularly so in *Letting Go, When She was Good, and Portnoy's Complaint.*

Indeed, *Portnoy's Complaint* can be viewed as the first volume in a Rothian "Trilogy of Desire" also including *My Life as a Man* and *The Professor of Desire*. These novels, perhaps more emphatically than any other in his canon, reflect Roth's ongoing preoccupation with, in his own words, "the struggle to accommodate warring (or, at least, contending) impulses and desires, to negotiate some kind of inner peace or balance of power, or perhaps just to maintain hostilities at a low destructive level, between the ethical and social yearnings and the—Singular lusts of the flesh and its pleasures. The measured self vs. the insatiable self. The accommodating self vs. The insatiable self."[13] In *Portnoy's Complaint,* the major social issues of ethnic identity, cultural assimilation, and family tensions are clearly present, and function as basic themes. But their primary purpose is to provide a setting in which to examine Portnoy's sexuality. In fact, Portnoy or his erotomania dominates the social content and overshadows it (although Portnoy believes the opposite to be true). He thereby engages our attention, becoming an extreme but recognizable embodiment of the universal implacability of the flesh and herein lies its psychological significance and complexity.

The same might be said of the wife hating Peter Tarnopol in *My Life as a Man,* except that the stridency of his narration renders him finally boring rather than interesting in "the battle of the sexes." Yet *My Life as a Man* is not Roth's most effective treatment of the love marriage theme. The novel contains several finely wrought sections ("Salad Days," for example, is an impressive performance), but many of the insights tend to slip out of focus, overpowered by the sheer redundancy of their dissection and the cloyingly self-justifying tone of the delivery.

Tarnopol's story is actually Roth's vehement gesture of retribution toward his own late wife, and the personal animus motivating the work finally undermines it. Of course, *My Life as a Man* is not mere transcription. Much constructive fabrication surrounds this treatment of Roth's marriage, and the book's whole conception is quite consciou·'y "literary," particularly with regard to form. Perhaps the most immediately noticeable of the novel's various interesting features is its reflexive structure, an experimental format that constitutes a variation on the Kunstlerroman. What makes the book somewhat unusual although not unique is that it extends the parameters of that genre to become not just a novel about a fictional artist, but, ostensibly, a collection of that author's work. The first section, "Useful Fictions," consists of two short stories ("Salad Days" and "Courting Disaster") supposedly written by Tarnopol.

My Life as a Man is structurally challenging then, and addresses significant issues. Moreover, it records that particular point in his life. Nevertheless, the novel is disappointing, primarily because the narrator's splenetic ravings are too unrelieved. Roth practically grants this, as he has Tarnopol quoting Flaubert's letter to his mistress, Louise Colet, concerning her poetic attack on Alfred de Musset: "You wrote with a personal emotion that distorted your outlook and made it impossible to keep before your eyes the fundamental principles that must underlie any imaginative composition—you have turned art into an outlet for passion, a kind of chamber pot to catch an overflow. It smells bad; it smells of hate!"[14]

Tarnopol admits that "all I can do with my story is tell it. And tell it. And tell it. And that's the truth."[15]

But this is a truth in which the reader soon loses interest. Although the events of Tarnopol's tumultuous life are potentially quite absorbing, Roth's inability or unwillingness to treat his intensely personal subject matter somewhat more dispassionately results in a narrator protagonist whose struggles with the erosagape self and others' conflicts soon seem to lose significance, for he appears to wallow in, and almost to relish, defeat.

This is the most immediately recognizable difference between Tarnopool and Portnoy, a contrast that sharply reveals the latter's greater substance as a fictional creation: Portnoy is engaging in a way that Tarnopol never is. Of course, this is largely because Portnoy is immensely entertaining, and because his egocentricity is continually undercut by his own sense of comic self-deflation. Hence he remains somehow appealing, even at his most vile level. No matter how desperate his plight becomes, he never loses his theatrical impulse or his awareness that he is dramatizing himself. There is something redeeming about this.

Despite the seriousness of Portnoy's neuroses as typified by his self-hatred he possesses throughout, even in the catastrophic scenes involving Israel with Naomi, a certain manic appeal. He has, to coin a phrase, an "immoral fiber" that Tarnopol lacks, which induces us to tend to take more seriously his attempts to resolve the sexual conflicts that beset him. Essentially, Portnoy's difficulty is the same as that of most of Roth's protagonists: he is unable to reconcile the diametrically opposite demands of the superego and the id. Roth's puritanical hedonists are all at war with their own dual natures, futilely striving to effect a truce between incompatible urges. Perhaps the most telling example is David Kapesh, protagonist of the *The Professor of Desire*. This is among the most satisfying of Roth's novels because here he managed to fuse Portnoy's appeal and Tarnopol's sobriety, creating in Kapesh one of his most credible narrators. A typically urbane and sophisticated Rothian protagonist, Kapesh presents the detail of his plight in a polished, controlled, and wryly amusing manner. Eschewing the caustic self-righteousness of Neil Klughman, the stuffy solemnity of Gabe Wallach, the erratic histrionism of Portnoy, and the shrill lugubriousness of Tarnopol, he states his case in a voice that is eminently suited to the book's themes. It is Roth's most convincing attempt so far to create the illusion of extemporaneous first-person narration.

In *The Professor of Desire,* Roth retained all the strength of *My Life as a Man* while avoiding that book's weakness. He continued to perfect not only the narrative voice, but also those other facets of fictive creation that had always been his virtues: the capacity for sharp evocations of setting through selective description and allusion, the ability to portaiture, an almost preternatural sensitivity to the distinctive qualities of realistic dialogue, and a highly developed sense of the absurd as it manifests itself in the everyday lives of his characters. Interestingly, *The Professor of Desire* largely retains *My Life as a Man's* concern with the despised spouse, but in the more recent novel Roth is always in control of his material. Therefore, this subject does not dominate the book, but simply serves as one of several that are pursued for the purpose of revealing the intricacies of the protagonist's inner workings.

In its handling of the theme of interpersonal responsibility and guilt, then, *The Professor of Desire* is the most convincing of the "Trilogy of Desire" novels, the one broadest in its applications. Kapesh's difficulties are akin to those of Portnoy or Tarnopol, but his particular case is more persuasively delineated and more convincingly stated than those of the other two, because it is presented with so much more artistic detachment and reserve, which characterise Kapesh's personality.

Dr. Klinger (who plays Spielvogel to Kapesh's Portnoy) says that for Kapesh, "moral delinquency has its fascination."[16]

This is obvious even at the outset of the novel, as Kapesh devotes the opening pages to a celebration of Herbie Bratasky, a childhood hero who had been "social director, bandleader, crooner, comic, and m.c."[17] of the Catskills resort hotel run by young Kapesh's parents. What most fascinates David about

Herbie is that, in short, he is "Crazy enough for anything that's his whole act"[18] For example, he can vocally imitate the entire range of bathroom noises "ranging from the faintest springtime sough to the twenty-one gun salute with which mankind emits its gases"—he can also "do diarrhea."[19] That such talents should intrigue a school aged child is not surprising, but Kapesh's admiration for Herbie's mimetic virtuosity is simply the first in a series of adulatory attachments that through out his life will reveal his split personality: the wild, libidinous, self-indulgent side vs. the serious, responsible, scholarly component. In college, for example, Kapesh explains the apparent dichotomy between his "high grades and—base desires" by quoting Byron "Studious by day, dissolute by night."[20]

Later, as an academic, Kapesh aligns himself with poet in residence Ralph Baumgarten, a notorious Lothario whose poetry and private life alike reveal that "for him flagrance appears to be much of the fun."[21], and finally earn him ostracism. Although he himself is outwardly sober and conventional, Kapesh is repeatedly drawn to arrantly flamboyance of the repressed side of his personality, his more unseemly and lubricious and actually dominant aspect.

It is in Kapesh's relationship with women, though, that this tendency is most evident, and it is around these relationships that *The Professor of Desire* really revolves. As numerous critics have mentioned, women in Roth's trilogy are seldom presented as fully rendered characters in their own right, but fall in to three rather reductive categories determined almost exclusively by their relationships to the male protagonists. Briefly stated, these classifications are as follows: the "lascivious girl" whose sexual abandon at once enthralls and unnerves the protagonist; the castrating "bitch" who seeks to master the protagonist; and the "nice girl" who, despite her obvious attractions (including a "normal" degree of sexual gusto), ultimately bores the protagonists. In each of the "Desire" novels, there is at least one example of each type.

In *Portnoy's Complaint*, for example, the "lascivious girl" appears in imaginary form as Thereal McCoy and in actuality as "The Monkey." The critic Martin Amis has poined out that the emasculating woman in *Portnoy's Complaint* is not immediately identifiable for she appears not as one of Portnoy's lovers, but as Sophie Portnoy, the stifling yiddish mama. And the "nice girl "role is shared by "The Pumpkin" and "The Pilgrim." In *My Life as a Man,* Sharon Shatsky is the wanton, Maureen Johnson Tarnopol is the "ball breaker," and Susan Seabury McCall is the "nice girl." In *The Professor of Desire,* the three categories are represented by lascivious Birgitta Svanstrom, emasculating Helen Baird Kepesh, and "nice girls" Elisabeth Elverskog and Claire Ovington.

In attempting to evaluate his dealings with these women, Kapesh realizes that he is blocked by a basic contradiction. He desperately yearns for sexual abandon, but whenever he embraces it as with Birgitta and Helen) his consequent guilt feelings drive him toward less sensual, more conventional women (Elisabeth and Claire); ironically, he then loses interest in those women and his guilt is increased, resulting in impotence and melancholia. Helen accuses Kapesh of being a "young fogy"[22] and of despising "fun"[23] but really that is not his problem.

Rather, the opposite is true. He is not stuffy or strait-laced, but is actually a libertine; paradoxically, he cannot accept that fact. In the final analysis, Kapesh is too fun oriented. Always, though, Kapesh is aware of the tension between the two sides of his personality, so that whichever aspect he is embracing at any given moment, he is never at peace. When he indulges his earthy impulses he often feels that he is in a state of "contamination,"[24] yet with the wholesome Claire he cannot repress the nagging feeling that there is something too "perfect" about her. In less guarded moments, when he is not deliberately trying to need his own "better judgement," his feelings toward her are negative:

> Anger; disappointment; disgust, contempt for all she does so marvelously, resentment over that little thing she will not deign to do. I see how very easily I could have no use for her. The snapshots. The lists. The mouth that will not drink my come. The curriculum review committee. Everything.[25].

The problem is that for Kapesh, 'Birgitta' and 'more' are just different ways of saying the same thing, while 'Claire' and 'enough' they, too, are one word,"[26] but for Kapesh "enough" is not enough.

Hence he envisions a situation of hopelessness, a quandary in which there is no solution: "I am ready to think it is something about me that makes for the sadness; about how I have never quite pleased anyone, including myself; how, hard as I have tried, I have seemed never quite able to be one thing or the other, and probably never will be."[27]

As discussed earlier, the elder Kapesh is indeed the most affectionately drawn of Roth's many fathers, and here even the "Jewish mother," certainly a figure of derision in Roth's *Portnoy's Complaint,* emerges in a fully sympathetic light. There is abundant humour as well. But the humour in *The Professor of Desire* is seldom belittling or raucous, as in *Portnoy's Complaint;* it is gentler, more subtle, more akin to the comedic elements in Roth's "I Always Wanted You to Admire My Fasting'; or Looking at Kafka," another of his most accomplished works.

All this serves to create a more balanced total impression than in any of Roth's previous novels. It is in this sense quite mature, as it not only probes the underside of interpersonal culpability, but also celebrates the more positively reinforcing aspects of interdependency, commitment and love.

The sections that chronicle Kapesh's and Claire's idyllic existence at their summer hideaway are among the most lyrical in recent fiction, creating a feeling of peaceful reconciliation reminiscent of that evoked by the closing Ludeyville passages in Bellow's Herzog. Indeed, Roth has publicly acknowledged his admiration for Bellow's work (in the dedication to *Reading Myself and Others* and elsewhere), and *The Professor of Desire* owns much to the older writers's work and his more considered viewpoint that Roth first evinced here (and largly retained in the "Zuckerman" novels) reminds one of Bellow's sagacious tentativeness, his poignant ambiguity. There are specific referents, as well. Kapesh's habit of vacillation followed by ill-advised choice recalls Tommy Whilhelm's in *Seize the Day,* as a comparison of the following two passages illustrates:

> In addition, Kapesh's habitual cry of "I want somebody"[28] echoes Henderson's almost identical "I want" in Bellow's Henderson the Rain King. A Bellow novel is actually mentioned when Kapesh refers to "Herzogian helplessness."[29]

There is considerable humour throughout. But it is low key as often as it is uproarious. True, certain touches are typically

Rothian: Kapesh's oddball mentors (Herbie, Jelinek, and Baumgarten) provide quite a few guffaws, as do the remembered snippets of resort hotel life; the ludicrous "Wally" scenes generate more belly laughs, as a persistent homosexual harasses the beleagured Kapesh via the apartment buililding intercom; and the dream sequence involving Kafka's whore is as bizarrely comical as anything in "On the Air." Generally, however, Roth's humour is noticeably subdued in this novel. The scenes toward the end, in which Kapesh's recently winnowed, hyperactive father attempts to conceal his glee over the son's apparent decision to "settle down" with Claire, are exemplary. Although comic touches abound, there is also a pervasively somber undertone that consistently informs the text, creating an unmistakably tragicomic dimension. This, too, is Bellowian.

Ultimately, *The Professor of Desire* is one of Roth's best books. The intricacies of interpersonal responsibility and guilt are never oversimplified (as they sometimes are elsewhere in his corpus), mainly because Roth is more reluctant here to pass moral judgments. Even where guilt is clearly proven, the blame is withheld. Roth seems to suggest that Kapesh's problems are not the fault of his or anyone else's shortcomings, but are a condition of life itself. Even the rigidly "proper" Arthur Schonbrunn, Kapesh's stuffy department chairperson, reveals by his attemps to seduce Kapesh's beautiful wife, Helen, that he too has his hedonistic, irresponsible facet. The obvious implication is that everyone has seamy side of conduct, and that this is what makes "normal" living with its restraints, strictures, and responsibilities frustrating and ultimately unsatisfying. To this degree, Kapesh is Everyman, except that his situation is exaggerated, as is usual in Roth's fiction. Kapesh's frustrations are not unlike those depicted in the Chekhov stories to which he alludes.

Certainly, this is the purpose of the numerous literary references that appear so often in the text: to reinforce and lend authority to the novel's basic suppositions. This device is entirely appropriate, for Kapesh, as a university professor of literature, would be apt to think in such terms. The numerous allusions to Chekhnov, Kafka, Dostoevsky, Flaubert, Mann, Tolstoy, and others serve to support the novel's basic assertion that, as one of his students writes on her final examination, "We are born innocent, we suffer terrible disillusionment before we can gain knowledge, and then we fear death and we are granted only fragmentary happiness to offset the pain."[30]

As Kapesh envisions it, the disillusionment, fear, and consequent anguish are largely the result of people's inability to perceive how they stand in relation to themselves and to their antithetical moralistic and prurient urges. And of course, this is by implication related to the whole larger issue of interpersonal relationships and existential dilemma. This is the dichotomy innately embedded in the human psyche.

He seems to imply that the large problems of responsibility and guilt are essentially enigmatic, that there is something in human nature that renders final judgments on such issues impossible. Hence, in Roth's work these questions are left unanswered, creating a sense of irresolution and ambiguity that evokes the perplexing tentativeness of life itself. Despite their desperate efforts toward reconciliation, the characters in Roth's fiction seldom reach that goal. At best, they achieve qualified adjustment, and only partial self-understanding.

Among Roth's protagonists are a librarian (Neil Klugman), a high ranking bureaucret (Portnoy), a whole gallery of professor writers (Gabe Wallach, Peter Tarnopol, David Kapesh, and Nathan Zuckerman), and if we include the collected short fiction an army officer (Nathan Marx), a businessman (Lou Epstein), and an attorney (Eli Peck) But despite their various levels of professional status and the fact that practically all of these characters are at least reasonably successful at their jobs, most of Roth's protagonists seem to derive only moderate satisfaction from their work. They do them; usually, though, there is scant conviction in their actions, and little real dedication.

In a less negative but decidedly unenthusiastic vein, Gabe Wallach confides that his career is of secondary importance to him. He admits that he teaches "out of neither spiritual nor financial urgency," and that "in the end I knew it was not from my students or my colleagues but from my private life, my secret life, that I would extract whatever joy or whatever misery was going to be mine."[31]

The bitingly sarcastic view of academy that emerges from Gabe's comments has been frequently cited as a masterpiece of "academic satire." Yet Gabe's comments are unwittingly ironic, for his personal life is not only disappointing in itself, but eventually affects his professional life as well. This is equally true of Roth's authors. In *My Life as a Man,* Tarnopol, whose early enthusiasm for writing and teaching is seemingly unbounded, ultimately becomes "blocked", and confesses that his "Writing was wholly at the mercy of marital confusion"[32] and that he has become "hopeless at my work[because] miserable in marriage".

Aware of his schizophrenic weakness and the resulting hypocrisy that it engenders, Portnoy is left in a state of ambivalence toward his job. Although by day he is an able and respected public official, privately he is a slavering hedonist rather like David Kapesh of *The Professor of Desire.* This conflict gives rise in the imagination of David Kapesh to fantasies of public revelations of his true nature, as in the comical headlines that he envisions: "Asst. Human Opp'y Commish Found Headless in go go Girl's Atp!"[33] and "Asst Human Opp'y Commish Flogs Dummy, Also lives in sin, Reports Old School Chum."[34]

In short, Portnoy is stymied, caught in a love hate relationship with his job, and of course this dilemma serves as an effective metaphor for his larger predicament. In Roth, the protagonists' dilemmas must finally be seen as resulting from their own emotional and psychological confusions.

In parts of *Portnoy's Complaint, Our Gang, The Breast,* and his baseball extravaganza, *The Great American Novel,* he seems to be celebrating the sheer playfulness of the artists, an almost egoless condition. But he also seems to be intensely moral in *Letting Go, when She was Good* and in much of *My Life as a Man.*

It seems as if his fascination with comedy is only a reaction against this other aspect of his personality or is it something permanent? But the reality is: "Sheer playfulness and Deadly Seriousness are my closest friends;... I am also on friendly terms with Deadly playfulness, playful playfulness, serious playfulness, serious seriousness and sheer sheerness."[35]

Before *Portnoy's Complaint,* Philip Roth had become a well-known writer. *Portnoy* made him famous all over the world, and in America he became a star. In the late sixties, sex was being touted as the thing: the heart of life, the redeemer, etcetra. *Portnoy's Complaint,* with its obsence language and erotomanical candor, appeared to many to be sympathy with that viewpoint.

But the reality is that:

> I would never have written a book as farcical as "Portnoy's Complaint" if I had any devotion to the cause of sex; causes don't thrive on self satire. Causes expel you for self-satire. Nor was I a soldier in the cause of obscenity. Portnoy's obscenity is intrinsic to his situation, not to my style. I have no case to make for dirty words, in or out of fiction.[36]

He also says: "Obscenity can bring a refreshing sense into the language that would be acceptable even in polite society, but it must be used with great care."[37]

Philip Roth is considered in France as an American-Jewish writer—even as a member (along with Bellow and Malamud) of so-called New York-Jewish school. Only Malamud came from New York and spent his childhood there, in a poor neighborhood in Brooklyn. Virtually all of Malamud's adult life has been spent far away from New York, teaching at colleges in Oregon and Vermont.

Bellow was born in Montreal and has lived almost all of his life in Chicago, eight hundred miles west of New York, a city widely different from New York. Roth was born in newark, New Jersey. He lived in a lower middle class Jewish neighbourhood in New York until he was seventeen and went off to a small college in small Pennsylvania.

He spent the year after college in graduate school at the University of Chicago, then went to Washington. D.C., in 1956, he returned to Chicago to teach at the university for two years. So the Jewish background is a major source of inspiration in his work. Like Bellow and Malamud Roth was born to Jewish parents and raised self-consciously as a Jew. He lived in a predominantly Jewish neighbourhood and attended public schools where about 90 per cent of the pupils and teachers were Jewish. The disparity between this tragic dimension of Jewish life in Europe and the actualities of daily lives as Jews in New Jersey was something that he had to puzzle over himself. Being a Jew in New Jersey was comical just because it was somehow bound up with these ghastly events.

Now the question arises—what does America mean to Roth? He replies:

> America allows me the greatest possible freedom to practice my vocation.... America is the place I know best in the world. It's the only place I know in the world. My consciouness and my language were shaped by America, I am an American writer in ways that a plumber isn't an American plumber or a miner an American miner or a cardiologist an American cardiologist; Rather, what the heart is to the cardiologist, the coal to the miner the Kitchen sink to the plumber, America is to me.[38]

But it doesn't mean that Roth has forgotten his native place, Newark as he says: "But going to Newark is very different from going anywhere else, because it resonates with personal history. Newark for me is at once a presence and an absence."[39]

He also added: "New Jersey figures strongly in *Goodbye Columbus*, *Portnoy's Complaint* and the autobiographies, but not in the rest of my work."[40]

He also says: "Where I live now is immaterial, where I grew up is not. Americans tend to be layered people, don't they? They begin in one place and lay down the first geological layer. Then they are educated somewhere else, and that's a second geological layer. Then they marry someone who has his or her own geological layering, and all of that tends to get laid over theirs. Then they get a job somewhere else, and that continues another geological layer. So they have numerous layers, but the one at the bottom doesn't necessarily get buried."[41]

Roth is very engrossed in writing as he says:

> Once I'm writing, I don't want to go anywhere.. writing is problem-solving. Everyday there are a series of problems I have to solve. I solve them as best I can, and that leads to new problems.... I'm a realistic novelist and a realistic autobiographer.[42]

He also says: "Updike and Bellow hold their flashlights out into the world, reveal the real world as it is now. I dig a hole and shine my flashlight into the hole."[43]

In 1880, Newark was a city of approximately 100,000 people, most of them of British stock as Roth says: "And then between 1880 and First World War 250,000 immigrants came, two and a half times the population."[44]

They came at a moment when Newark was "undergoing a powerful and dynamic transformation", and they helped it to boom. And as the city grew, the next generation, the children of these immigrants, took on another task, fought another struggle: the Americanization of their children. "They had a particular task, an American task, and a particular cultural burden," he says. "Newark is the battleground, one of many cities in this country, on which the struggle took place. The job they had was to stand between the European family of their immigrant parents and the American realities of their young children. They were a generation of negotiators, of constructors, with the tenacious, stubborn will of the constructor."[45]

And, Roth says, they succeeded, but not without a lot of pain. "They took blows from both sides", he says, "from the parents who clung to the rigorous orthodoxy and from the children who wanted to be rid of all that because they sensed immediately that it was useless in this society. The cultural struggle was bruising. The homes were full of conflict and tension; when you negotiate, there is always tension. And it created a lot of neurosis too."[46]

It is a neurosis that Roth has creatively mined for more than 30 years, a neurosis without which much of his art would not exist. He wanted something difficult and dangerous to happen to him. He wanted a hard time. And he got it. In his early twenties, he wanted to prove to himself that he wasn't afraid of all those things.

From 1962 to 1967 was the longest period he had gone, since becoming a writer, without publishing a book. Alimony and recurrent court costs had bled him of every penny he could earn by teaching and writing and hardly into his thirties, he was thousands of dollars in debt to his friend and editor, Joe Fox. The loan was to help pay for his analysis, which he needed primarily to prevent him from going out and committing murder because of the alimony and court costs incurred for having saved two years in a childless marriage.

Ever since some of his first stories were collected in 1959 in a volume called *Goodbye, Columbus*, his work has been attacked from certain pulpits and in certain periodicals as dangerous, dishonest and irresponsible. Many editorials and articles were published in Jewish community newspapers condemning these stories for ignoring the accomplishments of Jewish life or, as

Rabbie Emanuel Rackman recently told the convention of the Rabbinical Council of America, for creating a "Distorted image of the basic values of Orthodox Judaism".

Among the letters he received from readers, there have been a number written by Jews accusing him of being anti-Semitic and "self-hating" or at least tasteless.

It is also charged that such criticism as he makes of Jews or apparent criticism is taken by anti-Semites as vindication of their attitudes, as "fuel" for their fires, particularly as it is a Jew himself who seemingly admits to habits and behaviour that are not exemplary or even normal and acceptable. When Roth speaks before Jewish audiences, invariably there have been people who came up to him afterward to ask:

> Why don't you leave us alone? Why don't you write about the Gentiles? Why must you be so critical? Why do you disapprove of us so? It is difficult, if not impossible, to explain to some of the people. They are ashamed of what I see no reason to be ashamed of and defensive where there is no cause for defense.[47]

They look at fiction in terms of "approval" and "disapproval" of Jews, "positive and negative" attitudes towards Jewish life—they are likely not to see what it is that the story is really about.

To give an example, a story Roth wrote called "Epstein" tells of a sixty-year-old man, who has an adulterous affair with the lady across the street. In the end Epstein, who is the hero, is caught, caught by his family and caught and struck down by exhaustion, decay and disappointment, against all of which he had set out to make a final struggle.

Some people may experience Epstein as a cheat and nothing else, he usually experiences himself as something more. And generally speaking, what draws most readers and writers to literature is this "Something More"—all that is beyond simple moral categorizing. It is not Roth's purpose in writing a story of an adulterous man to make it clear how right we all are if we disapprove of the act and are disappointed with the men. Fiction is not written to affirm the principles and beliefs that every body seems to hold, nor does it seek to guarantee the appropriateness of our feelings. The world of fiction, in fact, frees us from the circumscriptions that society places upon feeling. One greatness of the art is that it allows both the writer and reader to respond to experience in ways not always available in day to day conduct; or if they are available, they are not possible or manageable or legal or advisable or even necessary to the business of living.

He is writing a story of a man who is adulterous to reveal the condition of such a man. If the adulterous man is a Jew, then he is revealing the condition of an adulterous man who is a Jew. Infact, people of all faiths have sought pleasure—or freedom, or vengeance, or power, or love, or humiliation. Roth questions: "Do you call Raskolnikov a balanced portrayal of students as we know them? Of Russian students? Of poor students? What about those of us who have never murdered anyway, who do our school work every night?"[48]

Roth's works are critique of his own ideas as he says:

> This is not to say that you leave your intellectual baggage at the door when you sit down to write, or that in your novel you discover that you really think just the opposite of what you' ve been telling people—if you do, you're probably too confused to be producing good work.[49]

He intended to write a critique of nobody's ideas but his own. A novelist doesn't persuade by what he is "trying to say", but by a sense of fictional authenticity he communicates, the sense of an imagination so relentless and thoroughgoing that it is able to convert into its own nonconvertible currency whatever the author has absorbed through reading, thinking and raw experience.

He says: "What's frustrating me is very like what's killing Kapesh. I wish I had thought to give Professor Kapesh those words to speak: 'On the metaphorical level the fantasy remains rather opaque.' [50]

References

1. Roth, Philip. *Reading Myself and Others*. New York: Vintage, 2001, pp.23-24.
2. Roth, Philip. *Portnoy's Complaint*. New York: Random, 1969, p.30.
3. Cooperman, Stanley. "Philip Roth: 'Old Jacob's Eye' With A Squint," *Twentieth Century Literature* 19, no. 4 (1973): 213.
4. Roth, Philip. *The Professor of Desire*. New York: Farrar, 1977, 247.

5. Roth, Philip. *Letting Go*. New York: Random, 1962, p.5.
6. Ibid., p.28.
7. Ibid., p.33.
8. Ibid., p.39.
9. Ibid., p.487.
10. Roth, "Document Dated July 27, 1969,". in *Reading Myself and Others*, 26.
11. Roth, Philip. *Portnoy's Complaint*. op.cit., pp.10-11.
12. Granville Hicks, "A Bad Little Good Girl," review of *When She was Good, New Statesman*, 17 June 1967, 25-26.
13. Roth, "On *The Breast*," in *Reading Myself and Others*, 70.
14. Roth, Philip. *My Life as a Man*. New York: Holt, 1974. p.238.
15. Ibid., p.231.
16. Roth, Philip. *The Professor of Desire*. op.cit., p.102.
17. Ibid., p.3.
18. Ibid., p.5.
19. Ibid., p.6-7.
20. Ibid., p.17.
21. Ibid., p.123.
22. Ibid., p.71.
23. Ibid., p.60.
24. Ibid., p.135.
25. Ibid., p.162.
26. Ibid., p.165.
27. Ibid., p.222.
28. Ibid., p.106.
29. Ibid., p.157.
30. Ibid., p.94.
31. Ibid., pp.229-230.
32. Roth, Philip. *My Life as a Man*. New York: Holt,1974, p.104.
33. Roth, Philip. *The Professor of Desire*. op.cit., p.161.
34. Ibid., p.175.
35. Roth, Philip. *Reading Myself and Others*. op.cit., p.97.
36. Ibid., p.99.
37. Raymont, Henry. "TO Philip Roth, Obscenity isn't a Dirty Word". *The New York Times*.
38. Roth, Philip. *Reading Myself and Others*. op.cit., p.110.
39. Keyishian, Marjorie. "Roth Returning to Newark to Get History Award", Oct 4, 1992.

40. Ibid.
41. Ibid.
42. Ibid.
43. Ibid.
44. Ibid.
45. Ibid.
46. Ibid.
47. Roth, Philip. *Reading Myself and Others*. op.cit., p.194.
48. Ibid., p.199.
49. Roth, Philip. "On the Breast", *Reading Myself and Others*. op.cit., p.62
50. Ibid., p.60.

6

Conclusion

An intensely private man, Philip Roth is one of America's greatest writers. He is dedicated, even obsessive about his work but loathes the fame that attends it. After spells in Eastern Europe and the UK, his return to New York marked a period of creative renewal as he reflected on the US through the lens of history.

Philip Roth has had the grandest prizes available to an American writer. He has been to the white house to have the National Medal of Arts pinned on him by former president Bill Clinton. For the last decade, at an age when most writers are beginning to lose interest, Roth has produced a series of books he has written before, and he shows no signs of slowing down.

"Even now, he doesn't relent", says Aaron Ascher, Roth's old friend and editor. "This is a 70 something-years-old writer who is still going uphill and keeps getting better. He has back problems which give him great pain, yet he's always working. He never stops, even in his worst periods."[1]

He has always believed in the separation of life and art. He keeps his private life stri tly to himself and prefers not to work where he lives. In Connecticut, his studio is back in the trees away from the house. Why is Philip Roth so great? Amidon breaks his answer down into bite-size sections:

> "Philip Roth is male", "Philip Roth is Jewish", "Philip Roth is American", "Philip Roth is Nathan Zukerman", "Philip Roth is kidding", "Philip Roth is Divorced", "Philip Roth is His Mother's Son", "Philip Roth is prolific", "Philip Roth is mortal", "Philip Roth is immortal". Roth has been twice divorced, and it's difficult to judge which break-up was nastier or more influential. He separated from his first wife, Margaret Martinson, in 1963. Their train-wreck marriage

> provided material for several novels. Martinson inspired "The Monkey" (Marry Jane Reed) in "Portnoy's Complaint" and Maureen Tarnopol in "My Life as a Man", the latter a monstrous man-wrecker who tricks her writer husband into marriage (something Roth swears Margaret did to him by buying urine from a homeless woman before her pregnancy test). In 1990, he married the British actress Claire Bloom, his long time companion, though the couple divorced five years later, in a split so acrimonious that Bloom felt compelled to write a scathing account of the marriage, "Leaving a Doll's House" (1996). In it she describes Roth as a controlling, misogynistic monster who forced Bloom's 18-year-old daughter out of the house because her conversation bored him. In response, Roth created the spoilt actress Eve Frame in *I Married a Communist,* a social climber who ruins her husband's life by writing a tell-all autobiography.

Family relations have always stood at the heart of Roth's work. Portnoy describes his over-bearing mother, Sophie, as "The Most Unforgettable Character I've Met" and it's safe to say that Roth feels the same about his own over-weaning mother, Bessie, though she is more saint to him than monster: "My mother was one of those devoted daughters of Jewish immigrants who raised housekeeping in America to a great art.) (Don't talk to anyone in my family about cleaning—we saw cleaning in its heyday.)"[2]

His father, Herman, an insurance salesman, looms equally large in the author's imagination, inspiring *Patrimony (1991*), a deeply moving account of the elder Roth's last days.

Roth's monkish routine is at odds with what he once called his "reputation as a crazed penis" bestowed on him by *Portnoy's Complaint,* his great panegyric to the comedy of sex. When Portnoy was published in 1969, it seemed to epitomize the anarchic spirit of the decade. Maybe it did, but the author himself was a product of the 1950s.

The last generation of well-behaved, sterniy educated children who believed in high culture and high principles and lived in the nuclear shadow of the cold war until their orderly world was blown apart by birth-control pills and psychedelic drugs. *Portnoy* was considered outrageous when it appeared, but the real outrage was Roth's and he was outraged because he couldn't help being a good boy however much he yearned to be bad.

Like most Jewish families, Roth's was clear-knit, affectionate and tempestuous; his father, Herman, was a passionate New Dealer, a forceful indignant man, who worked for Metropolitan life insurance company and rose to be a district manager. Putting pressure on people and facts and his own experience is one of the many solutions Roth has come up with for the problem to which he has devoted his life: how to transform and transmute life into art.

> I have to have something to do that engages me totally, without that, life is half for me. I can't be idle and I don't know what to do other than write... the crude cliché is that the written is solving the problem of his life in his books. Not at all what he's doing is taking something that interests him in life and then solving the problem of the book—which is, how do you write about this? The engagement is with the problem that the book raises, not with the problems you borrow from living.[3]

Voice is the vehicle by which a writer expresses his aliveness and Roth himself is all voice. Style, in the formal, flowery sense, bores him: he has, he once wrote, "a resistance to plaintive metaphor and poeticized analogy". His prose is immaculate yet curiously plain and unostentatious, as natural as breathing. Reading him, it's always the story that's in your face, never the style. His voice rounds so spontaneous that the lazy reader might suppose he is listening to conression rather than reading a work of fiction.

Roth first tangled with the bitch when *Goodbye, Columbus* provoked rabbis to denounce him as "a self-hating Jew" and he responded by writing *Letting Go* the most conventional of his novels, asif to show that he was indeed as serious and worthy as authors were expected to be in the 50s. Being a good boy, however, did not sit easily either with his surreal comic inventiveness or with the troubles he was having in a difficult first marriage to Margaret Williams.

When he finally yoked comedy and rage together to produce *Portnoy's Compliant*, the serious writer again came face to face with the bitch publicity and this time she didn't let him go.

"In 1969, I wrote Portnoy. Not only did I write it—that was easy—I also became the author of Portnoy's Complaint and what I faced publicly was the trivialization of everything."[4]

Instead of being read as someone playing brilliant games with reality in the tradition of Kafka and Gogol, Roth got scandal, outrage and best-seller celebrity in its most crummy form. According to Ascher, "The attacks were horrible and disheartening, especially from the Jews. He had to cope with the nightmare of a smash hit. It made him angry and defensive, so he closed up. But may be it did him good. The set back of great success changed and improved him. Without it, he'd have been different."[5]

Fiction is for him at once played hypothesis and serious supposition, an imaginative form of inquiry—everything that exhibitionism is not... contrary to the general belief, it is the distance between the writer's life and his novel that is the most intriguing aspect of his imagination. Most Roth critics (including Roth himself) have emphasized that his career has largely been constructed out of his creative and cultural conflict with his Jewish audience. Yet his wide audience does not consist only of Jewish readers. His characters have risked themselves in diverse locations such as New York, New Jersey, Chicago, New York, London, Prague, Jerusalem and Palestine.

His narrative strategies and literary models have been similarly varied: Henry James, Marcel Proust, James Joyce and Franz Kafka are clear influences on his work and his novels have employed the many different literary strategies found in the work of these great predecessors. He explores their practical consequences by rendering them (Americans) in fictional form. For Roth, the self takes its form through experimentation and should be perceived as a type of fiction. Asserting one's identity is, as he understands it, always a transgressive, act. This means that for him no form of identity—ethnic or otherwise—can ever be fixed.

To paraphrase what he once told Mary McCarthy, Roth is far more a novelist than he is a Jew. By 2001 when Roth published "The Human Stain", the story of a black man who passes for a white Jew, it was clear that much of the appeal of Roth's work has been its ability to portray not just American-Jewish experience in all its historical variety but to challenge in ways that are distinctively postmodern the meaning of identity altogether.

At the heart of both Roth's fictions and the realities of American culture are such subjects as intertwining personal and communal identities, sexual politics and practice, the post-modern world and the place of America in that world, self-invention in the context of human annihilation and acts of terror, and racial and cultural pluralism as well as the working of human psyche in such a complex and bewildering milieu and ethos.

To read Roth is to be challenged to risk that which Roth and his characters always risk: the premises that seem to define one's very self. Perhaps Malamud continued to attract Roth's critical gaze over twenty-five years because he, more than Saul Bellow or Ralph Elison, represented in his work the ethical stance, Roth most wanted to emulate but instead pretended to destroy through the acts of his shiksa—crazed, sex-crazed, family—betraying, Jewish-son-protagonists.

Transgression in Roth's fiction illuminates the details of many of his narratives. Roth's frustration with his sub cultural position as a Jew in American society is, in many ways, the irritant that produces his fiction. His irritation, however, is not simply the result of overt resistance by mainstream society. His frustration is also clearly determined by his position in Jewish American culture—by his embroilment in and rebellion against the world of his parents. In contrast with Norman Mailer, who is also fixed on transgression and is also Jewish (although scarcely involved in Jewishness), the origin of Roth's major theme is located and delineated in terms of cultural dynamics and sub cultural perspectives on mainstream existence. Where Mailer has been more politically radical and ideological and heroically disposed, Roth has shown himself, beneath the brittle surface of his social defiance, to be rooted in Jewish and European traditions and in feelings of vulnerability to persecution. Moreover, this substratum of Jewish feelings and ideas in Roth has resulted in a far more explicit burden of moral/ethical sensibility in his work through at the same time he has striven like Mailer to achieve authenticity and artistic power through cultural and psychological transgression.

Another fact of this ethical substratum in Roth the novelist is certain ambivalence about succeeding in the American mainstream. To transgress is to step across a boundary or cross a limit; and Roth's success in bursting the boundaries that confined his father's generation is rife with crosscurrents. A second-generation American from a lower-middle class Jewish home, Roth dramatizes in his fiction the arc of a career of a talented literary rebel who uses liberal times, the permission of his gift, and early success to express pentup Jewish ambition, appetite, and anger, and then to suffer the backlash, the countercurrent, of communal recrimination and psychological guilt.

Several of Roth's novels are written in the first person. And their heroes have lot in common with him. Portnoy is brought up in New York, much as he was; David Kapesh in *The Professor of Desire* is professor and teaches the same literature courses that Roth has taught at the University of Pennsylvania. But it doesn't mean that he has nothing to confess and no one he wants to confess to. One exaggeration gave birth to Portnoy, and we know his destiny; this character has become an archetype. Another exaggeration produced Maureen, the majestically deranged woman, the fury of jealousy and paranoia in "My Life as a Man". Roth had depicted a woman who was not good, who persecuted others and who exploited others and that spoiled everything. A woman without conscience, a woman who misused every power, a vindictive woman with limitless cunning and wild, unfocused hatred and rage—and to depict such a woman was contrary to the new ethics and to the revolution that espoused them. It was antirevolutionary. It was on the wrong side of the cause. It was taboo. It sounded misogynistic and anti-feminism.

Maureen buys a sample of urine from a pregnant black woman in order to pass the rabbit test and trick Peter Tarnopol into marriage. In another scene—their last brutal fight—when beaten by him, Maureen defecates in her pants, thus depriving them both of tragedy at the most painful moment of their marriage.

He was writing *Portnoy's Complaint,* a raucous, aggressive, abrasive book whose conception and composition were undoubtedly influenced by the mood of the times. Roth says:

> I don't think I would or would have written that book in that way a decade earlier, not only because of the social, moral and cultural patterns that prevailed in the fifties but because, as a younger writer still strongly involved with literary studies, I had pledged my loyalty to a more morally earnest line of fiction.[6]

Roth has written many of his novels in first person. For him it is a way of gaining stylistic freedom. He is able to use conversational tones and rhythms that give great expressive value and appeal. He can turn the volume up and down within a single sentence. He can slip in and out of the kind of colloquial talk and the kind of formal talk he is partial to.

And of course, it is the "I" who can be most intimate, who speaks in confidence, who tells us secrets, hate secrets, love secrets, family secrets, tribal secrets, the stuff of shame, embarrassment, humiliation and disgrace. There is blend of both realism and interior monologue in his psychological novels which explore both the unconscious and the real social milieu, the psychic layers as well as manness. He interprets social life under the glow of the psychic.

Roth is mainly concerned with depicting the individual's personal, inner directed anguish. Moreover, he almost always portrays a particular "type"—the sophisticated, urbane, Jewish American intellectual. Even Neil Klugman and Alexander Portnoy, who are not in fact writers or academicians, think and speak as if they were. Neil, a librarian, and Portnoy, a high ranking liberal bureaucrat, share the bookishness and glib articulateness of Roth's actual literati: Gabe Wallach, Peter Tarnopol, David Kapesh, and Nathan Zuckerman. Neil, a former philosophy major, is described by Mr. Patimkin as "a student or something like that."[7]

Portnoy has edited the *Columbia Law Review*, and is familiar with the work of Dos Passos, Freud, Kafka, Yeats, Dylan Thomas, and others. All Roth's major novels explore the agonized soul searchings or self-contemplation. It is no accident, for example, that Portnoy, Tarnopol, Kapesh, and Zuckerman are all engrossed in self-analysis; the novels in which they appear are in effect the transcripts of their psychological struggles.

Quite naturally, then, Roth in his "serious" works has tended to favour the first person participatory point of view. The relative advantages and disadvantages of this particular mode of narration are well known. Most obviously, it permits total access to the inner workings of the central character's mind, and psyche; and what is lost in "veracity" or accuracy" is compensated for by the insights that are afforded into the protagonist's personality. That Portnoy, for example, is guilty of certain confusions and delusions is not a problem. Indeed, the very raison de'tre of *Portnoy's*

Complaint is to explore Portnoy's lack of self-knowledge; his fretful introspection and vitriolic outbursts are not only tangible evidence of his "complaint," but constitute the most direct possible articulation of it. Although an "unreliable narrator," he is such because of the very disorientation that makes his case exemplary and worth of book length documentation.

What might be seen as something of a drawback to Roth's habitual use of first person narration, however, is a certain stridency to which more than a few critics have objected. Until recently there has been little distance between Roth's narrators and the events they describe, and his books have therefore exhibited an archly self-justifying tone. If Portnoy objects to what he imagines as the Jews' "sucking and sucking on that sour grape of a religion,"[8] a similar charge of obsessiveness could easily be levelled against him and the other Rothian narrators.

Although they maintain a tone of mocking, self-righteous condescension, at times they appear almost morbidly preoccupied with their individual trials. Roth's language is predominantly conversational, direct, uncluttered, and colloquial. Roth is a highly deliberate stylist whose quality of seeming spontaneity is actually the result of an entirely conscious design. Moreover, he has certain stylistic affinities. He freely employs the explict "vulgarisms" of contemporary American English, a tendency that underscores his shared preference for realistic dialogue.

Perhaps the most sensitive and thorough treatment of Roth's style is *About Portnoy*, by Patricia Meyer Spacks, who cites the highly accomplished tonal manipulation which, even more than the novel's subject matter, accounts for its special "personality." She stresses the very conscious stylistic awareness that underlies the book's illusion of extemporaneity.

The novel is, she says, "shaped by style, its language at times is identical with its substance." By this she means that the phraseology, the tempo of the sentences, and the choice of words reinforce the sense of comic incongruity that is so central a feature of the book. The novel's tone is carefully manipulated through language, as Roth selects a mode of expression that "enforces the reader's consciousness of the ludicrous with its incongruous conjections, its comic restoration of literal force to dead metaphor." Most importantly, however, Roth exercises a highly "literary" control over Portnoy's street-wise ideolect. "The calculated rhythms and ironies, the tonal mixture even the punctuation," Spacks says, "all suggest the formalities of written rather than oral communication the freedom of spoken language combines with the control of the written form."[9]

Among Roth's most highly developed skills is his ability to vividly evoke a sense of the physical surroundings within which his characters act out their personal dramas. Roth's evocation of detail is quite selective. Although Roth will often create a sharply visual representation and invest it with discrete particularity, he does so primarily to advance characterization.

Another interesting area of style in Roth is his adroit use of symbolism. He is accomplished in the manipulation of this device, and has applied it skilfully in some of his best works. The symbols that he creates are never farfetched or contrived, but are organic, growing out of the fundamental imperatives of the works in which they appear, rather like the "practical" or "natural" symbols of Hemingway: significant points of personal appearance add powerfully to the effectiveness of a scene. Roth also uses sports imagery adroitly to heighten the sense of disparity between suburbia and the inner city and Updike has remarked that his "deepest pride" as an author is in his "ability to keep an organized mass of images moving forward."[10]

Roth displays precision about his own future creative incarnations, this time as the author of *My Life as a Man* in his final comments on Gold. His "extravagant prose, his confessional tone (the article about divorce; then the several prefaces and appendixes about his own divorce; my ex-wife says this about me, etc; then finally the story about divorce-all of this seems to have meaning to me in terms of this separation... the not-so-friendly relationship between the writer and the culture... I must say I am not trying to sell selfishness."

For ten years following the appearance of *Goodbye Columbus* in 1959, Roth struggles to find a form that would contain and objectify his sternly adversary vision of American culture and in his two massive novels of the early and middle sixties, *Letting Go* and *When She was Good*, he experimented with greater effectiveness than is generally recognized with the traditional form of the realistic social novel. As a result, Roth found himself caught in a predicament that, to one degree or another, has confounded American writers ever since Melville: he had vast quantities of material but he could not discover or possess a subject. All he could do was to describe and document at infinite length the experiences of his characters, record every word of their interminable and mostly trivial conversations and in that way to produce a certain effect of life—busy, abrasive, vibrant but finally one-dimensional and incoherent. The form most congenial to Roth was the novel of narcissism, just as his strongest penchant was for the tragicomedy of paranoia and it happened that in *Portnoy's Complaint* he was able to coordinate form and penchant to extraordinary effect, enabling him to explore the psychology of sex with keen insight.

Roth is a fine stylist and may be the funniest serious, writer in America, he is gravely deficient in a sense of the novel form; he has no firm understanding of what his novels are supposed to mean and he has no subject matter except fanatical self-infatuation. His strategy in *My Life as a Man* is to try to convert these weaknesses into literary capital by making them part of the contrived architectual and thematic design of the novel. Roth divides his narrative into two sections, the first purporting to be a fictional account written by a young novelist named Peter Tarnopol of the adventures of a young novelist named Nathan Zukerman; the second presenting Tarnopol's autobiographical account of the actual experience of his own life from which some of the events of the first section have been distilled. Throughout this monologue Tarnopol speculates continually about the relationship between his own life and that of his fictional alter ego, expresses bafflement at the complexity of the problem and seems to be trying to create the impression that his novel is really about the effort of the novelist to define and explore the nexus between life and art. The life-art relationship is given dramatic objectification in the novel's two-part structure and his attempt to make fictional use of the materials of his life. There is actually no organic relationship between the fictional experiences of Zuckerman and the "real life" experiences of Tarnopol; hence, there is no thematic justification for the presence of both men in the novel. In addition to the complications of structure and the refracting perspectives of his fictional personae, Roth resorts to other devices in his effort to give the appearance of artistic deliberation to effects he seems to have sensed might be viewed as artistic flaws.

Throughout the novel, Tarnopol is repeatedly accused of fanatical preoccupation with his guilt, his Jewishness, his marriage and his ego. His psychiatrist, Dr. Spielvogel, who is cutely resurrected from *Portnoy's Complaint*, considers him to be "among the nation's top young narcissists in the arts" and diagnoses his troubles as stemiming from "narcissistic self-dramatization". He also writes to him a letter of criticism of the Zukerman stories. In fact, almost all the people in Tarnopol's life—his relatives, mistresses, students, wife—write him letters about the stories and they call attention to shortcomings that Roth has had ample opportunity to discover in his own writing. But it is, after all, Tarnopol's writing that is being criticized and because it is, Roth nearly succeeds in having it both ways. The trouble is that there is actually no discernible difference between Tarnopol and Roth, just as there is no discernible reason except perhaps a legalistic one why Tarnopol rather than Roth should be acting as narrator. Tarnopol is never evaluated by Roth even though he is criticized by almost everybody else, and Roth never achieves sufficient dramatic distance from him to make it clear what he thinks and therefore, what the reader is supposed to think about Tarnopol's character and behaviour. His is the only point of view in his story, and those moments when another perspective might become authoritative and contradictory of his own are never exploited—presumably because he and his creator are at all time in complete agreement. *My Life as a Man* is, in short, a totally solipsistic novel, which may very well make it a perfect expression of the times. Its form is the endless ranting monologue; its content is guilt, anxiety and acute paranoia; its appropriate setting is the psychiatrist's office where, as was literally the case in *Portnoy's Complaint*, the only sound is the sound of the narrator's voice. Nothing in the world is real except that voice, all our separate, complaining voices are mute. But Roth's problem is that he cannot function as his own psychiatrist. He cannot find the meaning of his anguish or his anger, hence, we cannot. All he can do is talk, talk, sometimes brilliantly, sometimes tediously, but always toward a point that is never reached because it does not exist. What he is really up to is to use his own phrase—a form of literary onanism.

A Jew in the post-holocaust decades has been identified in America with righteousness and restraint, with the just and measured response rather than with these libidinous and aggressive activities that border on the socially outrageous and may even constitute criminal transgression. It might be well to begin with the novels of Saul Bellow, by now the grand old man of American-Jewish writers, and to Roth, the country's most accomplished working novelist. His heroes are Jewish in vivid and emphatic ways when they are actors in dramas of conscience where matters of principles or virtue are at issue, but are by comparison only faintly marked by their Jewishness, if they are Jews at all, when appetite and Quasi—or outright libidinous adventure is at the heart of the novel.

Bellow's first Jewish Jew was Asa Leventhal in his second book *The Victim*. Bellow himself now judges this excellent novel a "proper" book. Then there is the next book *The Adventures of Augie March,* where surely the least important ingredient in the lively and seductive hero's make-up is his sense of himself as a Jew. While Bellow seems largely to locate in Leventhal's Jewishness the roots of his morbidity, gloom, uncertainty, touchiness and moral responsiveness, he connects Augie's health, cheeriness, vigour, stamina and appetite to his rootedness in a Chicago that is American to the core, a place where being Jewish makes of a boy nothing more special in the virtue department than any other immigrant mother's child.

The movement away from the obsessively Jewish Jew Augie culminates in Bellow's next big novel, *Henderson The Rain King,* whose hoggish and greedy hero is so much a creature possessed by strange gargantuan and ravenous hungers of the sense and the spirit that Bellow cannot see his way to making him even the most attenuated of Jews. Saul Bellow's longer works tend generally to associate the Jewish Jew with the struggles of ethical Jewhood and the non-Jewish Jew and the Gentile with the release of appetite and aggression.

In Malamud these tendencies are so sharply and schematically present as to give his novels the lineaments of moral allegory. For him, the Jew is innocent, passive, virtuous, and this to the degree that he defines himself or is defined by others as a Jew; the Gentile, on the other hand, is characteristically corrupt, violent and lustful particularly when he enters a room or a store or a cell with a Jew in it. His best book-containing as it does the classic Malamiundian moral arrangement is still *The Assistant* which proposes that an entombed and impoverished grocer named Morris Baber shall by the example of his passive suffering and his goodness of heart transform a young thieving Italian drifter named Frank Alpine into another entombed, impoverished and suffering Jewish grocer and that this shall constitute an act of assistance—or so the stern morality of the book suggests.

Redemption from what? Crimes of violence and deceit against a good Jewish father, crimes of lust against the father's virginal daughter whom the guy has spied upon naked and then raped. We might almost take what happens to the bad goy when he falls into the hands of the good Jews as an act of enraged Old Testament retribution visited upon him by the wrathful Jewish individual.

To see how still another kind of Jewish writer, Norman Mailer, might have recorded the implications of a story like *The Assistant* we can look to his famous essay *The White Negro* published first in *Dissent* magazine in 1957, the very year Malamud's novel appeared. Mailer none the less comes up with a scenario startlingly similar to the one with which *The Assistant* begins. *The Assistant* is a manifestation of ethical Jewhood with what one might legitimately call a vengeance.

And now we return to *Portnoy's Complaint* and the hero limned by this Jewish writer. Obviously the problem for Alexander Portnoy is that, unlike Arthur Fidelman, nothing inflames his Jewish self-consciousness so much as setting forth on a wayward libidinous adventure—that is, nothing makes it seem quite so wayward than that a Jewish man like himself should be hankering after the objects for which he is crazy. The hidden Jew is unmasked in him by the sight of his own erection. He cannot suppress the one in the interest of the other, nor can he imagine these contradictory urges in him living happily ever after in peaceful co-existence. Like the rest of us, he too has read Saul Bellow, Bernard Malamud and Narman Mailer. His condition may be compared to that of Frank Alpine who after his painful circumcision—had all at once found his old disreputable self, the un-circumcised dog end Mailersque hoodlum of the forbidden lusts and desires, emerging from solitary confinement to engage his freshly circumcised and circumscribed self in hand-to-hand combat.

In *Portnoy* the disapproving moralist who says "I am horrified" will not disappear when the libidinous slop shows up screaming. "I want!" Peter Shaw attacked *Portnoy's Complaint* for "fanaticism in the hatred of things Jewish." Both Roth and Updike can be most accurately described as social realists. They generally prefer the literal rendering of relatively commonplace actualities and avoid highly esoteric flights in the manner of, say, John Hawkes. Each has produced, however, a certain number of what might be called "experimental" fictions. Generally sportive and quirky, these idiosyncratic departures nevertheless tend in most cases to reflect the writer's ongoing concerns.

Roth's experimental ventures, for example, address such issues as Jewish-American identity, the relationship between artifice and truth (especially in the area of "official" versions of truth), and personal responsibility and guilt. Updike has also utilized experimental effects to pursue some of his dominant interests: the unique quality of American small town life, the tentative groupings of adolescence, and the undercurrent of sensuality that so largely motivates his characters' behaviour. The principal difference between the two writers' use of experimental approaches is one of proportion; Roth has indulged in the experimental impulse more often and to a greater extent than Updike, a fact that takes on added significance in view of Roth's smaller corpus. Whereas Updike has ventured into experimentalism in an occasional, intermittent sort of way, Roth in an extended period in his career embraced experimentalism exclusively, producing a whole series of unconventional works.

Portnoy's Complaint signalled a departure from Roth's accustomed mode of Jamesian realism, and the beginning of a five-year period of literary experimentation that was to produce two more novels, two short stories, and three political sketches. *The Breast* and *The Great American Novel; On the Air* and *Looking at Kafka;* and *Our Gang, A Modest Proposal,* and *The President Addresses the Nation.*

In any case, however, Roth's period of experimentation must be seen as a necessary, integral, clearly defined phase of his artistic development. Unlike Roth, Updike can be said to have utilized unconventional techniques simply to augment his more traditional skills, and at no point in his career has he yielded totally to the temptation of the experimental. Such effects operate in Updike's work to create an impression of literary counterpoint to the predominant realism of his novels and stories. Only in *A Month of Sundays* and the clearly unrepresentative *Other Modes* section of Museums and Women—in which he toys with a variety of avant-garde formulations in the manner of Donald Barthelme and other recent practitioners of highly innovative fiction—does he depart at length from conventional technique. Significantly, *A Month of Sundays* is one of Updike's least satisfying novels, and the *Other Modes* sketches constitute barely ten percent of his published short works to date. Usually, the experimental features of Updike's fiction function unobtrusively, as in *Bech: A Book, Rabbit Redux* and certain shorter works.

While Roth is completely at ease with—and remarkably skilled at—broad, burlesque farce and boisterous slapstick, Updike's humour runs more to witty repartee and intellectualized parody, the type of humour that characterizes his high verse. By conflating two worlds, that of ancient mythology and that of mundane actuality, Updike further develops the idea that contemporary existence is a disappointing proposition. It clearly illustrates, however, that Updike is at his most effective self when experimental innovation serves a basically, supplementary purpose, operating as an enrichment of—rather than as an alternative to—conventional realism.

Of all contemporary American writers, Philip Roth is arguably the most ambitious. Unlike many aging novelists, whose productive qualities wane over time, Roth has demonstrated a unique ability not only to sustain his literary output but even to surpass the scope and talent inherent in his previous writings.

As Roth has made abundantly clear in his fiction, how one represents his or her subjects is never an easy task. There are always a variety of variables, always a series of miscalculations, and always the chance that one just might not get it right. The act of writing becomes, in a sense, a crap shoot, an uncertain attempt by the author to be understood by his or her audience. Readers' expectations can have a profound effect on the writing's reception, as the character Philip laments in *Deception*:

> I write fiction and I'm told it's auto-biography, I write fiction, so since I'm so dim and they are so smart, let them decide what it is or it isn't.[11]

In approaching Roth's writings, such a sentiment resonates with significance. Roth's fiction seems most alive when his readers are "getting it wrong," frustrated in their attempts to secure an ultimate meaning or pin down an especially slippery passage. "Sheer Playfulness and Deadly Seriousness are my closest friends,"[12] he once perceptively told an interviewer, and in his novels there is always just enough of the former to upset any attempt at finding the latter.

But even this act of literary mischief is itself a profoundly "serious" matter, and the author acknowledges its gravity:

> As writer, of course, I have myself been not merely labeled mischief-maker but condemned by any number of affronted readers [...] In their eyes I commit not amusing mischief but serious mischief, not responsible mischief but irresponsible mischief; with a crazy intensity that is unremitting, I enact a farce about issues that are anything but farcical [....Readers] have reminded me more than once that my impertinence imposes on even our gravest concerns a demeaning and most ridiculous shape. Because of this my mischief making is something other than a relief. It is a menace and a scandal.[13]

Philip Roth has spent a career both justifying and rationalizing his writing of *Portnoy's Complaint* (1969). So maligned and criticized was he from all sectors of the Jewish community, including the American rabbinate, that his succeeding works seemed to be apologetic in nature; that is, they were written in defence of his craft. He took on an alter ego, Nathan Zukermen, who showed up as Roth's fictional protagonist, maintaining throughout that his life was not Philip Roth's. Philip Roth has inured us as an author by turning sentences around in his most interesting and almost always stimulating novels.

Roth is one of the most inventive Jewish authors of any period. He is a serious writer who has never been somber in print; his narrative voice is unique and so is the way he consistently wrings slapstick comedy out of the tics and obsessions of his characters. No one else writing today has been more amusing or more enlightening. Despite his denial many critics say that *Portnoy* was really autobiographical, how could Roth have created such a vividly possessive portrait of a man in hilarious turmoil except by actually being that man? Such a narrow conception of fiction and its imaginative resources annoyed and exasperated him.

He could have deflected these misreadings by following *Portnoy's Complaint* with a novel whose central character bore no surface resemblances to himself. With characteristic contrariness, he did the exact opposite Peter Tarnopol, the narrator of *My Life as a Man* (1974), is, unlike Portnoy but like Roth, a writer and one who has enjoyed early acclaim. Roth was hailed as "The Golden Boy of American Literature" (*New York Times Book Review*, September, 1959). Tarnopol's obsessive topic is his disastrous first marriage; that Roth had lived through such an experience was by then fairly common knowledge among his readers. By giving Tarnopol so many of his own biographical details, Roth seemed to be setting a trap for misinterpreters.

Roth has tirelessly insisted on the distinction between the raw material of life and the transforming power of fiction and his energy shows no signs of flagging. His office is a study on his Connecticut property about 60 yards, from his house.

"I work at my job the way most human beings work at jobs; I start mornings and quit evenings."[14] Bad reviews no longer bother him:

> I am sometimes frustrated by my own efforts but not by the public response. Once a book is out of your hands, readers make it what they will.[15]

Looking back, Roth sees a pattern to his work:

> Ever since *Goodbye Columbus*, I've been drawn to depicting the impact of place on American lives. *Portnoy's Complaint* is very much the raw response to a way of life that was specific to his American place during his childhood in the '30s' and '40s'. The link between the individual and his historic moment may be more focused in the recent trilogy, but the interest was there from the start.[16]

Roth's comedy and satire are often directed at Jews and their customs. His use of Jewish stereotypes for scathing humour has alienated and angered some members of the Jewish community shaken by the Holocaust. The eminent critic Irving Howe in *Philip Roth Reconsidered* called Portnoy's Complaint "a vulgar book"[17] and denounced Roth's shallow treatment of Jewish life.

Roth, like other post-modern novelists, uses comic irony to mock rational methods of solving contemporary problems, particularly problems with regard to traditional Jewish issues that people hold dear. In his world, it's the ones we know best and love most who are trying to oppress and destroy us: our parents, our friends and neighbours, our lovers, our children.

According to Levy Asher, Philip Roth's worldview is essentially childish. His most successful writings are about young people, but the formula turns sickly when his characters grow into adults because the existential self-actualization of a mature adult is beyond his scope. The classic Roth character is terrified, helpless and about to throw a big fit. By the time his characters get old and prepare to die, they may become resigned but there is little evidence that they ever become mature.

In this sense, there is a great difference between Roth and an author he is frequently compared to, John Updike. There are similarities as well—they both hit their stride during the Vietnam War era when Roth's *Portnoy's Complaint* and Updike's *Couples* perched on the bestseller list. Both writers carried forward the risqué literary tradition of D.H. Lawrence and Henry Miller, but the literary vision of Updike feels expansive while that of Roth feels repressive.

John Updike seems infused with generosity and curiosity. He publishes short stories and poems along with novels and he is also, by any measure, one of our top literary critics. His characters inhabit an amazing variety of cultural backgrounds. Philip Roth's fictional universe, on the other hand, is entirely peopled by Jewish families in Newark or Jewish families who left Newark. Then there are some characters who resemble Philip Roth.

But Roth is averse to readers drawing parallels between his life and those of his fictional creations. To do so, after all, belittles the importance of a novelist's imagination, and it also soils the stance of moral seriousness that Roth so deeply cherishes. Like Saul Bellow and a number of others, Philip Roth himself is essentially a social realist, a novelist of manners. Although his career has encompassed some experimental ventures, in his best and most representative works he has created strikingly vivid impressions of American society today.

In his major novels and stories he has convincingly captured the collective American personality and the dilemmas with which it grapples. He has addressed the same large social issues: ethnic identity, family relationships, individual moral responsibility and guilt, sexuality and romantic love, materialism, and social moods in general.

As a Jewish American artist, Roth evinces a prevailingly Jewish angle of perception. This is certainly not to suggest that he speaks for all Jewish Americans, or that his work constitutes a manifesto. But his protagonists, his principally urban backdrops, his use of language, and his thematic emphases all reflect the Jewish American experience. Among Roth's central concerns, for example, is the ongoing problem of cultural assimilation. Many of his protagonists struggle, in varying degrees, with the psychological conflicts that this adjustment engenders. They are also city dwellers, as is largely true of the actual Jewish American population, which has tended to cluster in and around the urban centres. Similarly, their language and that of their families and associates echoes actual Jewish American speech, by blending educated American English, and urban and Yiddish influenced-dialect patterns.

The most controversial feature of Roth's fiction has been the ambivalence with which many of his characters perceive their Jewishness. They seem to view themselves as at once both enhanced and diminished by their heritage. In treating this idea, Roth sometimes depicts a fundamental contrast between two opposed ways of life: the more traditional, European mode of Jewishness, and the secularized, "modern" existence embraced by the fully assimilated jews. Indeed, the resulting psychological and social tension is among Roth's most obvious concerns in his earlier work, particularly in *Goodbye,Columbus* and *Portnoy's Complaint*.

Like Roth's protagonists, Updike's "heroes" exist in a climate of adjustment, and in their own ways they confront various identity crises. But Updike's larger, overriding theme is that of cultural disintegration, motivating such diverse works as *The Poorhouse Fair, The Centaur, Couples, Problems*, and the *Rabbit* novels. Whether the protagonist is a rural, urban, or suburban character, the crises he encounters are invariably caused, at least in part, by a breakdown of the established order. Thus, Updike addresses many of our most pressing concerns: the luck of meaningful work, the negative effects of materialistic excess, the dissolution of marriage and family life, and even in *Rabbit, Redux* the conundrum of race relations. Roth chides his characters not for being Jewish, but for being, not Jewish enough.

While Updike adopts a broad, almost sociological approach, Roth tends towards a more introspective psychological handling of his material. His books are as much character studies of the protagonists as they are commentaries on the current scene. Accordingly, Roth's works are almost always written in the first person (spoken, as it were by their protagonists).

Members of a mistreated minority, Roth's characters are more concerned with personal survival than with the larger society that has excluded them. In short, Roth's characters are in search of a sophisticated, existential self knowledge that will enable them to function independently in a world where "the center cannot hold".

But this is not to say that Roth is concerned only with personality and Updike only with the social structure. From *Goodbye, Columbus* to Roth's latest books, the difficulties encountered by the Rothian protagonists are certainly not experienced in a vacuum and in fact are often exacerbated by what Roth terms the "Struggle going on today between self and culture." Similarly, Updike could hardly be accused of sacrificing character for theme.

Certainly his early work from *Goodbye, Columbus* which won him a national book award at the age of 26 in1959, to *When She was Good,* a studied account of a midwestern Joan of Arc bent on a moral crusade, reflected a preoccupation with civility and social obligations. The prose was refined, even fastidious, and it was informed by an earnest morality. At the time, Roth, who had grown up in Newark as the son of an insurance salesman, tended to regard fiction as "something like a religious calling,"an elevated notion, he once wrote, that "dovetailed nicely in my case with a penchant for ethical striving that I had absorbed as a Jewish child."

He approached his chosen vocation with high ideals and modest expectations.

> My expectation was that I would always have to teach at a university to earn a living.", he recalled, while talking with a visitor at the Algonquin. "Nor did I particularly just want to be a writer. There is a studious side of me that likes to read

and teach, and back then, $3,800 a year was quite enough for me to live on.[18]

By the mid-60's, however, things had changed. Roth had spent several years in psychoanalysis, he had been scarred by a bad marriage, not unlike the one depicted In *My Life as a Man* and he had begun to hunger after the success he saw such friends as John Updike and William Styron achieving.

He had also been criticized for being anti-Semitic, "self-hating" and tasteless, and had set for himself the odd goal, as he wrote in *Reading Myself and Others*, of "becoming the writers some Jewish critics had been telling me I was all along: irresponsible, conscienceless, unserious."

The result, of course, was *Portnoy*, which used to outrageous effect the raw, impassioned humour Roth's friends had been enjoying in private for years—humour that would be pushed to even greater lengths *Our Gang, The Breast* and *The Great American Novel*. The theme of *Portnoy* was the throwing off of duty, its hero's determined and futile attempt to free himself from responsibility and guilt.

With *Portnoy*, Roth got success he'd wanted and he got it in spades. Unlike his hero Zukerman, however, he did not stay in New York, but escaped his new found fame by moving first to Yaddo, the writer's colony, and after some time to an old farmerhouse in Connecticut, where he still spends half of every year. Like Lonoff, the reclusive author portrayed in *The Ghost Writer*, Roth has become "deeply skeptical of the public world" and now leads a wilfully quiet life. His days are spent "turning sentences around"; his evenings in reading novels, underlining important passages just the way he did when he was a graduate student at the University of Chicago many years ago: "What Do I Need the City For?"

"The concentration of writing requires silence", he says. "For me, large blocks of silence. It's like hearing a faint Morse code, a faint signal is being given, and I need quiet to pick it up. Besides, what do I need the city for? A little bit goes a long way. One week in New York will take care of me for a year."[19]

His novels explore the psychology of sex and the psychology of egocentricity or Narcissism. The psychoanalysis of *Portnoy's*

Complaint, wherein handcore fantasies and textbook explanations leapfrog each other; leads to relentless exploration of libidinal mysteries and repressed urges in his various novels, which can be categorized as first the symptomatic books and then the diagnostic ones. In his sixth and best novel *My Life as a Man* (1974) Roth goes beyond psychoanalysis which permeates *Portnoy's Complaint* and examines and explores the themes of female power and male subservience from shifting perspectives, which elevate this novel beyond the level of psychoanalysis and provide deeper and multilayered insight into the working of human psyche. *My Life as a Man* almost goes back to the uncertainties of *Letting Go* early which are however now held at higher levels and transcend the provisional certainties of *Portnoy*. Tarnopol is a character, not a case. Thus Roth committed as ever to psychoanalysis but disabused of the libidinal commonplaces of *Portnoy* managed in *My Life as a Man* to free himself to invent the world as he went along, and, through the play of perspectives of which psychoanalysis was just one of many, to produce the most richly exploratory and densely textured of all his books while *Portnoy* brilliantly applies the hackneyed jargon of Freud, Otto and other convenient sources, *My Life as a Man* perceptively indicates that there are no privileged explanation of authentic mysteries, only points of view. Thus *My Life* strikes deeper emotionally than *Portnoy*.

His early novels like *Letting Go* (1962) probe the psychology of repressed, inhibited and driven characters. *Portnoy's Complaint* (1969) is a remarkable Freudian novel, wherein psychoanalysis makes its debut as both narrative backdrop as well as mode of behavorial interpretation accounting for the violation of sex taboos as well as presentation of guilt as the slapstick of the superego. *My Life as a Man* (1974) is his magnum opus; its multi-layered texture views the theme of female imperiousness and male compliance from diverse psychological angles and is thus a complex and perspicacious psychological novel. *The Professor of Desire* (1977) is a novel which depicts erotic, emotion and psychic recuperation of David Alan Kapesh. But Roth is at his best when he delineates the psyche of his protagonists who are embroiled in crisis, catastrophe and debacle.

His function is thus preponderantly the tragic-comic exploration of human psyche immersed in the vortex of libido, confronted with the super-ego, burdened with a sense of moral responsibility, afflicted with guilt-consciousness, embroiled in Narcissism and egocentricity, rooted in jewish-American identity and yet seeking to transcend and at times transgress it.

References

1. Al Alvarez, "The Long Road Home." *The Guardian*: Saturday, September 11, 2004.
2. Garner, Dwight. "Philip Roth is His Mother's Son". *The New York Times*: Sep 24, 2007.
3. Al Alvarez, "The Long Road Home." *The Guardian*: Saturday, September 11, 2004.
4. Ibid. op.cit.,
5. Ibid.
6. Roth, Philip. *Reading Myself and Others*. New York: Vintage, 2001, pp.103-104.
7. Roth, Philip. *Goodbye, Columbus*. Boston: Houghton Mifflin, 1959, p.105.
8. Roth, Philip. *Portnoy's Complaint*. New York: Random, 1969, p.76.
9. Patricia Meyer Spacks, "About Portnoy," *Yale Review* 58, no.4 (1969). 628-631.
10. Samuels, "The Art of Fiction XLLIII: John Updike,"116.
11. Roth, Philip. *Deception: A Novel*. New York: Simon and Schuster, 1990, p.190.
12. Roth, "After Eight Books," Interview with Joyce Carol Oates. Ontario Review, 1974.Rpt. in *Reading Myself and Others*. op.cit., p.111.
13. Roth, Philip. "A Bit of Jewish Mischief." *New York Times Book Review*, 7 Mar, 1993, p.1,20.
14. Al Alvarez, "The Long Road Home." op.cit.,
15. Ibid.
16. Ibid.
17. Howe, Irving, "Philip Roth Reconsidered." *Commentary Dec* 1972. p. 77.
18. Al Alvarez, "The Long Road Home." op.cit.,
19. Ibid.

Bibliography

Primary Sources

A Philip Roth Reader. New York: Farrar, 1980.

American Pastoral. Boston: Houghton Mifflin, 1997.

Deception: A Novel. New York: Simon and Schuster, 1990.

Everyman. New York: Vintage, 2007.

Exit Ghost. New York: Houghton Mifflin, 2007.

Goodbye, Columbus. Boston: Houghton Mifflin, 1959.

I Married A Communist. New York: Vintage, 1999.

Letting Go. New York: Random House, 1962.

My Life as a Man. New York: Vintage, 1994.

Operation Shylock: A Confession. New York: Simon and Schuster, 1993.

Our Gang. New York: Vintage, 2001.

Patrimony: A True Story. New York: Vintage, 1996.

Portnoy's Complaint. New York: Random House, 1969.

Reading Myself and Others. New York: Farrar, 1975.

Sabbath's Theater. New York: Vintage, 1996.

Shop Talk: A Writer and His Colleagues and Their Work. Boston: Houghton Mifflin, 2001.

The Anatomy Lesson. New York: Vintage, 1996.

The Breast. New York: Vintage, 1994.

The Counterlife. New York: Vintage, 1996.

The Dying Animal. Boston: Houghton Mifflin, 2001.

The Facts: A Novelist's Autobiography. New York: Farrar, Straus & Giroux, 1988.

The Ghost Writer. New York: Vintage, 1995.

The Great American Novel. New York: Vintage, 1995.

The Human Stain. New York: Vintage, 2001.

The Plot Against America. New York: Houghton Mifflin, 2004.

The Prague Orgy. New York: Vintage, 1996.

The Professor of Desire. New York: Farrar, 1977.

When She was Good. New York: Random House, 1967.

Zukerman Unbound. New York: Vintage, 1995.

Secondary Sources

Allen, Mary." Philip Roth: When She was Good Was Horrified" *The Necessary Blankness: Women in Major American Fiction of the Sixties*. Urbana: University of Illinois Pr., 1976.

Alvarez, Al. "The Long Road Home." *THE GUARDIAN*, 11 Sept. 2004.

Asher, Levy. "Overrated Writers, Part One: Philip Roth." Brooklyn, 5 Jun 2006.

Baumgarten, Murray and Barbara Gottfried. *Understanding Philip Roth*. Columbia: U of South Carolina P, 1990

Ben Siegel, "The Myths of Summer: Philip Roth's The Great American Novel", *Contemporary Literature* 17, no. 2 (1976): 175-76.

Bloom, Harold, ed. *Modern Critical Views*: Philip Roth. New York: Chelsea House,1986.

Bloom, Harold. *The Anxiety of Influence: A Theory of Poetry*. Oxford United Press,1973.

Bourjaily, Vance. "The Professor of Desire." *The New York Times Book Review*, 18 Sept. 1977.

Bruce, Lenny. *How to Talk Dirty and Influence People*. New York: Simon and Schuster, 1992.

Cushman, Keith. "Looking at Philip Roth Looking at Kafka." *Modern Jewish Studies Annual IV* (1982); joint issue with Yiddish 4, no. 4 (1982): 12-31.

Deer, Irving and Harrier Deer. "Philip Roth and the Crisis in American Fiction". *Minnesota Review* 6, no. 4 (1966): 353-60.

Detweiler, Robert. " Philip Roth and the Test of Dialogic Life." *Four Spiritual Crises in Mid-Century American Fiction*. University of Florida Monographs, no. 4. Gainesville: Univ. of Florida Pr., 1963.

Dickstein, Morris."My Life As A Man" *The New York Times Book Review*, 2 June 1974.

Ditsky, John. "Roth, Updike, and the High Expense of Spirit". *University of Windsor Review* 5, no. 1 (1969): 111-20.

Donaldson, Scott. "Philip Roth: Days of Whine and Moses". *Studies in American Jewish Literature* 11, no. 1 (1970): 21-35.

Dowd, Maureen. "Roth's Real Father Likes His Books", *The New York Times*, 26 Oct. 1983.

Dwight McDonald, "Our Gang", *The New York Times Book Review,* 7 Nov. 1971, 31.

Edwards, Thomas R. "The Great American Novel", *The New York Times Book Review,* 6 May 1973

Freud, Sigmund. *Jokes and Their Relation to the Unconscious*. Trans. James Strachey and Angela Richards. Hammondsworth: Penguin, 1976.

Gardner, John. "The Breast." *The New York Times Book Review,* 17 Sept. 1972.

Garner, Dwight. "Philip Roth is His Mother's Son," *The New York Times,* 24 Sept. 2007.

Gogol, Nikolai. "Nena" (The Nose) *Pietarilaisnovellcja. Trans*. Into Finnish by Esa Adrian. Helsinki: Otava,1975. 15-50.

Gordon, Lois G. "PORTNOY,S COMPLAINT": Coming of Age in Jersey City". *Literature and Psychology* 19, nos. 3 and 4 91969): 57-60.

Granville Hicks, "A Bad Little Good Girl", review of *When She was Good, Saturday Review,* 17 June 1967, 25-26.

Grebstrein, Sheldon N. "The Comic Anatomy of Portnoy's Complaint". In *Comic Relief: Humour in Contemporary Literature,* edited by Sarah Blacher Cohen. Urbana: Univ. of Illinois Pr., 1978.

Green, Martin. Introduction. In *A Philip Roth Reader*. New York: Farrar, 1980.

Greenberg, Robert M. "Transgression in the Fiction of Philip Roth". *Twentieth Century Literature*: 43, 4 (1997):487.

Halio, Jay L. *Philip Roth Revisited*. New York: Twayne,1992.

Howe, Irving. "Philip Roth Reconsidered". *Commentary,* December 1972. 69-77.

Ireland, G.W. "The Voice of Philip Roth" *Queens Quarterly* 87, no. 2(1980): 286-92.

Jones, Judith Patersonand Guinevera A. Nance. *Philip Roth. Modern Literature Series*. New York: Ungar, 1981.

Junker, Howard. "Will This Finally Be Philip Roth's Year?" *New York,* 13 Jan. 1969, 44-47.

Kafka, Franz. "Metamorphosis". *Metamorphosis and Other Stories*. 1916. New York: Penguin,1984. 7-63.

Kakutani, Michiko. "A Postwar Paradise Shattered from Within". Rev. of American Pastoral. *The New York Times* 15 April 1997, late ed.:C11.

Kaminsky, Alice R. "Philip Roth's Professor Kapesh and the Reality Principle". *University of Denver Quarterly* 13, no. 2 (1978): 41-54.

Katukani, Michiko. "Is Roth Really Writing about Roth?" *The New York Times,* 11 May 1981.

Keyishian, Marjorie. "Roth Retuning to Newyark," *The New York Times,* 4 Oct. 1992.

Kilman, Bernice W. "Names in Portnoy's Complaint", *Critique* 14, no. 3(1973): 16-24.

______________ . "Women in Roth's Fiction". The Nassau Review 3, no. 4(1978): 75-88.

Lee, Hermoine. Philip Roth. *Contemporary Writers.* New York: Methuen, 1982.

Leshanski, Jonathan. "The Great American Novel", The Vintage Books, 9 May 2003.

Martin Amis, " No Satisfaction", review of *The Professor of Desire, New Statesman,* 13 Jan. 1978, 50.

McDaniel, John N. "The Fiction of Philip Roth". *Haddonfield,* N.J.: Haddonfield House, 1974.

Mehlman, Peter. "You Know How Philip Roth Does It?", *Santa Monica,* California, Monday, 14 Nov. 2005.

Melville, Herman. Moby Dick: or, *The Whale.* Ed. Charles Feidelson, Jr. New York: Macmillan, 1964.

Mikkonen, Kai. "The Metamorphosed Parodical Body in Philip Roth's *The Breast." CRITIQUE: Studies in Contemporary Fiction.*

Milowitz, Steven. *Philip Roth Considered: The Concentrationary Universe of the American Writer.* New York: Garland, 2000.

Nora Sayre, " Wild Pigs and Others", review of *When She was Good, New Statesman,* 2 June 1967, 770.

Ozick, Cynthia. Three letters (signed 16 June 1972, 19 June 1972, and 5 October 1972)to Holt, Rinehart, and Winston. Unpublished. Ken Lopez Bookseller, *Catalog* 126: R-S, Item 319.

Patricia Meyer Spacks, "About Portnoy", *Yale Review* 58, no. 4 (1969): 623.

Peter Prince, "Old Glories", review of *The Great American Novel, New Statesman,* 21 September 1973, 393.

Pinsker, Sanford. "Reading Philip Roth Reading Philip Roth." *Studies in American Jewish Literature* 3, no. 2(1977-78); joint issue with *Yiddish* 3, no. 1(19770: 14-18.

Pinsker, Sanford. Ed. Critical Essays on Philip Roth. *Critical Essays on American Literature.* Boston: G.K. Hall, 1982.

Pinsker, Sanford. The Comedy That "Hoits": An Essay on the Fiction of Philip Roth. *Literary Frontiers.* Columbia Univ. of Missouri Press, 1975.

Pinsker, Sanford. *The Schlemiel as Metaphor: Studies in the Yiddish and American Jewish Novel.* Carbondale: Southern Illinois United Press, 1971.

Plante, David."Conversation With Philip: Diary of a Friendship." *The New York Times Book Review,* 1 Jan. 1984, 3, 30-31.

Prescott, Orville. "Letting Go". *The New York Times Book Review,* 15 June 1962.

Roth, "I Always Wanted You to Admire My Fasting". *Reading Myself and Others.* New York: Farrar, 1975.

Rothstein, Mervyn. "To Newyark, With Love", *The New York Times,* 29 Mar. 1991.

Royal, Derek Parker. "Fouling Out the American Pastoral: Rereading Philip Roth's The Great American Novel." *Upon Further Review: Sports in American Literature.* Ed. Michael Cocchiarale and Scott D. Emmert. Westport, CT: Greenwood-Praeger, 2004. 157-68.

Safer, Elaine B. "The Double, Comic Irony, and Post-Modernism in Philip Roth's 'Operation Shylock'—Ethnic Humour." *Melus,* Winter, 1996.

Sale, Roger. "Reading Myself and Others", *The New York Times Book Review,* 25 May 1975.

Searles, George J. *The Fiction of Philip Roth and John Updike.* Carbondale: Southern Illinois UP,1985.

Searles, George J. "Philip Roth's 'Kafka': A Jeu-ish American Fiction of the First Order." *Modern Jewish Studies Annual* IV (1982); joint issue with *Yiddish* 4, no. 4(1982): 5-11.

Sheldon N. Grebstein., "Portnoy's Complaint (Philip Roth)", cassette recording (Deland, Fla:. Everett Edwards, 1973).

Stanley Cooperman, "Philip Roth: 'OLD Jacob's Eye' With A Squint", *Twentieth Century Literature* 19, no. 4(1973): 213.

Syrkin, Marie. "Philip Roth and the Jews: An Exchange." *The New York Times Books Review,* 3 Oct. 1974.

Thompson, Bob. "Some Quotes by Roth". Washington Post Staff Writer, *Sunday,* 12 Nov. 2006.

Weil, Henry. "Philip Roth: Still Waiting for His Masterpiece." *Saturday Review,* June 1981, 26-31.

Wood, Michael. "Hooked" Rev. of My Life As A Man. *New York Review of Books* 13 June 1974: 8-10.

Woolf, Virginia. *Orlando*: *A Biography.* 1928. London: Penguin, 1967.

Interviews

"An Interview with Philip Roth." *Reading Philip Roth.* Ed. Asher Z. Milbauer and Donald G. Watson. New York: St. Martin's, 1988. 1-12.

"Interview with *The London Sunday Times*", *London Sunday Times* 19 Feb. 1984.

"Interview with Alan Lenchuck", *New York Review of Books*: 19 Oct. 1972.

"Interview with The Paris Review". *Paris Review* 93 (1984): 215-47.

"It No Longer Feels a Great Injustice that I Have to Die." Krasnik, Martin. *The Guardian* 14 Dec 2005.

"Talk with Philip Roth." Davidson, Sara. *New York Times Book Review*, 18 Sept. 1977.